D1532027

Intellectual Property in the Information Age

Intellectual Property in the Information Age

The Politics of Expanding Ownership Rights

DEBORA J. HALBERT

Quorum Books
Westport, Connecticut • London

Library of Congress Cataloging-in-Publication Data

Halbert, Debora J. (Debora Jean)
Intellectual property in the information age : the politics of expanding ownership rights / Debora J. Halbert.
p. cm.
Includes bibliographical references and index.
ISBN 1–56720–254–3 (alk. paper)
1. Intellectual property—United States. 2. Information superhighway—Law and legislation—United States. I. Title.
KF2979.H35 1999
346.7304'8—dc21 98–23976

British Library Cataloguing in Publication Data is available.

Library of Congress Catalog Card Number: 98–23976
ISBN: 1–56720–254–3

First published in 1999

Quorum Books, 88 Post Road West, Westport, CT 06881
An imprint of Greenwood Publishing Group, Inc.

Printed in the United States of America

The paper used in this book complies with the Permanent Paper Standard issued by the National Information Standards Organization (Z39.48–1984).

10 9 8 7 6 5 4 3 2

Copyright Acknowledgments

The author and publisher gratefully acknowledge permission to use the following material:

Portions of the Introduction and Chapter 7 first appeared in Debora Halbert, "The future of intellectual property law," *Technological Forecasting and Social Change, 53* (1997): 147–160. Reprinted by permission of Elsevier Science.

Chapter 4 is a revised version of Debora Halbert, "Intellectual property piracy: The narrative construction of deviance," which first appeared in the *International Journal for the Semiotics of Law, X/28* (1997): 55–78, and is here reprinted with the permission of the publishers, Deborah Charles Publications.

Contents

Preface

This book is a product of the information age and is a testimony to much of what is said within its pages. After completing my dissertation at the University of Hawai'i, I was asked if I would follow my own advice and put the dissertation on the Internet, to which I answered "Of course." As soon as it was ready, I placed it in a subdirectory of the Hawaii Research Center for Futures Studies home page (http://www.hawaii.edu/~future/). Thus, the dissertation entered the ever-expanding web of knowledge available on the World Wide Web (WWW or Web).

It was not long before the advantages of such a direct form of communication became recognizable. I have had the opportunity to talk with the hackers about whom I had written, speak with other people researching similar topics, and get published in traditional journals because of the availability of my work on the Internet. Ultimately, this book is a result of placing my dissertation on the Web. Jeremy Geelan was one of the many who read the dissertation. He contacted me regarding a revised manuscript for publication. This volume is the result.

In another important way, this book is proof of my argument that there is no single author. Although my name appears on the cover, this book would not have reached completion without the help and support of many people. I thank my parents for their support. Thanks to Neal Milner, Kathy Ferguson, Michael Shapiro, Jim Dator, and Richard Vincent for reading and commenting on many drafts. I also thank Michael Sysiuk, Brian Richardson, Colleen Fox, Kennan Ferguson, Kerry Burch, Scott Daniels, Cindy Mackey, Jeff Heidrich, and Christen Hesselbacher for providing the intellectual and emotional support necessary for such a project. Additionally, I thank Allen Cooper for tirelessly reading the manuscript; Lucas Parra, whom I only know through e-mail, for his very important editorial comments. I also thank my research assistant, Jagady Blue, who was instrumental in providing much needed research and editorial skills and Otterbein College for providing the opportunity to apply for a National Endowment for the Humanities (NEH) grant that helped support the completion of this project. The support provided by the NEH grant came in the form of a subscription to Lexis-Nexis, a research tool no modern day researcher should be without. Finally, I thank Maurice Foisy and Tim Allen at Western Washington University for their mentoring and support over the years.

A book is never the work of one author and I owe an intellectual debt to many people. All errors, of course, are my own.

Introduction

The United States is in a legal feeding frenzy over intellectual property rights. As intangible items become commodified, everyone seems to want a share. There are legal controversies over who owns the images of the dead, over who wrote a phrase in a song, over reverse engineering of computer programs, over the use of the "look and feel" of a computer program, over ideas, over body parts, and over genetic material. Control over personal information is increasingly in the hands of database owners who compile information on everything from consumer tastes to medical histories.[1] Despite the dependency of ideas on borrowing, using, rephrasing, and appropriating the work of others,[2] the question is usually phrased as "How much can be owned?" not, "Should it be owned?"

When ownership of intellectual property is challenged, it is not questioned on the grounds that intellectual property should be a public good, but rather to what degree it can be property.[3] This distinction is important. When Pepsi trademarks the phrase "uh-huh,"[4] when Daffy Duck's intellectual property lawyer calls the local newspaper to tell them they cannot quote the duck,[5] and when a man's cancerous organ becomes the object of property,[6] the boundaries of intellectual property become so expanded as to be oppressive.

Our current framework of intellectual property, while being enormously beneficial to the large information brokers of our time, is detrimental to the free exchange of information as well as to the ability of a world citizenry to participate in its own future. But this notion of the individual author who is in control of his or her creative work successfully conceals the larger political and economic implications of the intellectual property system where major owners such as Microsoft can own as well as control information systems and the information itself. The author as the owner of a copyright is the exception, not the norm. If an employee leaves a company for another, his or her ideas remain the property of the past employer who can sue to regain them.[7] To publish, an author will have to sign the copyright over to the publisher. There are even property rights in images. Elvis' image is not only popular but lucrative. Colonel Tom Parker, Elvis' manager was the lucky owner of the copyright on Elvis' image. Elvis' family does not own his image and cannot control its use.[8] Jimi Hendrix's image is another example. His father says he was unaware he had sold his rights to Hendrix's image and music, and now he wants them back.[9]

Two things about the history of intellectual property need to be kept in mind. First, the concept of *intellectual property* and the corresponding notion of *originality* stemming from a person's intellect are not natural, nor have they been universally embraced. They are the outgrowth of economic interests and legal definitions within a specific historical context. That historical context is the 18th-century struggle over copyright ownership and the development of a concept of *proprietary authorship*.[10] Second, intellectual property, specifically copyright, is designed to benefit the publishers who hold the copyrights, not the authors themselves.[11] Copyright usually belongs to the company for which the author works or the publisher who publishes the work, not the author. With each new technology, such as photography, television, photocopying, and computer programming, the concept of intellectual property is challenged due to the new relationships made possible. Each time a technology disrupts the intellectual property law, the law has been revised to include the new technology in a manner that keeps the basic relationship between author and copyright owner intact. The discourse on intellectual property obscures the relationships of power that develop between authors and copyright owners, corporations and the public.

A lack of understanding of copyright rules may lead the average American citizen to mistakenly believe they can communicate, exchange, and share information freely. Anyone who has copied computer software knows the reproduction is an exact duplicate of the original. Anyone who has used a VCR knows television programs can be taped with the press of a button. Anyone who has read an interesting article and forwarded it over the Internet to a friend knows that the copyright notice can be ignored. The Internet provides the possibility for uncontrolled exchange of information and new ways of distributing everything from books to music to art. Nevertheless, making a copy of a computer program, taping a program in order to keep it permanently, or forwarding an article to a friend are illegal acts—even though they are committed casually by virtually everyone.

We are witnessing the expansion of copyright law to include new dimensions of ownership previously considered unimportant. For example, in the early 1980s, software was given away without a thought to copyright protection. By the 1990s, software companies closely guarded their copyrights to the point where businesses and individual homes were raided to halt piracy.[12] Copying is difficult to control because of the ease in which products are copied, and so copyright owners are attempting to establish new property boundaries via legal and legislative means.

In addition to legal avenues, property owners have utilized public relations and education as tools for compliance with conventions governing intellectual property. It has become important to convince citizens that behavior that seems natural, like sharing a magazine article with a friend, is illegal. Convincing others of the illegality of "natural" forms of behavior (such as exchange via the Internet) is accomplished by passing laws that enforce specific property relations and criminalize the exchange of certain types of information. It is also done through manufacturing stories about the bad guys, stories that make them evil, dangerous, and of course, criminal. These stories are also conveyed by equating moral action with preserving intellectual property and immoral action with violating copyright.

In a digital environment, sharing information is copying information. Instead of recognizing that the usefulness of copyright law has virtually ended, those interested in protecting this abstract property right are weaving webs of ownership that make the exchange, sharing, and creation of new expressions more difficult and the punishments for not complying with the law more severe. The lack of security in ownership of intellectual property caused by the digital revolution has led to an enormous push in legislative efforts aimed at solidifying the notion of intellectual property and expanding it to include all aspects of a creative product.

Intellectual property can be divided into four basic categories: patents, copyrights, trademarks, and trade secrets. Each category is protected by legal rules bound by assumptions about creation, productivity, and innovation. This book is primarily concerned with copyright. A study of copyright in the information age is important for several reasons. First, regardless of how we feel about computer technology, it is here to stay. Second, new technology is making copyright an obsolete concept and, therefore, it may be more useful to replace this centuries old idea instead of investing more time and money into enforcing laws not fit for a digital world. Copyright as a conceptual tool has been a 200-year ideological struggle designed to draw territorial boundaries around cultural goods. In the new information age, 18th-century notions of copyright are inadequate for governing the exchange of information, and effectively thwarts the potential of information technology.

Third, if we do not watch carefully how information and technology as property are constructed, we will find ourselves in a future of Orwelian proportions. The balance between innovation as a social good versus a private benefit codified in the U.S. Constitution is being replaced with the language of ownership. The balance advocated by the U.S. Constitution between protection and access is tilting in favor of tightly controlled property rights. We should think very carefully about a system that takes property relations and applies them to the realm of ideas. How far ownership can go needs to be debated vigorously. Copyright is the tip of a larger intellectual property iceberg that ultimately leads to questions about who should own life and knowledge.

Finally, copyright is important because the potential is there for technology to radically transform the way we think, create, and exchange information. The Internet, for example, provides an outlet for unbridled exchange of information, a place to attempt collaborative projects, and a place to creatively develop new ideas. Technology premised on the notion of copying, which all computer technology assumes at its most basic level, can be used to develop new methods for sharing knowledge and making progress in the arts and sciences.

This book is written to illustrate how the narrative process is used to extend the law of copyright to ever broader realms of protection. Narrative analysis is an important conceptual tool. Clearly, narratives have an immediate impact on the individuals involved because they often describe the actions of real people. The narrative paradigm also uncovers hegemonic processes. As Sara Cobb and Janet Rifkin stated, "The storytelling metaphor allows the hegemonic processes in discourse to come into focus."[13] Furthermore, the notion of neutrality in narratives needs to be challenged. Stories have political impacts and once we begin evaluating how narratives affect our perception of events, these impacts become more visible. On another level, once it is understood that stories are strategic, the need to create alternative stories becomes more clear. Again, Cobb and Rifkin are enlightening: "Unless alternative stories are elaborated, persons are co-opted into identities they did not author and cannot transform."[14] Finally, the ability to interpret a narrative event is an important critique of power that clarifies the underlying assumptions in the dominant narrative. Ultimately, narratives serve as boundary markers—they authorize actions and stake out limits that cannot be crossed.[15] Using a narrative approach, it is possible to excavate how power operates in the intellectual property narrative.

Stanley Fish noted, "Change is produced when a vocabulary takes hold to the extent that its ways of elaborating the world become normative and are unreflectively asserted in everyday practices . . . change just creeps up on a community as a vocabulary makes its unsystematic way into its every corner."[16] Change begins with problematizing what goes as unquestioned. This type of change, the type that creeps into our dialogue, is beginning to appear as a result of computer technology and is elaborated on throughout the pages of this book.

In working through the layers of narrative created in the copyright story, it is important to document the types of stories that are being told about intellectual property and who is telling these stories. The narratives that have been created to entrench private property in the information age present multinational corporations as victims, teenage hackers and developing countries as villains, and involve the government as both a peacekeeper and enforcer. This narrative process serves to establish property lines in new technology and socializes the average citizen to an understanding of what is and is not acceptable. If the copyright message can be uncritically passed on through narratives to the general population, then the property rights of current owners will be reinforced. If copyright cannot be embraced, then more individuals will find themselves facing criminal charges until a new concept of private property is accepted. This book is about how the conceptual fences of private property have been drawn around the intangible technological objects that make up our current economy—software, information, and even entertainment.

This study is guided by two levels of analysis. The first looks at the discourse that constitutes intellectual property—its historical roots, its modern manifestations, and its applications to computer technology. I follow this discourse through a variety of texts in order to illustrate how property lines are created in technological intellectual property as this form of property becomes increasingly important to the U.S. economy. The first six chapters follow this theme. The second level of analysis has to do with how authorship is used to define territory and how technology subverts the authorizing function and provides for possible alternatives to authorship. Chapters 7 and 8 begin to address this second issue.

Chapter 1 narrates the construction of a traditional copyright story. Copyright has evolved in many ways; it incorporates a far broader spectrum of work and is significantly different today than it was in the 18th century. However, we owe our assumptions about copyright, and our general approach to authorship, to 18th-century law. Building on the work of Mark Rose, this chapter sketches the emergence of copyright law in 18th-century England. Similar copyright movements were occurring in Germany and France at the same time and these approaches are also discussed. Finally, this chapter follows the copyright movement across the ocean to the United States and highlights the important aspects of U.S. copyright law. This chapter is an assessment of copyright history and describes the transition from European copyright law to U.S. law. Here, the "traditional" copyright story as told in the United States is outlined. My purpose is to provide a reading of the history that focuses on the rhetorical construction of copyright.

Chapter 2 begins the process of describing how copyright is currently used to expand the scope of knowledge ownership to copyright technology generally and the Internet specifically. This chapter focuses on policy recommendations and Congressional action regarding computer technology. It describes how computer technology was first incorporated under copyright law and evaluates key policy recommendations to Congress on how to deal with technology.

Chapter 3 considers the way courts have interpreted copyright law. The history of case law is one of ever-widening circles of protection. The United States has gone from being one of the world's most prolific pirates to copyright's most dedicated defender. Obviously, greater protection reflects the United States' current dependence on intellectual products for its economic success. It could also be argued that greater protection of intellectual property is necessary as technological developments make possible greater exchange. How modern technology influences intellectual property exchange should give us an idea for how the law will interpret new challenges to property rights. This chapter briefly traces this history and discusses the major decisions that have shaped law in the area of technology.

Chapter 4 begins to describe the "dark side" of information technology. Once clear definitions of property have been created, it becomes possible to identify the criminal element that emerges when new forms of property capable of being stolen have been created. This chapter explores the issue of international piracy of copyrighted materials. It follows the debate on this issue through a decade of government hearings and into the recent TRIPs agreement. Along with intellectual property products, the United States exports its concept of intellectual property. U.S. insistence that the rest of the world follow its intellectual property story has created a problematic environment for the rest of the world. This chapter assesses our approach to international protection for copyright law and argues that the construction of pirates is ultimately a strategy for forcibly imposing on the world our understanding of copyright. Pirates help define what is inappropriate behavior in the information age.

Chapter 5 again goes to the dark side of the information age and takes up the issue of the hacker. Like the pirate, the hacker helps construct the debate over information technology and intellectual property by providing publicly recognized villains who can be fought. This chapter traces the development of the hacker from harmless teenage "nerd" to the evil terrorist who could bring the entire country to its knees. In the name of protecting "legitimate" owners from the illegal actions of these villains, the boundaries of intellectual property are carefully and uncritically drawn around new technology. In the case of the computer hacker, we can also begin to understand the larger threat to the United States via terrorism that must be met with harsh penalties. Ultimately, both pirates and hackers define intellectual property boundaries. They help illustrate to everyday citizens what is inappropriate in an information age. In the process, questions about ownership of information and who benefits from such information are lost.

Chapter 6 discusses the technological transformation of authorship. Copyright cannot exist outside some sort of understanding of authorship. The type of author with which copyright was designed to deal is the individual proprietary author. Although it is questionable whether such a creation ever existed, technology certainly makes possible new approaches to authorship. Copyright law cannot deal with notions of hypertext, multiple or collaborating authors, or computers that can create "art." Thus, there is great potential for authorship once it is unhinged from the law of copyright. This chapter begins to outline this potential.

Chapter 7 begins with a critique of copyright law. It takes apart many of the assumptions on which the law is based and evaluates its merits. This chapter begins to evaluate possible scenarios for the role of intellectual property in the future. The future scenarios detailed in this chapter include those that are both probable and utopian. They begin with our most likely future, where we continue to allow copyright and intellectual property laws to be expanded unhindered, thus allowing for the further commodification of life and knowledge. This commodification obviously has serious repercussions for the exchange of ideas and human freedom. A second position that can be explored as a future possibility is the perspective of the hacker where the ownership of information is problematized. The final scenario goes further to suggest we can move away from the concept of property as it applies to creative work and develop an alternative method based on sharing knowledge.

Some will not be comfortable with my approach. After all, how is it possible for me to sympathize with thieves and dangerous criminals? For me, this is not the question. How these particular individuals are constructed as thieves and criminals is what interests me. In an effort to create a more secure system, insecurity has been manufactured. Yes, there are people who do harm to others. However, what is happening now is a struggle to control property ownership, a form of ownership established through 18th-century notions of authorship, creativity, and originality. These concepts ensure that creative work continues to be looked on as the product of individuals when, in fact, this is rarely true. The current struggles over intellectual property advance the economic dominance of powerful industries at the expense of opening creative exchange up to the public.

Technology has the potential to transform our understanding of property, authorship, the production of knowledge, and our identities as citizens. How new technologies will be protected and defined in an information age has much larger implications than who will benefit. How boundaries in intangible property are defined, how we are defined as citizens, what is defined as ethical and unethical behavior, and the extent to which we wish to see our ideas and minds commodified stand in the balance of this debate.

There has never been universal consensus about the extent of intellectual property protection, despite government and business attempts to tightly control it. However, the tension between ownership of information and freedom of information is intensifying as information becomes commodified and the object of an international economy. The rhetoric about individual ownership is heated as new technology makes it easy to copy information and freely share it. This is a contest that transcends a boring recounting of the history of copyright. This contest is about how we will be defined as citizens, what will be owned, and how we will produce and exchange knowledge in the future.

NOTES

1. A. Branscomb, *Who owns information? From privacy to public access* (New York: Basic Books, 1994).
2. "Everyday life invents itself by *poaching* in countless ways on the property of others." See: R. Coombe, "Objects of property and subjects of politics: Intellectual property laws and democratic dialogue," *Texas Law Review, 69* (1991): 1853.
3. T. M. Horbulyk, "Intellectual property rights and technological innovation in agriculture," *Technological Forecasting and Social Change, 43* (1993): 259–270.
4. Just look on any can of Pepsi with the "uh-huh" slogan and you will see the TM sign. This means "uh-huh" is now the equivalent of any brand name and cannot be generically used by other companies.
5. "Ducking the issue of the little black duck," *Honolulu Advertiser*, 21 February 1995, p. B1.
6. J. O'C. Hamilton, "Who told you you could sell my spleen?" *Business Week*, 23 April 1990, p. 38.
7. J. Bennet, "Who owns ideas and papers, is issue in company lawsuits," *The New York Times*, 30 May 1993, p. 1, 27.
8. "Presley's relatives, however, are not necessarily realizing the profit or controlling the uses to which the image is put. Prior to his death, Presley had conveyed the exclusive right to exploit his name and likeness to a corporation controlled by Colonel Tom Parker, his manager, in exchange for royalties. Factors Etc., Inc., is an assignee corporation controlled by Parker who is presumably free to exploit the Presley image in any manner. Once exclusive rights to attributes of the persona are assigned, they may be utilized without regard for the sentiments and sensibilities of heirs." R. J. Coombe, "Author/izing the celebrity: Pub-

licity rights, postmodern politics, and unauthorized genders," *Cardozo Arts and Entertainment*, 1992, p. 373 fn. 24.

9. C. Fleming, & J. Giles, "Jimi, rest in peace," *Newsweek*, 16 January 1995, pp. 64–65.

10. M. Rose, *Authors and owners: The invention of copyright* (London & Cambridge: Harvard University Press, 1993).

11. As Mark Rose and Lyman Ray Patterson explained, copyright did not emerge to protect the author from exploitation. Rather, copyright emerged in order to protect publishers' rights to the copies and their ownership of the "copyright." The legal battles of the 18th century relied on a discourse about proprietary authorship of ideas. The debate over copyrights and authorship culminated in the landmark case, *Donaldson v. Beckett*. The case found that an author of literary text had a common law right of ownership that was held in perpetuity, however, the Statute of Anne (the first copyright law) restrained, or pre-empted this common law right, and limited an author's right to statutory ones. L. R. Patterson, *Copyright in historical perspective* (Nashville: Vanderbuilt University Press, 1968), 175. This decision to award statutory protection was designed to break the London bookselling monopoly by limiting the number of years copyright could be privately owned. A second implication of this case, and the most significant thing to emerge, was that intellectual property becomes a creation of the author's intellect. . . . Rose, *Authors and Owners*. However, the beneficiaries were ultimately the publishers. See also: E. Earle, The effect of romanticism on the 19th century development of copyright law, *Intellectual Property Journal, 6* (1991): 278.

12. A. S. Bauman, "Only police may search your home, right? Guess again," *Seattle Times*, 24 October 1995, p. A1.

13. S. Cobb, & J. Rifkin, "Neutrality as a discursive practice," *Politics and Society* (1991): 81.

14. Ibid., 74.

15. M. De Certeau, *The practice of everyday life* trans. S. Rendall, (Berkeley, Los Angeles, & London: University of California Press, 1984), 123, 125.

16. S. Fish, *Doing what comes naturally: Change, rhetoric, and the practice of theory in literary and legal studies* (Durham & London: Duke University Press, 1989), 24.

1

The Historical Construction of Copyright

The 18th-century copyright story is one repeated so frequently that it has become conventional. It is a story complete with victims, villains, and heroes with continued relevance into the late 1990s. Before I address the implications of the changing copyright environment, it is important to understand the historical context of the traditional copyright story. This chapter summarizes the history of copyright and outlines the copyright story used to structure debates and assumptions important to modern copyright law. Copyright has evolved in many ways; it incorporates a far broader spectrum of work and has changed significantly since the 18th century. However, we owe our assumptions about copyright, and our general understanding of authorship, to 18th-century law.

This chapter focuses on the construction of copyright through discursive negotiations regarding ownership and exchange. Michael Shapiro conceptualized the tension that emerges when sovereignty systems (ownership) are pitted against exchange systems (advocating the relaxation of control). Shapiro defined these systems in terms of their relation to each other: "The opposition between flows of exchange and the inhibitions of sovereignty is oriented around issues of selfhood and location and consequently involves an emphasis either on ownership and the maintenance of authority and control or on reciprocity, substitutability, and the relaxation of control in order to produce expanded domains in which things can circulate."[1] Copyright battles reflect the mutually exclusive desires to maintain authority and control, and the necessity to relax control to facilitate circulation. The position a person takes in this debate is dependent on his or her economic incentive to either share or control information.

The sovereignty–exchange dynamic is an important conceptual tool for understanding the history of copyright. As Shapiro noted, sovereignty systems focus on ownership and maintenance, but of course have elements of exchange. Exchange systems tend to focus on circulation, but also have elements of sovereignty. Problems arise in sovereignty systems when tendencies toward greater exchange disrupt the authority of the status quo. The history of copyright follows this conceptual model.

Producing sovereignty models involves a narrative process: "The process of asserting or making sovereignty models, as well as that of challenging them, involves active, interpretive struggles."[2] This chapter highlights the interpretive historical struggle over copyright law, dealing specifically with the English, German, Italian, and U.S. stories. Later chapters deal with modern interpretive struggles.

English copyright history illustrates how authorship has been used to enclose "new territories" under the rubric of private ownership.[3] It is often forgotten that what appears to be a solid foundation is actually a social construction.[4] Specifically, copyright is a socially constructed discourse that has become a powerful social myth.[5] This myth, constructed over the past 200 years, has taken on the power of truth in which its assumptions and history are ignored.

Brad Sherman and Alain Strowel noted in the introduction to their collection of essays on copyright that copyright is a body of law that has yet to be put "in context," meaning it is only now being subjected to the historical scrutiny other aspects of law have already undergone.[6] Changes made to copyright because of technology, new cultural forms (like digital sampling), and international agreements have sparked growing interest in this field.[7] In order to understand its present manifestations, we must first understand copyright's history.

HISTORY OF COPYRIGHT: THE ENGLISH EXPERIENCE

In discussing the history of copyright, we need to start with authorship because copyright and authorship go hand in hand. Copyright protects the property of an author. In Paul Goldstein's words, "copyright, in a word, is about authorship."[8] Although this statement appears unproblematic, a brief history illustrates the energy and political debate involved in creating copyright and the proprietary author. The emergence of copyright in 18th-century English law serves as a point of departure.

In 1476, the printing press was introduced in England. The printing press made several innovations possible. First, duplications became easier and more accurate. Second, mass distribution became viable. The printing press revolutionized information storage, retrieval, and usage. "Printing, unlike writing, allowed a society to build on the past with a confidence that each step was being made on a firm foundation. Printing generated confidence that new information was an improvement over the old. The revolution in the ability to accurately reproduce works fostered an understanding that progress can occur through a process of revision and improvement."[9]

Thus, printing made possible the modern book, as well as concepts of progress and scholarship. Before printing, the oldest written copy was considered the most correct because inaccuracies tended to develop with each hand-copied work. Written texts evolved based on who was doing the copying and which parts were of interest to them. The increased accuracy and rapidity of the newer editions, which resulted from the printing press, made recent editions more valued than older ones. Printing provided a mechanism through which a larger reading public developed, thus contributing to an emerging public sphere.[10] Eventually, because of increased access to printed material, a literate public emerged that consumed printed matter. Who owned information and profited from printed work became crucial questions as this market developed.

Starting in 1529, laws were passed requiring manuscripts to be licensed with the Stationers' Company. An important consideration, at least for the Crown, were the numerous dissident tracts made available through the printing press. Consequently, copyright was a controlling mechanism for the British government.[11] Copyright during the 16th and 17th centuries was more a matter of censorship inhibiting publication than a matter of protection for author's rights. It wasn't until later that authorial protection moved to center stage.

In order for an intellectual property system to be realized, Mark Rose argued several criteria needed to be met. First, "a sufficient market for books to sustain a commercial system of cultural production" had to exist.[12] Second, "the concept of the author as the originator of a literary text rather than as the reproducer of traditional truths had to be more fully realized."[13] Third, "there had to be an adequate theory of property, or, more precisely, an adequate mode of discourse about property, a language in which the idea of the proprietary author could [be] elaborated," a discourse realized with John Locke's theory on property.[14] The printing press and the corresponding expansion in literacy and writing created the market necessary for Rose's first criteria. Next, the author had to be linked to the text as owner of the text. This crucial step was done throughout the stories told about authorship, creativity, inspiration, and ownership.

The 1688 revolution in England provided an opening for the emergence of a debate on liberty and property. Rose noted that after the 1688 revolution there was a stronger emphasis on liberty and property in the public discourse. Although not complete, this new discourse helped build foundations for the author as proprietor in the early 18th century.[15] Corresponding notions of rights in tangible property facilitated this discourse. Making the link between tangible and intangible property was a critical aspect of the emerging discourse over proprietary authorship.

The metaphors employed were useful in analyzing the copyright story. Metaphors were used to make familiar the unfamiliar and provide a conceptual framework for action. A variety of metaphors were tested in the rudimentary stage of this discourse in order to make the best possible case for protection. In an effort to establish who the good guys were, the author was depicted as shepherd, vessel of divine inspiration, magician, and monarch during the 16th and 17th century. Paternity became a common metaphor as well.[16] Eventually, the metaphor of a landed estate was favored. The author, in this final metaphor, worked at a literary creation. The value he added made the work his property. Rose explained: "The figuration of the literary work as a form of estate would be reiterated and elaborated, and it contributed to a new way of thinking about literature."[17] The landed estate metaphor brought to intangible property the characteristics of tangible property. Thus, the narrative emerging was one that privileged authorship as proprietary.

During the late 18th century, private property rapidly replaced the English commons, as exemplified by laws being passed prohibiting peasants from catching fish or killing deer. The landed property metaphor was a powerful tool for understanding how one could own ideas, as well as land.[18] By aligning the author in this emerging drama with landed estates, the people engaged in this discourse could easily draw on images of theft and hardship related to loss of property. The idea of the author as the owner of ideas emerged as a concept equally threatened by trespassing as the landed property owner. Thus, understanding the author as a property owner was best explained by using the metaphor of a landed estate and equivocating land with ideas—both could be owned.

Prior to the Statute of Anne, or the Copyright Act of 1709, printed matter was controlled via the Licensing Act, which allowed authorities to prohibit publication of anything dangerous. The Licensing Act, repealed in 1694, mandated all books be licensed by registering them with the Stationers' Company. Once registered with the Company, the work became the "copies" of the Stationers' Company.[19] Registration occurred when the book was entered into the register. The Company recorded who owned the "copyright."[20] The Stationers' Company, the body established to censor printed material by the Crown, had a virtual monopoly over all printed matter. The emergence of the "copyright" endorsed the Stationers' Company right to copy rather than the author's right to own.

Logically, one might expect that the booksellers would lobby for the Statute of Anne because the elimination of the Licensing Act left them without protection for their copyrights and thus vulnerable to illegal reproductions.[21] However, both Rose and Peter Prescott explained why this did not occur. As Prescott argued, the Stationers' Company was not immediately affected by the loss of the Licensing Act because they were, essentially, a book cartel. The Stationers' Company controlled prices, determined what was published, and excluded outsiders. Working as a guild, the booksellers of London effectively excluded outsiders from competing in the London market. The guild was replete with a mandatory 7-year apprenticeship and each member was required to follow guild rules.

Within the printing monopoly, licensing was merely a helpful, but not essential, way of controlling the publication of books. The monopoly could be maintained because the names inscribed in the stationer's ledger were not the names of authors, they were the names of printers. Authors sold their books to printers, usually for a flat fee, thus giving up rights to publication and any further royalties, even if the book was popular. Generally, once entered into the ledger, this "copyright" was respected by the other members of the guild. Within the guild, the "copyright" to books written by individuals who had died hundreds of years ago (and thus no longer subject to protection) were still bought and sold. The printer who owned the copyright for these older manuscripts was the only one who could "legitimately" reproduce the book in question for sale.

The Statute of Anne was not intended as a copyright protection act, but as a trade-regulation act. Its principle function was to regulate the book trade.[22] Among other things, the Statute of Anne reduced the copyright term to 14 years, with a possible renewal for another 14 available to the author. It made statutory copyright protection available to anyone, not just the stationers. Finally, copyrights in already published material were extended 21 more years, but then would enter the public domain. This last provision specifically addressed the concerns of the London booksellers and their already existing copyrights.

The 21-year extension of copyrights created for the London booksellers a buffer that explains why the two important landmark cases on English copyright did not occur until later. As Patterson noted, "Although the Statute of Anne was enacted in 1709, it was 1774 before it finally reached the House of Lords for a definitive construction. Events and circumstances of the sixty-five years since its enactment had obscured both the background of the legislation and its antecedents. Fundamental changes had occurred between the enactment of the statute and its construction by the Courts."[23] The Statute of Anne was created to prevent monopolies in the book trade. Thus, with the prospect of the monopoly tumbling, booksellers began developing arguments to justify their continued control.

During this period it was customary for the author to sell his or her work to the bookseller who then reprinted it at will. The author, however, maintained some basic rights to the text. The bookseller could not change the words, or add to the text. The booksellers began building a common law approach to copyright to address the "rights" authors continued to hold after they sold books to publishers. These rights included the right to sell the work, thus protecting the publisher, too.

As Patterson attested, "Although the author had never held copyright, his interest was always promoted by the stationers as a means to their end."[24] With the end of the 21-year extension, the London booksellers began what has become known as the "Battle of the Booksellers" where they campaigned for perpetual copyright. By presenting this controversy as a battle, a narrative with clear actors, heroes, and villains was created. This battle used the assertion of an author's right as its standard. In this battle to form a coherent rhetorical community, the author became the hero in desperate need of protection from those who stole the author's work.

The London book cartel called these villains *pirates*. These pirates were guilty of printing books belonging to the London cartel.[25] This controversy sparked heated debates, letters, articles, and narratives about piracy and more generally the rights of authorship.[26] The London booksellers detailed the tragic story of piracy with their personal horrors. Piracy, it was told, was ruining the lives of honest businessmen and their families. The copies (books) were the inheritances of these innocents, and thus pirates were deftly stealing from the mouths of babes.[27] The story told by publishers about piracy was appropriated by those advocating authors and used to illustrate the problems with lax protection for authors. These personal tragedies established the narrative tone for policymaking. Although these pathetic narratives were not the only factor influencing decision making, they did help obscure the more powerful logic of profit.

In 1769, the publishers won a victory in *Millar v. Taylor*. This decision, which was overturned 5 years later by *Donaldson v. Beckett*, succeeded in fixing the idea of copyright as an author's right.[28] Even though *Millar* was overturned, it conceptually created author's rights in their work. Future law, even though it limited this right, began with the assumption that authors had rights invested in their work. In a somewhat tricky maneuver, this coup ultimately benefited the booksellers. Patterson explained:

> The change, however, was less a boon to authors than to publishers, for it meant that copyright was to have another function. Rather than being simply the right of a publisher to be protected against piracy, copyright would henceforth be a concept embracing all the rights that an author might have in his published work. And since copyright was

still available to the publisher, the change meant also that the publisher as copyright owner would have the same rights as the author.[29]

Even though the booksellers failed to establish a perpetual copyright in *Millar*, they succeeded in establishing the natural right of the author as proprietor. This right transferred to the publisher on purchase of the copyright. The booksellers helped solidify a way of thinking about authorship beneficial to those owning the copyright to authorial works.

It must also be recognized that the Statute of Anne was passed almost immediately after the unification of England and Scotland. Scotland had a printing trade, but no law of copyright. In 1707, England and Scotland united. In 1709, the Statute of Anne was passed. There is, in fact, a connection between these two events. The booksellers in London had other means of protecting their monopoly and were not worried until it became clear Scottish booksellers were competing with London booksellers. Scottish booksellers, in the 18th-century battle of the booksellers, were the pirates used to justify new copyright law. Scottish booksellers would print texts at much lower prices than their London competitors. This practice, of course, became extremely controversial. Thus, the intent of the Statute of Anne was twofold: First, to protect against future monopolies in the bookselling trade and, second, to draw Scotland under some form of copyright law. Of course, in reacting to the latter and wishing to avoid the former, the Statute of Anne succeeded in conferring all rights in a book to publishers for a limited amount of time instead of some rights for an unlimited amount of time.

After 70 years and numerous arguments about the natural rights of an author, *Donaldson v. Beckett* became the landmark case. *Donaldson v. Beckett* addressed common law versus statutory author's rights. The case found that an author of a literary text had a common law right of ownership that was held in perpetuity. The Statute of Anne restrained, or pre-empted this common law right, and limited an author's right to statutory ones.[30] Patterson argued this decision was rendered to break the bookselling monopoly. However, although copyright had been transformed from a publisher's right to an author's right, the publisher was still the beneficiary. The Battle of the Booksellers may not have provided publishers with a perpetual copyright, but it served its function by creating the proprietary author and the literary work as legal concepts that defined the "center of the modern literary system."[31]

Within the cultural framework of 18th-century England, the battle over copyright raged.[32] The concept of the *modern proprietary author* was used as a weapon in the struggle between the London booksellers and the booksellers of the provinces.[33] Clear victims and victimizers emerged, as did a general understanding about the necessity to protect an author's rights. The narrative was successful in establishing the rights of authors as filtered through booksellers. The economic benefits gained by advocates of an author's right ensured a strong defense of copyright in the future.

Over the next 100 years, the text became defined more clearly as a bounded entity instead of a speech act. Rose stressed that in the early modern period texts were thought of as actions instead of things. In part, the move toward proprietary authorship transformed texts-as-actions into texts-as-things that through labor an author had created.[34] The author became the focal point instead of the relationship between the text and author or the text as an act. What is unique about the *Donaldson* decision is the "development of 'intellectual property' as a creation of the author's intellect."[35] Prior to this approach, the author was firmly associated with the past and with the scholarship on which he relied.[36] However, assigning ownership is critical in a discourse emphasizing sovereignty. The author as boundary between texts instead of engaged in a dialogue with the text became the primary paradigm. Although author's rights were the London publisher's tool to maintain strict control over copyrights, the result was a profound impact on how literary works and intellectual property were perceived. This new social relation also transformed the way society perceived the ownership of knowledge.

HISTORY OF COPYRIGHT: THE GERMAN EXPERIENCE

Whereas Rose focused on England, Martha Woodmansee studied the emergence of the proprietary author in Germany. Although there are differences between German and English copyright protection, a similar discourse on authors developed. In Germany there were no copyright protections. Authors sold their books at a flat rate to publishers who then profited by reproducing them. No law protected German booksellers. Piracy became widespread as protection remained minimal while literacy increased.[37] The only protection available to German booksellers was the "privilege."[38] The book privilege, like the English Statute of Anne, was created to protect the rights of printers, not authors.

However, wrapped within the publisher's desire to protect its copyright was a fundamentally new way of understanding authorship. As the economic advantages of authorship grew, the author was able to sell his ideas in the marketplace instead of relying on patronage. A radical transformation in authorship was underway as the printers vied for better copyright protection. Instead of ideas originating with God, the concept of *original genius* developed: "That is, inspiration came to be regarded as emanating not from outside or above, but from within the writer himself. 'Inspiration' came to be explicated in terms of original *genius*, with the consequence that the inspired work was made peculiarly and distinctively the product—and the property—of the writer."[39] Inspiration became central in understanding how the creation of ideas occurred. As inspiration was centered, it transformed the writer into a unique individual responsible for a unique product.[40] Consequently, 18th-century theorists re-made the author.[41] By making ideas the original creation of an author, it became logical that the author could own the resulting work.

Of course, there were still problematic aspects of this new form of authorship. If the author can be assigned ownership of a book, then how can the author turn this book over to the publisher to publish? Within the 18th century, theorists made the distinction between the physical object of a book and the expression of the ideas within the book. The first was not the property of the author, but the "original creation" of the ideas could remain personal property.[42]

Both Rose and Woodmansee developed a perspective with far-reaching implications for authorship. The transformation of the author during this period was fundamental for understanding modern authorship. And, of course, the understanding of authorship emerging in the 18th century best served the booksellers.

The book as property passed from author to publisher quickly. It was the publisher that reaped the vast majority of the profits.[43]

Because the booksellers were privileged by this new economic relationship, "the goal of protecting the rights of the creative author is proudly asserted even as the notion of author is drained of content."[44] What is concealed is who benefits from such a movement toward sovereignty.

HISTORY OF COPYRIGHT: THE FRENCH EXPERIENCE

The development of authorship described by Woodmansee and Rose does not stand uncontested. Carla Hesse studied the emergence of authorship and copyright in 18th-century France. Although not rejecting Rose and Woodmansee's conclusions, she argued that the French revolution provided a distinctly different starting point for the debate over authorship. Two authorship stories emerge in the French debate in comparison to the monological discourse identified by Rose and Woodmansee. As Hesse noted, "The French Revolution offered the occasion for an unusually explicit and fascinating debate in France about the identity and role of the author in modern life, a debate whose legal resolution continues to provide the foundation for French copyright law. A closer examination of this debate and its resolution throws into question some of the historical claims of Foucault and his successors, and thus their characterization of modern cultural life as well."[45] In France, two discourses of authorship emerged. One was similar to the English and

German experiences—that ideas originate in the individual mind "and not acquired through appropriation or labor, are the most natural and inviolable form of property."[46] This argument, Hesse agreed, is consistent with Rose's genealogy.

France diverged from Germany and England because a viable second position on authorship was advanced by Condorcet. Condorcet argued against the individual claim to knowledge as property. "He imagined an authorless world of free manipulation and circulation of information and ideas."[47] At this point, Hesse argued, Foucault's position (emulated by Rose) needed to be revised because in France two discourses on the nature of the author emerged. The discourses constituted a tension between the enlightenment view of ideas as property and Condorcet's notion of knowledge as communitarian. In France, the Crown endorsed the notion of ideas as property, whereas the will to overthrow the absolute author was the position of the French revolutionaries. Hesse's point is that the emerging discourse on authorship was unstable from the beginning.[48]

Although the emergence of the author was significantly different in France, the same tensions emerged. These tensions were between greater sovereignty over the idea and greater exchange. Yes, the French were more concerned about the public good at this moment in history, whereas the English did not find a notion of public good as compelling. However, even with the greater influence of the public good argument, the tendency toward greater control over ideas remained visible in the French debate. Ultimately, the notion of the public good became crucial to understanding copyright law. So was the notion of the proprietary author. These two tensions became the heart of modern copyright. What Hesse did was provide another side to an ongoing struggle between sovereignty and exchange. However, as Rose pointed out, his story is also one of irresolution and speaks to the ongoing struggle between sovereignty and exchange. The struggle to fix literary property continues today.[49]

What Hesse illuminated is the political struggle between contending discourses on authorship. At any point in history, one will prevail over the other. Rose argued that a discourse favoring publishers was the result of the English experience. It is clear that these tensions continue to prevail today.

HISTORY OF COPYRIGHT: SYNTHESIZING THE ROLE OF THE AUTHOR

Pamela O. Long turned to 13th-century Italy for a different interpretation of the development of intellectual property and authorship. Long criticized Rose, Woodmansee, and Hesse for taking too narrow a view of copyright and its relation to authorship. She stated:

> The work of these scholars constitutes significant and sophisticated analysis of 18th-century copyright issues. In my view, however, they oversimplify the prior history of intellectual property and authorship. They are able to do this by defining copyright too narrowly as the moral right of authors over their own literary productions within the framework of Lockean notions of natural rights, and the 18th-century commercial book market. Yet copyright concerns the notions of intangible property, limited monopoly, social utility, and the prerogatives of authors over their writings before John Locke's formulation of natural rights, as well as the issues noted above. Even for the 18th century, as the legal historian Jane C. Ginsburg has demonstrated, author's rights do not always occupy a central place within legal history.[50]

Long's critique about focusing too narrowly on copyright as literary work is well taken. However, construction of an author's moral right is not the only issue. An equally important issue is the development of a significantly different approach to knowledge production that depends on authors as owners. The text is redefined as a bounded entity that is no longer an act, but an object. This is an important transformation.

Prior to the 18th century, proprietary authorship was far from accepted in England or Germany. Although a market economy emerged earlier for tangible objects, a book market was late in arrival. Woodmansee and Rose would probably agree that the invention of the printing press several centuries earlier was critical in the developing discourse on authorship. It was only at the moment when author's rights could be used instrumentally by the booksellers that they became an issue. This crucial watershed was reached when printers realized they could no longer maintain a monopoly over printed work, which happened in England with the passage of the Statute of Anne. It is important to remember that copyright emerged because of the economic interests of the booksellers. The emergence of print as a significant social medium allowed for the debate over economic controlling forces to be played out in the 18th century. The tension between sovereignty and exchange emerged, especially in France, and was settled in favor of sovereignty. The notion of the proprietary author emerged as victorious, resulting in better protection for the booksellers.

The impact of the discourse of original genius and authorship obscures that "cultural production is always a matter of appropriation and transformation."[51] Instead, authorship is isolated as "original" and literary works are separated from each other because they are written by distinct authors. Appropriation and transformation as a more appropriate description of authorial work is the subject of much modern literary theory, and I return to this issue in later chapters.

Copyright lacks a strong conceptual history because it emerged as a legal framework with a specific task. Although it draws on the philosophy of the time, including Locke and Hegel, copyright generally was designed with a utilitarian function in mind. In creating such a utilitarian law, however, those arguing for strong protection produced the proprietary author that failed to reflect the manner in which written work is produced. It is a concept used strategically over the centuries to produce favorable results for its beneficiaries. There is a large gap between legal definitions of authorship and literary definitions.[52] The U.S. situation does nothing to diminish this gap, rather it reproduced the assumptions of authorship.

AMERICAN COPYRIGHT LAW

By the time America began thinking about intellectual property, much of the narrative work had been developed and the resulting discourse was accepted uncritically as truth and factual. Property rights were a central issue in the emerging American states. Justin Hughes wrote: "Ideas about property have played a central role in shaping the American legal order. For every Pilgrim who came to the New World in search of religious freedom, there was at least one colonist who came on the promise of a royal land grant or one slave compelled to come as someone else's property."[53]

Concern over property was evidenced in the constitutional debates between the Federalists and the Anti-federalists.[54] The American founders were primarily concerned with tangible property, meaning land, businesses, and even people. However, Americans also brought with them a notion of intellectual property that was quickly codified.

Paul Goldstein's *Copyright, Patent, Trademark and Related State Doctrines* provides specific cases that have led to an understanding of how copyright is interpreted in the United States. This record demonstrates that it was the English copyright system that was adopted by the American colonies.[55] When the notion of an author's right crossed the ocean, so did the tension between sovereignty and exchange.

Patterson broke U.S. development of intellectual property law into four stages, each of which emphasizes a different perspective on copyright. American copyright includes state copyright statutes, a constitutional provision, the federal Copyright Act of 1790, and the precedent-setting case of *Wheaton v. Peters* in 1834.[56] The four ideas and corresponding protections were: "The idea that copyright is primarily for the benefit of the author was central to the state statutes; that copyright is necessary for learning was central to the constitutional provision; that copyright is a government grant (or statutory privilege) was central to the first federal copyright act; and that copyright was to prevent monopoly was central to the *Wheaton* case."[57] Through a variety of different channels, Americans incorporated all the perspectives of copyright within the newly created U.S. law.

Every state had written provisions to grant copyright protection to authors who were citizens of the United States prior to the U.S. Constitution.[58] Even though Americans were suspicious of monopolies, this limited form of monopoly was granted to protect the public interest "by encouraging literary and mechanical innovation."[59] Later, copyright was written into the U.S. Constitution, "[t]o promote the progress of science and useful arts, by securing for limited times to authors and inventors the exclusive right to their respective writings and discoveries."[60] One of the few powers to regulate commerce initially granted to Congress was the ability to grant patents and copyrights.[61]

The first federal Copyright Act passed on May 31, 1790. This act was designed to protect printed work from piracy and protected maps, books, and charts for a 14-year term. A 14-year renewal was provided for living authors.[62] The law conveyed a statutory privilege, not a right. This statutory privilege mirrored the decision in *Donaldson v. Beckett* where author's common law rights were superseded by statutory rights. Additionally, it appears the founders of the U.S. Constitution were less willing to confer a natural rights philosophy to intellectual property. Most notably, Thomas Jefferson explicitly wrote there was no natural right in inventions or ideas. Jefferson believed that:

> "Ideas should freely spread from one to another over the globe, for the moral and mutual instruction of man, and improvement of his condition. . . ." This is why nature made ideas, "like fire, expansible over all space . . . and like air . . . incapable of confinement or exclusive appropriation." Societies may choose to protect the property of ideas in order to encourage useful inventions. Elsewhere, Jefferson indicates that he approves of such protection, but there is no natural right to the protection of this form of property.[63]

Because a natural rights philosophy held little weight, and indeed an attitude of exchange was supported, protection in the United States became exclusively statutory. Authors had a statutory right to protection in order to provide incentive for innovation. But there was no moral or natural right. This is a divergence from the English law that continued to be persuaded by a common law author's right, even if statutory law took precedence.

The Copyright Statute of 1790 was amended in 1802 to allow, among other things, protection for prints. It was amended in 1831 to extend protection to musical compositions and extended the term of protection to 28 years. It was amended again in 1834.

The first important copyright case was *Wheaton v. Peters* in 1834. This landmark decision closely mirrored *Donaldson v. Beckett*. The Court concluded there was no common law copyright and that statutory protection could only be obtained by adhering to the 1790 act.[64] The Court confirmed that copyright was a privilege, not a right.[65] This case was about protection against monopoly and established the English precedent in the United States. Although the United States rejected what later became an author's moral right, it affirmed the economic rationale for copyright. The proprietary author unproblematically found its way into U.S. copyright law.

Today, the growing trend in property rights discourse is toward intangible forms of property. As Hughes noted, "A less frequently discussed trend is that historically recognized but nonetheless atypical forms of property, such as intellectual property, are becoming increasingly important relative to the old paradigms of property, such as farms, factories, and furnishings."[66]

In part, this trend reflects the commodification of abstractions such as music, art, literature, and ideas. Where once a discourse of tangible property developed in order to protect the interests of those in the position to acquire property, now a discourse of intangible property is used to privatize the intangible. The discourse of private property is used to expand the scope of what can be owned or, in other words, to extend sovereignty.

The law has undergone numerous changes in order to expand protection to music, paintings, drawings, motion pictures, sound recordings, and most recently computer software. The Copyright Act of 1976 was signed into law by President Gerald Ford and marked the most recent statutory manifestation of copyright. In 1989, the United States joined the Berne Convention for the Protection of Literary and Artistic Works.

Even though the United States joined the Berne Convention, it explicitly rejected the moral rights position on copyright in favor of utilitarian rights of authorship. Although the Berne Convention protects moral rights, the United States, in a departure from European law, understands copyright as utilitarian.[67] The Berne Convention in Article 6[bis] gives the author "the right to claim authorship of the work and to object to any distortion, mutilation or other modification, of, or other derogatory action in relation to, the said work, which would be prejudicial to his honor or reputation."[68] This moral right of authorship relies on the natural right notion of property.[69] As previously discussed, the United States rejected the natural rights philosophy as it applies to intellectual property.

I assert, however, that the rationale for rejecting a natural rights philosophy today is significantly different than the 18th-century reasoning. The 18th-century reasoning was reliant on a belief in exchange of ideas for the promotion of a better society—the enlightenment ideal. Today, the United States is concerned with protecting an economic system. Our intellectual property system, like the London booksellers, uses the author as justification for continued support of copyright law. The traditional story of copyright as protecting the individual creative author is endlessly repeated in order to affirm the commonly shared rhetorical vision of copyright. The claim is constantly made by U.S. industries that without copyright protection, authors would lack incentive to produce creative work. The repetition of the copyright story ensures its continued acceptance as new generations of government officials and businesspeople uncritically accept the assumptions of intellectual property without knowledge of its specific historical context.

AUTHORSHIP AS MALE

It is not possible to understand the historical construction of copyright law without understanding its gendered dimensions. The philosophy of intellectual property has its roots in Locke and Hegel and hinges on the definition of intellectual work as private property.[70] The combination of Locke's theory of property, the patriarchal environment of the late 17th and early 18th century, and the characteristics of the book market, created a discourse on copyright that was masculine in nature. Both Locke and Hegel have been the subject of extensive feminist critique that I will not repeat here.[71] However, the link between feminism and intellectual property deserves some space.[72]

Intellectual property is about masculine creation. Ideas, expressed through the labor of an author, become property that can be possessed. Property generally, and authorship more specifically, are seen as masculine domains. Women, whose status as authors was problematic long before the institutionalization of intellectual property laws, were discouraged from writing and from participating in public life.

Women who published faced a twofold problem. First, they were discouraged from printing because it did not fit with the accepted feminine ideal. As Wendy Wall stated,

> Women in early modern England faced tremendous obstacles in establishing themselves as public figures of any kind. Literary and historical scholars have dramatized these prohibitions quite glaringly in past years, as they have documented restrictions on female education; the link between public speech and harlotry; the definition of the woman's domain as that of domestic piety; the identification of silence as a feminine ideal; and the mastery of rhetoric as a male puberty rite. Constrained by the norms of acceptable feminine behavior, women

> were specifically discouraged from tapping into the newly popular channel of print; to do so threatened the cornerstone of their moral and social well-being.[73]

A second problem for female authors was the reliance on a discourse that masculinized publication and feminized that which was published.

> By using the female body as a metaphor for the newly commodified book, both became defined as unruly objects in need of supervision and governance. When they imagined the female body as a medium for articulating power, whether dismembered in poetic fragments or as a corporeal sign for the text, writers consolidated their shaky social status as publishing writers. One result was the creation of a masculinized notion of authorship. . . . If women were tropes necessary to the process of writing, if they were constructed within genres as figures for male desire, with what authority could they publish? How could a woman become an author if she was the "other" against whom "authors" differentiated themselves?[74]

Thus, once booksellers got around to institutionalizing property rights in published works, women were already virtually excluded from authorship.[75]

This discourse, which emerged when regulation for the book trade was needed, was premised on male creation and birth. It was necessary to mark intellectual property through authorship and creativity. In Hegel's philosophy, property became an expression of one's will and personality.[76] Literary property was "original" because it originated from the uniqueness of a person's mind.[77] Many metaphors were utilized in an effort to describe the act of authorship and legitimate ownership of the ideas.

> The metaphors in which these earliest discussions of authorial property are couched reveal something about the sources of a new discourse of authorship. In the sixteenth and seventeenth centuries, various figures were employed to represent the author's relation to his writing, including the author as singing shepherd, tiller of the soil, vessel of divine inspiration, magician, and monarch. But the most common figure in the early modern period is paternity: the author as begetter and the book as child.[78]

All the metaphors were masculine ones. Each conceptualized writing as masculine. The paternity metaphor is significant for understanding copyright from a feminist perspective. It speaks to male creation and to the larger issue of legitimacy. Copyright invited the author to own his work. The work was not only the child of the author, but his property. Men were concerned with paternity. Authorship was a method for establishing paternity over a text, the male creation. Eventually, the metaphor of book as child became problematic once authors wanted to sell their labor in a marketplace. The metaphor broke down because if books are children, and children are to be valued not sold, why would authors sell their work? The "book-as-child" metaphor gave way to the book as a form of landed property. However, the paternity metaphor helped illustrate what later metaphors served to conceal—literary creation is masculine creation.

Although women still became authors, Wall suggested they did so either at great expense, or by appropriating specific genres of writing considered acceptable for women. An acceptable genre for women was the will, because it was societally acceptable for a dying woman to leave instructions to her children. Women appropriated this genre as an avenue into the public sphere as authors. Wills became subversive avenues into the largely male-dominated public sphere.[79]

Intellectual property emerged from a distinctly masculine history. Women writing during the Renaissance did so at their own risk. However, by appropriating forms of authorship, women continued to write legitimately. One cannot discuss the emergence of the proprietary author without noting that this is a male construction and as such holds yet another dimension of power that must be considered.

CONCLUSION: THE TRADITIONAL STORY OF COPYRIGHT

By the traditional story of copyright I mean the reasons given for why copyright exists and works. The law helps spread this story as truth by providing an avenue of action and a form of punishment for those who disobey. Thus, although a story such as copyright begins as a localized (or specialized) discourse, it becomes something everyone must pay attention to when the law brings it into contact with our everyday lives.

It is a simple story with only a few parts. First, an author is inspired by an idea. Second, the author expresses this idea in a tangible form. Third, the idea is the proprietary work of the author, meaning no one else can copy, distribute, or borrow from the work. Fourth, the author is protected via copyright, which provides the atmosphere in which creation can take place. As the author is creating, there are numerous villains waiting to pounce on the new idea and use it to benefit themselves. These villains include plagiarists, thieves, and pirates who have no respect for author's rights.

Jeremy Waldron did an excellent job of encapsulating the traditional story:

> The reasoning goes like this. The overall social good is served by the progress of science and useful arts. The progress of science and useful arts is served by the encouragement of authors. The encouragement of authors is secured by providing them with the incentive of legally secured monopoly profits from the sale and circulation of their works over a limited period of time. Incentives work by conferring benefits on those whose activity we are trying to encourage. Such a benefit may be seen as a reward for their efforts. Rewards are what we characteristically provided for moral desert; we reward the deserving and penalize the undeserving. Therefore, authors deserve the intellectual property rights that are secured to them in the name of social policy. The thought moves from *encouragement* to *incentive* to *benefit* to *reward* to *desert*, so that something which starts off as a matter of desirable social policy ends up entrenched in an image of moral entitlement.[80]

Missing from the traditional story is the step where authors transfer their bundles of sticks to the publisher who then holds sole proprietary interest over the work and continues to profit with very little going back to the authors.[81] This story is the result of years of energy directed at producing a mechanism through which to define and control literary property. It continues to take narrative energy to exist, as is illustrated in later chapters.

What would an alternative story look like? Much of chapter 8 is dedicated to this proposition. However, keeping in mind that copyright is a tension between sovereignty and exchange of ideas, an alternative story might place more emphasis on creation and less on ownership. Authors, poets, musicians, artists, and academics are rarely motivated solely by economic incentives. Only through a process of commercialization has copyright come to mean protection for economic gain. Thinkers such as Condorcet and Jefferson embraced the enlightenment tradition of the free flow of ideas. The exchange of ideas, if given precedent over the ownership of ideas, establishes a distinctly different framework through which to view property. It is the free exchange of ideas that is the premise of an alternative story. The issues and premises of an alternative story of intellectual property are discussed in later chapters. It is mentioned here in preview form only in order to establish the tension that can exist between copyright and its alternatives.

In this chapter, I have attempted to provide an overview of the traditional copyright story. Critical to the traditional story is the concept of a proprietary author, the original genius working as an individual unit to produce creative work. The next two chapters bring us into the present, where new technology is challenging the assumptions of the traditional story by providing avenues for actions that subvert the control of copyright. These chapters illustrate how new technology is gradually being incorporated into the traditional story in an effort to avoid the possible transformation that can occur if information is allowed to flow freely. The traditional copyright story, which emphasizes sovereignty, tends to transform citizens who care little about ownership of creative work and information into good consumers of information who will respect the boundaries of intellectual property.

NOTES

1. M. J. Shapiro, "Sovereignty and exchange in the orders of modernity," *Alternatives, 16* (1991): 448.
2. M. J. Shapiro, *Reading "Adam Smith": Desire, history and value* (Newbury Park, CA, London, & New Delhi: SAGE Publications, 1993), 38.
3. M. Rose, *Authors and owners: The invention of copyright* (London & Cambridge, MA: Harvard University Press, 1993), 133.
4. The larger question of social construction as always framing our realities is taken up by Pierre Bourdieu and Peter Burger and Thomas Luckman. See: P. Bourdieu, *Outline of a theory of practice,* trans. R. Nice (Cambridge: Cambridge University Press, 1977); see also: P. Berger, & T. Luckman, *The social construction of reality: A treatise in the sociology of knowledge* (Garden City, NY: Doubleday, 1996).
5. "We reach here the very principle of myth: It transforms history into nature." See: R. Barthes, *Mythologies,* trans. A. Lavers (New York: Hill & Wang, 1972), 129.
6. B. Sherman, & A. Strowel, *Of authors and origins: Essays on copyright law* (Oxford: Clarendon Press, 1994), 1.
7. Ibid., 1–2.
8. P. Goldstein, "Copyright," *Law and Contemporary Problems* (Spring 1992): p. 80.
9. M. E. Katsh, *The electronic media and the transformation of law* (New York & Oxford: Oxford University Press, 1989), 34.
10. J. Habermas, *The structural transformation of the public sphere: An inquiry into a category of bourgeois society*, trans. T. Burger, (Cambridge, MA: MIT Press, 1989); B. Anderson, *Imagined communities: Reflections on the origin and spread of nationalism,* 2nd ed. (London & New York: Verso, 1991).
11. For this brief history see: D. Lange, "At play in the fields of the work: Copyright and the construction of authorship in the post-literate millennium," *Law and Contemporary Problems* (Spring 1992): 140.
12. M. Rose, "The author as proprietor: Donaldson v. Becket and the genealogy of modern authorship," *Representations, 23* (Summer 1988): 56.
13. Ibid.
14. Ibid.
15. Rose, *Authors and owners,* 37.
16. Ibid., 38–39.
17. Ibid., 41.

18. For a description of the "Black Act," the act that made "taking of rabbits from a warren, fish from a pond, or deer from a forest, as well as the cutting of any tree" punishable by death see: M. E. Tigar, "The right of property and the law of theft," *Texas Law Review, 62*(1984): 1443–1475.

19. For more information see: E. Earle, "The effect of Romanticism on the 19th century development of copyright law," *Intellectual Property Journal, 6* (6 September 1991): 269–290.

20. The preceding information comes from P. Prescott, "The origins of copyright: A debunking view," *European Intellectual Property Review* (1989): 453.

21. This is the analysis offered by Peter Prescott. I find it to be a clearly stated version of the politics leading up to the Statute of Anne. See: Ibid., 453–455.

22. L. R. Patterson, *Copyright in historical perspective* (Nashville, TN: Vanderbilt University Press, 1968), 143.

23. Ibid., 144.

24. Ibid., 147.

25. Rose, *Authors and owners,* 11–12.

26. For a description of the debates that raged, see: Ibid.

27. "So too the London booksellers and printers had regularly couched their pleas and petitions to Parliament in pathetic domestic terms, complaining that they, their wives, and their children were being utterly ruined by piracy. Their copies were their legacies, dowries, and estates." Ibid., 40.

28. Patterson, *Copyright in historical perspective,* 15.

29. Ibid., 151.

30. Ibid., 175.

31. Rose, *Authors and owners,* 91.

32. Rose, "The author as proprietor," 56.

33. Ibid.

34. Rose, *Authors and owners,* 13.

35. Earle, "The effect of romanticism," 278.

36. I use the pronoun "he" to refer to authors not as a generic noun, but because authors during the 18th century were almost exclusively male. I deal with this aspect of authorship later.

37. The notion of a pirate, a key villain, is discussed in chapter 4.

38. M. Woodmansee, "The genius and the copyright: Economic and legal conditions of the emergence of the author," *Eighteenth Century Studies, 17* (Summer 1984): 437.

39. Ibid., 427.

40. Ibid., 429

41. Ibid., 442.

42. "If a book could be reduced to its physical foundation, as he suggests, then of course it would be impossible for its author to lay claim to peculiar ownership of it, for it is precisely the book *qua* physical object that he turns over to the publisher when he delivers his manuscript and that, in another format, is eventually purchased by his readers. To ground the author's claim to ownership of his work, then, it would first be necessary to show that this work transcends its physical foundation. It would be necessary to show that it is an emanation of his intellect—an intentional, as opposed to a merely physical object." Ibid., 443.

43. Rose, *Authors and owners,* 120.

44. Ibid., 136.
45. C. Hesse, "Enlightenment epistemology and the laws of authorship in revolutionary France, 1777–1793," *Representations, 30* (1988): 111.
46. Ibid., 114–115.
47. Ibid., 116.
48. Ibid., 130.
49. Rose, *Authors and owners*, 8.
50. P. O. Long, "Invention, authorship, 'intellectual property,' and the origin of patents: Notes toward a conceptual history," *Technology and Culture* (October 1991): 847.
51. Rose, *Authors and owners*, 135.
52. M. E. Price, & M. Pollock, "The author in copyright: Notes for the literary critic," In *The construction of authorship: Textual appropriation in law and literature*, eds. M. Woodmansee & P. Jaszi, (Durham & London: Duke University Press, 1994), 441.
53. J. Hughes, "The philosophy of intellectual property," *The Georgetown Law Journal, 77* (1988): 288.
54. See: J. Nedelsky, *Private property and the limits of American constitutionalism: The Madisonian framework and its legacy* (Chicago & London: University of Chicago Press, 1990). Additionally, for general approaches to property, the constitution, and U.S. democracy see: A. Reeve, *Property* (London: MacMillan, 1986); D. A. Schultz, *Property, power, and American Democracy* (New Brunswick, NJ & London: Transaction Publishers, 1992); E. F. Paul, & H. Dickman, eds., *Liberty, property, and the foundations of the American Constitution* (Albany: State University of New York Press, 1989).
55. P. Goldstein, *Copyright, patent, trademark and related state doctrines: Cases and materials on the law of intellectual property*, 3rd ed. (Westbury, N.Y.: The Foundation Press, 1993); Lange, "At play in the fields of the word,"139–140.
56. Patterson, *Copyright in historical perspective*, 180.
57. Ibid., 181.
58. Ibid., 183–192; J. W. Ely, *The guardian of every other right: A constitutional history of property rights* (New York & Oxford: Oxford University Press, 1992), 32–33.
59. Ibid., 33.
60. U.S. Constitution, Article I § 8, clause 8.
61. B. H. Siegan, One people as to commercial objects, in *Liberty, property, and the foundations of the American Constitution*, eds. E. F. Paul, & H. Dickman, (Albany: State University of New York Press, 1989), 111.
62. Patterson, *Copyright in historical perspective*, 197–198.
63. J. Yarbrough, Jefferson and property rights, in *Liberty, property, and the foundations of the American Constitution*, eds., E. F. Paul, & H. Dickman (Albany: State University of New York Press, 1989), 67.
64. Ely, *The guardian of every other right*, 80; Patterson, *Copyright in historical perspective*, 203–212.
65. Patterson, *Copyright in historical perspective*, 205.
66. Hughes, "The philosophy of intellectual property," 288.
67. This is different from protecting utilitarian works. U.S. copyright law ex-

plicitly states that utilitarian works are not protected. *Mazer v. Stein*, 347 U.S. 201, 74 S.Ct. 460.

68. P. Goldstein, E. Kitch, & H. S. Perlman, *Selected statutes and international agreements on unfair competition, trademark, copyright and patent* (Westbury, NY: The Foundation Press, 1994), 338.

69. See: D. Vaver, Some agnostic observations on intellectual property, *Intellectual Property Journal, 6* (6 September 1990): 125–128.

70. Hughes, "The philosophy of intellectual property," 287–366.

71. For a general feminist critique see: M. A. Butler, Early liberal roots of feminism: John Locke and the attack on patriarchy, in *Feminist interpretations and political theory*, eds. M. L. Shanley, & C. Pateman (University Park: The Pennsylvania State University Press, 1991), 74–94. Butler argued there was room in Locke's notion of individuality and liberalism for some equality for women. Although he did not explicitly endorse a firm patriarchal system, which was at odds with his notion of liberalism, Locke recognized that his audience at the time, a male audience, did not want to hear that women were equals (p. 88). In Locke's theory, women were "capable of earning through their own labor, of owning property and of making contracts" (p. 90). So, presumably, they were able to own literary works and be authors as well. However, what Locke wrote and how society interpreted Locke (which was to see only men as having equal weight) are two different matters.

For a critique of Hegel see: S. Benhabib, "On Hegel, women and irony," ibid., 129–145. With Hegel, Benhabib argued, there is a clear assertion of the inferiority of the female gender. "Hegel rejects that differences between 'men' and 'women' are naturally defined, and instead sees them as part of the spirit of a people (*Volksgeist*), he leaves no doubt that he considers only one set of family relations and one particular division of labor between the sexes as rational and normatively right. This is the monogamic sexual practice of the European nuclear family, in which the woman is confined to the private sphere and the man to the public. To justify this arrangement, Hegel explicitly invokes the superiority of the male to the female while acknowledging their *functional complementarity* in the modern state" (p. 133). Once confined to the private sphere there is no chance of emerging as an author in the public one.

72. For more information on feminism and intellectual property see: D. Halbert, Poaching and plagiarizing: Intellectual property and feminist futures, in *Perspectives on plagiarism and intellectual property in a postmodern world*, eds. A. Roy, & L. Buranen (New York: State University of New York Press, in press).

73. W. Wall, *The imprint of gender: Authorship and publication in the English Renaissance* (Ithaca & London: Cornell University Press, 1993), 279–280.

74. Ibid., 282.

75. Wall made the argument that women subverted the masculine construction of authorship and published by taking advantage of genres considered specifically feminine, such as letters to children and will making. However, as a general rule, women were not considered authors during this time frame. See: Ibid., 283–340.

76. Hughes, "The philosophy of intellectual property," 333.

77. Rose, Of *authors and owners*, 120.

78. Ibid., 38.

79. Wall, *The imprint of gender*, 282–283.

80. J. Waldron, "From authors to copiers: Individual rights and social values in intellectual property," *Chicago-Kent Law Review, 68* (1993): 851.

81. Elvis is a case in point. His will did not confer the property in his image to his family. Thus, they cannot control how Elvis is portrayed. Additionally, when the town in which Elvis grew up wanted to erect a statue in honor of the performer, the owner of the copyright on Elvis refused to let it be built. The moral: Once you have sold your copyright, you have lost any rights you once had in the work. See: R. Coombe, "Author/izing the celebrity: Publicity rights, postmodern politics, and unauthorized genders," *Cardozo Arts and Entertainment* (1992): 373.

2

Controlling Technology: Political Narratives of Copyright

In 1976, the National Commission on New Technological Uses (CONTU) recommended that computer programs be included as "literary" works under the Copyright Act, making them subject to copyright law. With no legislative debate, Congress amended Section 102 of the Copyright Act to include computer programs as "literary" works.[1] Although the courts were left to determine the applicable degree of protection, the CONTU report set the stage for the absorption of new technology under copyright law. Much has happened since the CONTU report, including the development of the Internet. The Internet represents the most significant challenge to property rights in this century and the CONTU report provides an integral framework for understanding how this challenge will be confronted.

President Bill Clinton and Vice President Al Gore made the construction of a National Information Infrastructure (NII) a priority for their administration during the 1990s. Among the important issues associated with the NII are privacy rights, who should regulate and own the NII, obscenity, and the applicability of the First Amendment. When Congress became obsessed with the issue of children's access to pornography via the Internet, public attention turned toward issues of censorship.[2] The debate over privacy rights, security, and encryption technology has been highly politicized and is of great concern to those interested in the future of the Internet. However, while public attention has been turned toward pornography and encryption technology, an equally important aspect of the NII has failed to garner much public interest. This debate concerned the recommendations of the working group on intellectual property presented in July 1994 and the subsequent treatment of intellectual property issues as they relate to the Internet. These recommendations helped define the debate over the extent to which we will be able to exchange information using the Internet. The recommendations were introduced as legislation in the form of the NII Copyright Protection Act of 1995.

In 1976, it was not possible to envision the types of exchange that would be possible in the 1990s. Congress has been in a reactionary mode, attempting to make copyright law protect new technology. Instead of rethinking the meaning of intellectual property in an information age, Congress has opted to supplement the civil and criminal copyright codes in order to provide increased ability to punish infringers. Ultimately, these legislative acts help clarify the importance of intellectual property to the U.S. economy and are vital in the narrative of property rights.

It is instructive at this point to review why intellectual property evolved in the United States in the manner it did. As discussed in chapter 1, intellectual property in the United States was designed to protect copyright owners. Granting such temporary monopolies over intellectual property was considered a necessary evil in order to promote the arts and sciences. This monopoly right was not always as extensive as it is today. At one point, a person could display a book, read from it publicly, or write other books based on it without violating copyright. Copyright was interpreted quite strictly to mean only the direct plagiarism of a work, and most creative activity surrounding a given work was considered legitimate.[3] As protection became the central focus of copyright law, the range in which one could use a text was slowly limited.

The expansion of intellectual property rights has served to protect the right of the owners from unauthorized use. The control and dominion of new conceptual territories is a significant aspect of the sovereignty system explained by copyright. The rapid growth of the Internet jeopardizes this sovereignty system that is protected by copyright. It is difficult to impede the flow of information on the Internet because it cannot easily be contained. The 1990s marked the beginning of a period when copyright was legally brought into the context of digital information and the Internet.

The Internet threatens copyrights because it provides a method for authors to bypass publishers, for readers to bypass both authors and publishers, and for copyrighted information to roam freely in an atmosphere where property rights are difficult to protect. On electronic networks, it is easier to make copies of copyrighted work, to appropriate portions of text without crediting the author, and, because electronic text is easily changed by each reader, it is more difficult to validate a text as belonging to a particular author. These threats were recognized by the National Writers Guild as issues that must be dealt with before the Internet is "safe" for intellectual property.[4]

The old sovereignty system where authors were paid by publishers who then owned the copyrights is undermined by this new form of circulation because it defies traditional control. Although the language of public policy and publishers suggests that authors are injured by the possibilities of the Internet, thousands of "authors" daily communicate via these electronic channels. As Shapiro noted, "polities whose sovereign surfaces appear smooth and untroubled contain dormant resistances below the surface, which can be awakened when various unleashed forces disturb the inscription process that is responsible for smoothing the surface."[5] In effect, the Internet is producing resistance to an unquestioned version of copyright and authorial integrity.

The NII Task Force helped redefine copyright for the Internet. The NII Copyright Protection Act of 1995 incorporates some of the task force's recommendations into new legislation designed to control the Internet.[6] Together, these actions constitute sovereignty maintenance tactics used to thwart the rapid circulation of ideas made possible by the Internet. These documents, and several others I discuss here, are sovereignty narratives. They are interpretive events designed to provide a common narrative of how copyright should be used in the information age.

In structuring these sovereignty narratives, the exchange between authors, publishers, and audiences is considered legitimate as long as it follows the rules of copyright. The uncontrolled exchange of ideas and documents, as practiced on the Internet, is thus labeled *illegal*. Despite obvious evidence to the contrary, the Internet is conceptualized as a place without "content" that will only become a meaningful aspect of our economic and educational life if property rights are strictly enforced.[7] Thus, the narrative Congress and policymakers endorse is one where copyright is uncritically extended to the information age and seen as the only legitimate tool for providing meaningful information on the Internet.

The new exchange system made possible by the Internet is not without its sovereignty function. Authors have become concerned with authentication and ensuring they are appropriately compensated. However, the exchange and discussion of information appears to be a more important consideration. For a large number of authors, circulation on the Internet takes precedence over ownership. Anyone can receive or download papers that indicate that they may be freely distributed as long as they are not used commercially. This noncommodified authorship on the Internet, while a positive and beneficial phenomenon, is disruptive of traditional forms of ownership and commercial authorship.

There are two important issues posed by this disruption: The first is determining how property rights will be defined in this new information age. The second is how exchange of already existing forms of intellectual property such as books and musical recordings will be regulated via a media that circumvents control. A strong narrative already has developed that assumes strict protection is desirable for both issues. This chapter more closely analyzes this narrative as well as the public policy recommendations emanating from this narrative. First, I review the 1985 Office of Technology (OTA) Report on technology and intellectual property. This report and the NII Task Force Report have many similarities, but possess a significant difference. A comparison of these reports makes clear that between 1985 and 1994 a desire to increase control over intellectual property developed.

THE 1985 OTA REPORT

The OTA wrote an extensive report in 1985 detailing the impact of technology on intellectual property. This report began by describing intellectual property law as the outgrowth of 18th-century technology. It also defined intellectual property rights as "dynamic" in nature, in effect shifting in response to social, cultural, and political circumstances.[8] This perspective, unlike the CONTU perspective that solidly places new technology under the laws of intellectual property, found that:

> At a basic level, the very definitions on which intellectual property rights are based take on new meanings, or become strained and even irrelevant, when applied to the context created by new technologies. They raise questions, for example, about what constitutes a "derivative work" when works are made available through intangible electronic waves or digital bits; about what constitutes a "work"; and about who owns the rights to it when it is interactive, and when creators have combined their efforts to produce it.[9]

These new circumstances meant technology was creating opportunities that previously had not existed. These opportunities were economic, political, and cultural in nature and were responsible for more information and better access to cultural goods.[10] Despite the opportunities provided by these new technologies, conflict was emerging as an increased emphasis on profit and ownership began to clash with the increased ability to exchange information.[11] These opportunities, and the potential for clashing interests, led the OTA group to claim that economic incentives may not have the desired effect, or might not create an environment for creative activity, because they could pit one interest against another. Given the traditional assumption that copyright is supposed to inspire creative work by providing an economic benefit, the OTA acknowledgment that economic incentives may actually hinder creative work is quite radical.

When evaluating authorship, the OTA report highlighted some of the new possible relations. Unlike the CONTU report that clearly designated computers as objects and rejected the claim that they could have a stake in authorship, the OTA report willingly looked at the ability of technology to produce new forms of authorship. For the OTA group, the possibility of interactive computing constituted a new form of authorship.

> In many cases, as with word processing programs, the machine contributes little to the creation of a work; it is "transparent" to the writers creativity. But with some programs, such as those that summarize (abstract) written articles, the processing done by the computer could constitute "an original work of authorship" if it were done by a human being. Indeed, the machine itself is at once a series of processes, concepts and syntheses of human intelligence—so mixed that it is difficult, if not impossible, to separate its parts from the whole.[12]

The OTA report left room for the claim that authors/creators may not be as distinct from the user as originally thought. In the case of interactive computer technology, the user became an author because the program was established to blend the author's ideas and the user's ideas. The OTA report took into consideration the fluidity of the boundary between authors and users. The computer was seen as a tool that could blend these distinctions into new possibilities.

Given the acknowledgment of the potential for new technology, the recommendations of the OTA group were rather mundane. Instead of embracing new possibilities, they concluded that Congress should either expand the existing agencies or create a new central agency to deal with intellectual property issues: "Such an agency's mission might include monitoring technological change and assessing how the law might deal with it, providing the necessary expertise to deal with complex technological issues, and collecting and analyzing data about information markets and use. Such an agency might also assume additional regulatory functions, such as distributing rewards or adjudicating disputes. Finally, it might coordinate intellectual property policy with policy in related areas."[13] These proposals obscured the potentially radical nature of this new technology and illustrated that the OTA was willing to embrace the traditional story and its form of protection before it endorsed the exploration of alternatives to intellectual property rights.

Like the 1994 report, the OTA recognized that enforcement of any new legislation was impossible without the willing participation of the public. The report observed that, "As technology makes the enforcement of intellectual property rights more difficult, public support for these rights becomes all the more critical."[14] Crucial to this form of enforcement was strong public relations, or "education," on the part of intellectual property industries and the government. This public relations blitz focused on persuading citizens to participate in the property boundaries that the industries wished to impose. In contrast, the general public, while acknowledging that piracy should not be condoned (i.e., illegally profiting from copyrighted work), saw nothing wrong with the personal use and appropriation of copyrighted work.[15]

Convincing people they have no right to use the products they buy is a difficult task. Developing criminal sanctions is important in convincing the general public they should not exchange products or information. By establishing who is a "criminal" and what type of activity will be criminalized, as is discussed in chapters 4 and 5, appropriate behavior in the information age can be described. However, before criminals can be created, it is necessary for policymakers and Congress to set the groundwork in the form of laws and policy papers. The strategy involves several interrelated steps. First, problematic behavior must be identified, in this case software pirates and general copyright infringers. Second, Congress and law enforcement must be convinced that this type of behavior is wrong and should be stopped. Third, criminality can be established and the laws can be enforced. The success of this narrative is crucial to getting property rights firmly established in a medium that has radically opened up the exchange of information.

The need to convince citizens that they cannot use copyrighted works however they please emerged because of a shift in the intent of copyright protection. There was a transformation of intellectual property law toward tighter control that coincided with emerging new technologies. This transformation evolved from the granting of the "right to copy" in the 1909 Act.[16] The right to copy changed the intent of the copyright act from: "*the right to control the use of copyright for commercial profit* (vis-à-vis competing publishers) to *the right to control the copyrighted work itself* (vis-à-vis the user of the copyrighted work)."[17] This expansion of copyright power permitted a copyright owner to control the commercial use of their property, as well as how people could use this property personally. It became legitimate to control the private use of copyrighted materials, assuming the law could be enforced.

Although the OTA recognized and advocated that intellectual property concerns were now linked to all areas of policymaking, its recommendations did little but offer an extension of the system. The OTA was careful to say it was too early to make strong regulations. The OTA report was delivered to Congress and it was in this presentation that their more radical tint became prominent.

OTA REPORT TO CONGRESS

The Subcommittee on Patents, Copyrights and Trademarks of the Senate Committee on the Judiciary joined with the Subcommittee on Courts,

Civil Liberties, and the Administration of Justice in April 1986 to hear the final report of the OTA on Intellectual Property Rights in an age of Electronics and Information.[18] The subcommittees were aware of the transformative effects of new technologies on the way information was communicated, as well as how science is done, and how ideas are exchanged. They were also aware of the economic advantage intellectual property brought the United States. It was with these important facts in mind that the subcommittees heard the final report.

D. Linda Garcia's presentation to Congress was more political than the report itself would have us believe. She commented that any new system would have to take into account that its structure would "determine not only which individuals and groups benefit from these new opportunities, but also in what ways and to what extent we, as a society, might exploit these technologies."[19]

Garcia informed the committee that, "OTA found, first of all, that the changes being wrought by the new information and communications technologies are as far reaching as those brought about by the printing press. Like the printing press, the new technologies are changing the way people work and conduct their business; how they interact and relate to one another; the way they learn, create, and process information; and the needs and expectations that they have."[20] The OTA presentation to Congress argued that consideration be given to determining who will benefit from the elaboration of an intellectual property system designed around new technologies. The report suggested that new technology problematizes, among other things, authorship, private use, intangible works, educational use, and the ethical dimensions of intellectual property use.[21] Perhaps the greatest difference between the 1985 report and the 1994 working group report is that in 1985 the new dimensions of authorship were not billed as threats to property and ownership, but seen as challenges and opportunities.

Some legal scholars disagreed with the conclusions of the report, arguing that the intellectual property system is flexible enough to adapt to new technologies (the conclusion of CONTU). One such view came from a member of the OTA advisory board, Paul Goldstein, who had some misgivings about the report. The OTA report argued new technologies are substantially different from previous ones. By contrast, Goldstein believed, "that the challenges presented differ little—certainly not in kind, and only slightly in degree—from the challenges that such technologies as radio, television, motion pictures, semiconductor chips—and, indeed, the printing press—have posed in the past."[22] His statement undermined the OTA conclusions by claiming that current law was adequate to the task. In effect, fitting new technology under old laws was a process of domestication through which we stifle the radical potential of a new technology in favor of more mundane uses. As Jane M. Gaines said, "new technologies may 'surprise' old categories, but only to be reformed according to existing conceptions of the world."[23]

Authorship is at the heart of Goldstein's disagreement with the report. The report stated that, "Copyright law, based on originality of works and individual authorship, may become too unwieldy to administer when works involve many authors, worldwide collaboration, and dynamically-changing materials."[24] The OTA seemed to see promise in this potential, especially if one reads the introductory paragraph of Garcia in which she stated the following:

> Our report is a product of the times; it is a jointly authored work, which has benefited from the collaboration, comments, and review of over three hundred people. These contributors have come from all over the country, and they represent a wide variety of perspectives. Included among them were representatives from affected industries, lawyers, educators, artists, musicians, writers, computer programmers and other creators, scientists and engineers, marketing experts, economists, young people, and academics from many disciplines.[25]

Garcia did not mention proprietary ownership of the report (it was a government report), nor did she mention the importance of the individual creator. Instead, she embraced the possibility of collaborative work. In such a scheme, identifying the input of any individual was impossible—the sum was greater than the parts. Allocating property rights would be difficult. As she noted, this is a sign of the times and an excellent example of the collaborative nature of authorship, a value embraced through exchange of ideas instead of strict control over them.

Goldstein, in his testimony, showed his inability to let go of the concept of the autonomous, individual author. He stated, "in speaking of 'authorship,' the Report's concern seems to be that interactive uses of computers, and networking of computer uses, will make it increasingly difficult to identify who the author of a particular work is."[26] Although this was certainly one interpretation, the report seemed to be celebrating the potential of multiple authorship even though Goldstein perceived it as a problem. Goldstein's words conformed to a sovereignty impulse. He spoke from his position within a strong copyright narrative where the inability to assign an individual author was problematic and undesired. Goldstein proposed to domesticate this new technology to old systems by creating programs to "trace sources and allocate royalties."[27]

The OTA report remained inconclusive on many points. It ultimately recommended that a reserved attitude toward technology be adopted because too much would change over the next decade. As Garcia told another group, the final recommendation was that, "as a society we are only at the beginning of a technological revolution and so the problems for the intellectual property system are long term. We told them that, while they might adopt some piecemeal measure now to deal with the situation, they would probably have to revise these mechanisms or completely change them over the next decade."[28] The OTA report was unpopular in both legal and business circles because it was ambiguous about how to protect intellectual products.[29]

Transformative possibilities were quickly traded for a smoothly working intellectual property law that fit the new technology to the law instead of the law to the technology. With the expansion of an information economy, information once shared as a common resource was now treated as a consumer item. The further one moves into an information economy the less chance one has to access information for free. The governmental recommendation for the new NII and intellectual property was an indication that we were heading toward stronger protection.

THE NII AND INTELLECTUAL PROPERTY

The progress of the NII Task Force, a group responsible for suggesting regulations for the emerging NII, can be found on the Web.[30] The "Preliminary Draft of the Report of the Working Group on Intellectual Property Rights" (the green paper) was finalized in September 1995 with the publication of the final report, called the white paper. The white paper articulated the vision of how intellectual property should be dealt with in the NII. This paper excellently illustrated the sovereignty maintenance tactics of traditional copyright supporters. What is most interesting about these recommendations is the manner in which the experts interpreted and asserted intellectual property as it was used and created on the Web. In making their recommendations, the group clearly sided with the traditional copyright interests and ignored the potential for new types of information exchange. In their eyes, the only way valuable content could be made available was if strong copyright protection existed. It is important to evaluate the working group's final draft and assess the property narrative that emerged.

The green paper faced criticism for virtually eliminating fair use in the electronic environment and for overregulating the use of copyrighted information on the Internet.[31] After the preliminary recommendations, the working group held public hearings in three cities and received more than 1,500 pages of written comments by more than 150 individuals and organizations.[32] These hearings were said to reflect the input of "a broad spectrum of interested parties; including various electronic industries, telecommunications and information service providers, the academic, research, library and legal communities, and individual creators, copyright owners and users, as well as the computer software, motion picture, music, broadcasting, publishing and other information and entertainment industries."[33] The white paper backed away from some of the working group's more controversial proposals, but generally restated the findings in the green paper. Most of the white paper recommendations were defined as alterations in a coat that was getting too tight.[34] The task of the white paper was to adapt copyright law to the Internet and ensure that copyrighted work was protected by the resulting legislation.

The white paper developed some important definitions and proposals that are worth discussing. First, the white paper defined *transmission* as a form of distribution because of the ease with which copyrighted work can move through the Internet.[35] This definitional move was important because distribution rights belong to the copyright owner and if transmission is a form of distribution then electronic exchange is subject to copyright owner approval. In Goldberg and Bernstein's words, "the Copyright Act [will] be broadened to encompass transmission of the work, in addition to the sale, rental, lease and lending of hard copies."[36]

This new "right" constituted a significant expansion of the copyright owner's control and clearly represented a sovereignty move. In the "real" world, such a standard would make loaning a book a copyright violation. The definition of transmission was qualified by the "to the public" clause, which meant it may not necessarily be illegal to transmit copyrighted work via private e-mail because such a use would not entail public viewing.[37] However, the meaning of "public" was also up for reinterpretation in the report. The task force defined public viewing in relation to the NII as the act of an individual user browsing a copyrighted document.[38] This meant if an individual looks at someone's home page, he or she has engaged in a public viewing and, through the process of viewing and thus caching the site, has engaged in a transmission (*caching* is an automatic function of most Web browsers where the cite is saved in order to make a second viewing a more efficient process). Both these actions would be illegal if copyrighted work was involved. The redefinition of both transmission and public viewing constituted a significant expansion in copyright scope.[39]

The second aspect of the white paper worth discussing was its position on the "first sale" doctrine. The first sale doctrine traditionally gave the buyer of a product control over its destiny. The copyright owner, unless the rights were specifically retained, lost rights to what happens to the product after the first sale.[40] According to the green paper, the first sale right would not apply to electronic transmissions because a copy remained with the original owner.[41]

The white paper argued that current law would meet the needs of a digital world because the doctrine of first sale applies only when the seller loses possession of the copyrighted work to the buyer. Thus, a copyright violation takes place if a person "sells" a product and continues to retain a digital copy. The definition of transmission ensures that an illegal sale would be a copyright violation. The property rights were extended by reinterpreting the status quo to deal in a more expansive manner with how the work might be used.

The third important aspect of this report was the approach to fair use that might be applied to the Internet. Fair use doctrine protects users of copyrighted works by allowing for some types of exchange that do not violate copyright. For example, fair use lets individuals quote from copyrighted materials, or use the material in its entirety as long as the use is for noncommercial or educational purposes.[42] The green paper limits the concept of fair use in the NII setting, essentially abolishing fair use as a meaningful concept.[43]

This treatment of fair use was one area where public testimony had an impact. The white paper convened a Conference on Fair Use responsible for drafting fair use guidelines for the Internet.[44] Of course, the working group continued to adhere to its belief in strong protections against overly broad fair use guidelines.[45] Additionally, the Conference on Fair Use was unable to reach agreement on what types of guidelines should be used when dealing with the Internet. Internet users thought all suggestions were too restrictive and copyright owners thought the proposed regulations were too lax.[46] The summary of the conference suggested that only an "end run" was possible, where users must pay for everything they use. The question then becomes how much a use will cost, not whether it is fair use.[47] The Conference on Fair Use (CONFU) officially ended May 18, 1998. CONFU was unable to make any strong recommendations because the tensions between the publishing industry and the library interests were too great to overcome.[48]

A fourth aspect of the report that needs mentioning is the liability issue. Online service provider liability appeared as an issue in the white paper. This issue had become more controversial because of litigation regarding the liability of online service providers.[49] The white paper refused to limit the liability of these service providers and argued they were in a better position to police traffic on their networks than copyright owners. "The Working Group believes it is—at best—premature to reduce the liability of any type of service provider in the NII environment."[50] This opinion was immediately used by Church of Scientology representatives in lawsuits they had pending against critics of their church.[51] The issue of online provider liability looks as if it is about to be resolved. The House and Senate recently passed the Digital Millennium Copyright Act of 1998 which, among other things, limits the liability of online service providers in some circumstances.[52] Such legislation will hopefully end suits like those filed by the Church of Scientology.

Ultimately, the white paper provided the groundwork for bringing a more powerful version of copyright onto the Internet than had existed to protect traditional copyrighted works. There was no time wasted in introducing these recommendations as legislation. In November 1995, a Joint Hearing of the Courts and Intellectual Property Subcommittee of the House Judiciary Committee and Senate Judiciary Committee met to discuss the copyright bills introduced simultaneously in the House (by Representative Carlos Moorhead) and in the Senate (by Senator Orrin Hatch.)[53] The resulting legislation was the NII Copyright Protection Act of 1995. Hatch acknowledged that we "are embarking upon a historic undertaking, establishing the 'rules of the road' for the information superhighway."[54]

The legislation followed the recommendations of the white paper and would have amended the Copyright Act in several key ways. First, it redefined public distribution to include transmission of copyrighted work.[55] It expanded the numbers of electronic copies libraries could make for archival purposes.[56] It provided improved access to copyrighted works in Braille. Additionally, it made it illegal to use, create, or exchange devices that could bypass technological protections for copyright owners, and provided remedies against those who "knowingly alter or disseminate false copyright-management information." It also increases criminal penalties for copyright violations.[57]

The issues raised by the NII Copyright Protection Act of 1995 continue to be debated. There are several more recent bills addressing the same copyright issues. These include: The Digital Copyright Clarification Act (S. 1146), The Digital Era Copyright Enhancement Act (H.R. 3048), The WIPO Copyright Treaties Implementation Act (H.R. 2281), and The On-Line Copyright Infringement Liability Limitation Act (H.R. 3209).[58]

THE NII SOVEREIGNTY NARRATIVE

The white paper began by enumerating the benefits of the NII. These benefits, however, would not be certain unless there were mechanisms for protecting copyrighted works in the "electronic marketplace."

> Thus, the full potential of the NII will not be realized if the education, information and entertainment products protected by intellectual property laws are not protected effectively when disseminated via the NII. Creators and other owners of intellectual property rights will not be willing to put their interests at risk if appropriate systems—both in the U.S. and internationally—are not in place to permit them to set and enforce the terms and conditions under which their works are made available in the NII environment.[59]

This language illustrated the concerns copyright owners had for an "unprotected" NII. The task force could not have been more clear about its vision: "The Internet, for instance, could continue to serve as a communications tool and resource for Government, public domain and works of willing authors. However, unless the framework for legitimate commerce is preserved and adequate protection for copyrighted works is ensured, the vast communications network will not reach its full potential as a true, global marketplace."[60] The intent of producing a global marketplace where content was provided by legitimate commerce was, in fact, the explicit goal of the NII Task Force.

The justification for the marketplace rhetoric was that it would provide better content to NII users and that ultimately these strong protections were in the public interest.

> While, at first blush, it may appear to be in the public interest to reduce the protection granted works and to allow unfettered use by the public, such an analysis is incomplete. Protection of works of authorship provides the stimulus for creativity, thus leading to the availability of works of literature, culture, art and entertainment that the public desires and that form the backbone of our economy and political discourse. If these works are not protected, then the marketplace will not support their creation and dissemination, and the public will not receive the benefit of their existence or be able to have unrestricted use of the ideas and information they convey.[61]

The report argued, "just one unauthorized uploading could have devastating effects on the market for the work."[62] This heavy reliance on the assertions of the traditional copyright story was indicative of the analysis provided by the task force on why copyright protection was needed.

A different market analysis could have been offered, one that suggested the type of free-flowing discussion that was taking place on the Internet was a true "marketplace of ideas," but this type of exchange was ignored by the task force. The charm of the Internet, and therefore the threat to traditional copyright owners, was that anyone could publish and be heard without the censoring impact of publishers. What traditional copyright owners feared was not the loss of a marketplace of ideas but the loss of ownership over the ideas that were exchanged.

The task force assumed that the only marketplace was one where traditional copyright owners would be in control. Nowhere was it questioned that authors might have deeper motives than making money via copyright or that poets might write poems because of a creative drive rather than an economic drive. The NII Task Force reiterated the traditional legal story in order to reaffirm the legitimacy of the story for copyright adherents. This traditional story was also important because it provided the legal framework within which to understand the NII. The task force never challenged the applicability of copyright law to the NII. The applicability of copyright was assumed and its extension to the NII was also assumed.

What the task force only partially obscures was that it was writing these words for the specific benefit of the many "intellectual property" industries that provided Americans with jobs. In fact, the task force specifically linked intellectual property rights with the national interest because of the employment it provided U.S. citizens: "In addition, people of all ages should recognize that millions of U.S. workers are employed by industries that rely heavily on intellectual property protection, and that intellectual property rights are truly a matter of national interest."[63] These industries, driven only by the profit motive, had a significant amount of interest in strict copyright laws, whereas the authors who work for them benefited only indirectly at best from such provisions.

The problem before this working group was not one of balancing the rights of copyright owners with the public interest, but was one of how to render the online world a market in which owners of information could enjoy exclusive and total rights to their property. This working group was about transforming the Internet into a shopping network where users were valued as customers and strict control over information was maintained. The proposals were akin to a virtual land grab. This point was well argued by Pamela Samuelson in her critique of the report:

> It [the report] downplays the extent to which the changes it recommends would, in fact, bring about a radical realignment in the historical balance between publisher interests and the public interest in access to information products, pushing the law in a direction that would favor publisher interests to the detriment of the public interest. It would abolish long-standing rights that the public has enjoyed to make use of copyrighted works, rights that have been consistently upheld in courts and in the copyright statute. . . . To put the point plainly, let me say that not since the King of England in the 16th century gave a group of printers exclusive rights to print books in exchange for the printers' agreement not to print heretical or seditious material has a government copyright policy been so skewed in favor of publisher interests and so detrimental to the public interest.[64]

The rhetoric of copyright often refers to the balance between the producer's rights and the public interest. It is one of the mainstays of the traditional copyright story that the public interest is served by our system of copyright. However, the new definition of public interest supported by the NII, appeared to emphasize the creation of jobs through intellectual property industries and not the promotion of the arts and sciences.

Because the NII was meant to provide the traditional printing, music, and telecommunications industries with a mechanism for getting their goods to consumers, it neglected the already existing community on the Internet that was engaged in creative discussions, scientific research, and projects of all sorts. As Samuelson pointed out, the Internet was providing the type of progress in the arts and sciences copyright was designed to protect.

> People have flocked to the net by the hundreds of thousands not because their favorite movies or books may be available there in another five to ten years, but because a wide variety of resources are available there already. Since its inception, the Internet has greatly facilitated and enhanced communication and learning of the very sort that copyright law is supposed to promote. It has enabled researchers to gather and share data more easily, to engage in collaborative work at remote locations, to criticize and refine one another's work, and to make research results and the like available at ftp sites, thereby enabling those interested in these results access to them. A large number of newsletters, journals, and listservs have sprung up and serve as forums for discussion of public policy and research issues in a wide variety of fields. Debate on the Internet could hardly be more robust.[65]

As one writer put it, the Internet was "a never ending world wide conversation."[66] Today, the Internet represents a source for substantive discourse and research that bypasses geographical and territorial constraints. If the Internet becomes a place dominated by the commercial interests of the telecommunications and entertainment industries, a vibrant source of exchange could be lost.

The Internet as a vast network of exchange defies the commercializing assumptions held by the task force. People do create, discuss, and exchange information, ideas, and literary texts absent monetary incentive and strong copyright protection. This perspective, however, is ignored by the NII Task Force. By transforming the Internet into a market, not only are citizens transformed into information consumers, but the language of supply and demand replaces the language of discourse networks and democratic communication.

Shapiro pointed out that, "it is necessary to raise the question of value, for value is always at least implicitly implicated in the sovereignty–exchange nexus."[67] Value is important because the manner in which the Internet is regulated means millions of dollars for publishers and other industries, not to mention the vast advertising power made available if security can be guaranteed. The problem rests in the fact that the Internet is hard to regulate, and that circulation occurs without difficulty. For information owners this is problematic because as Shapiro noted, "*value* emerges precisely at the point at which flows are inhibited."[68] If the ground rules created favor the major industries, then the free flow of information can be significantly curtailed and value sustained. As the white paper illustrated, the task force was willing to establish ground rules that privilege traditional copyright owners. It is yet to be seen how successful such sovereignty practices will be when put to the test.

In attempting to cement the sovereignty practices of the market economy the task force also dealt with the spatial representations through which the Internet is addressed. The market economy sovereignty system was jeopardized in ways not before possible by nature of the speed and multilocality of Internet communication. As Shapiro noted, "In a world based more on time than on territory, distance, in the old sense, is displaced by speed and acceleration. As a result, the inhibition of flows must involve modifying pace and trajectory rather than simply containing things. Sovereignty maintenance tactics must therefore change."[69]

The task force is an excellent source of answers to how sovereignty maintenance tactics can be employed. First, the rhetoric of cyberspace as being its own sovereign space was rejected and denounced. The task force did this early in its report:

> Finally, there are those who argue that intellectual property laws of any country are inapplicable to works on the NII or GII because all activity using these infrastructures takes place in "Cyberspace," a sovereignty unto itself that should be self-governed by its inhabitants, individuals who, it is suggested, will rely on their own ethics—or "netiquette"—to determine what uses of works, if any, are improper. First, this argument relies on the fantasy that users of the Internet, for instance, are somehow transported to "chat rooms" and other locations, such as virtual libraries. While such conceptualization helps to put in material terms what is considered rather abstract, activity on the Internet takes place neither in outer space nor in parallel, virtual locations. . . . Computer network transmissions have no distinguishing characteristics warranting such other-world treatment.[70]

The tone of this statement indicated the disregard the task force held for this alternative interpretation of space. Such new spatial practices were not to be allowed. In part, the recommendations of this task force and its accompanying legislation were designed to stabilize the flow of information spatially. As technology made the flow of information significantly easier, it was becoming necessary to create mechanisms for limiting the flow. The expansion of copyright and the inclusion of stricter guidelines was an effort to restrict the flow and to maintain a sovereignty system.

The working group offered nothing that was visibly radical. They advocated clarification and what they considered minor amendments to the Copyright Act. Besides the strengthening of the basic concepts, the working group focused on how it might be possible to convince the general public to adhere to copyright law. The public apparently did not immediately think of information and creative work as private property. After all, to get Europeans to adopt a private property system in its tangible form it was necessary to enforce harsh criminal penalties and engage in state-sponsored violence over several decades.[71] Thus, the task force recommended a course of public education regarding intellectual property.[72] Unless information owners could convince the public that ownership was legitimate, there was to be no protection because exchange would continue to occur, if only out of ignorance of the law. The educational recommendations of the task force are worth evaluating in greater detail.

It is unlikely that people used to sharing a favorite book with a friend, or passing on a used news magazine, or even photocopying a document, would accept assertions that this property deserves such strict protection. Even though a copyright owner owns the conceptual right, the buyer owns the tangible object—a book, a poem, or a tape recording. It is counterintuitive that such items, which are bought and paid for, are under the exclusive control of the copyright owner. It is easier to transfer habits of information sharing and exchange to an electronic realm (which is even less tangible) than to grasp an intellectually constructed justification for ownership of ideas. The task force understood this problem: "The average citizen has only the most general understanding that there are patents, copyrights and trademarks, let alone an understanding of the legal, economic and trade issues involved. . . . Most people do not have a very clear idea about the role of intellectual property law in encouraging creativity and the importance of intellectual property to our economic well-being."[73]

The public tendency to engage in discourse and exchange directly contradicted the capitalist tendency to own and control. Considering the ease with which information can be transferred, it is no wonder citizens not trained in intellectual property law "disrespect" the "rights of copyright owners." The public tends to adhere to an exchange discourse that facilitates their use and sharing of cultural products. Additionally, if the possibility of getting a cheaper version exists, what rational consumer would buy the more expensive product? One reason the moral claims of copyright ownership are important can be found in the fact that the rational consumer will buy the cheaper product, especially when it is identical to the more expensive product. Value for the user comes from uninhibited flows of products, not inhibited ones. Unfortunately, the prevailing discourse reduced the sharing of information to unimportant at best and criminal at worst.

The working group realized that the only way their recommendations would be workable was if most Americans (and global citizens) would agree on the definitions of property outlined in the Copyright Act. Thus, education was a critical element for success. They argued that, "Users must learn enough about this topic to appreciate just what respect for intellectual property laws can do for them, and why a seemingly harmless transaction on a computer network may have a great effect on the benefits they get from the intellectual property system."[74] The task force argued that users would ultimately benefit from the intellectual property system because "users are likely creators, too."[75]

In order to better educate the public, the task force initiated a Copyright Awareness Campaign in March 1995. Participants in this campaign developed guidelines for educating the public about intellectual property. The goal was to make intellectual property a "household word."[76] The task force recommended that this education begin at the elementary school level where "certain core concepts should be introduced."[77] These core concepts related to the "underlying notions of property—what is 'mine' versus what is 'not mine.' "[78] One can immediately note the lack of a category for things that are "ours" in this educational message. These concepts of property could then be extended to the Internet and copyright.

> Therefore, they should learn what one participant refers to as "electronic citizenship," including how to determine the owner of a work, and how to go about asking for permission to use it. Similarly, they should learn that the taking of someone else's property, including copyrighted works, without their permission is not right. Additionally, as noted previously, users will also be creators of copyrighted works, and therefore should know what their rights are and that they may expect those rights to be respected by others.[79]

Instead of teaching children how to share, how to create together and exchange ideas, the task force recommended we teach children to carefully guard their copyrighted work and establish economic relations not only to the work they might use, but with each other regarding creative work.

The goal of the task force was a positive one, they asserted. They wanted to educate people on the advantages of using the copyright system and the protection it could bring. They wanted a "just say yes" message to be heard through educational practices, one that showed "that works may be accessed and used, and that seeking permission is not an insurmountable barrier."[80] Of course, the task force had not read David Stowe's article in *Lingua Franca* where he described the insurmountable barriers to seeking permission for the use of copyrighted works. In some cases, permission was refused because it would make the company "look bad." In others, the costs were so large (up to $3,000 for a few lines of poetry) that it was a deterrent to use and/or authorized use.[81] Even using an online system through the library that will fax a full text version of the article for a fee plus a copyright charge can be prohibitively expensive. Educating people that they could overcome the barriers of authorization did not make it any more possible, especially as more and more copyright owners attempt to exact as much as the market would bear for their rights.

The educational agenda outlined by the working group illustrated an understanding of the importance of garnering public support for intellectual property. Through a narrative of intellectual property, brought to all children from kindergarten to college, the fences of intellectual property could be firmly established, perhaps without resort to violence or punishment. Getting the public to accept property rights in intellectual property was the goal of the variety of narratives we have analyzed, and it also illustrates why education was important in convincing people to follow the new rules. We are watching as new conceptual territory is being staked out by property owners and those of us used to understanding knowledge as communal will have to accept the new system or be transformed into criminals.

The changes to the copyright law recommended by the task force were designed to curtail private use of copyrightable materials that did not comply with copyright rules. As later chapters illustrate, the government and industries have taken to task commercial pirates and computer hackers via some strong-arm tactics. These tactics seek to create an atmosphere in which the average citizen can better understand the nature of intellectual property. The working group on intellectual property was responsible for the expansion of copyright law that directly affected the everyday person when they borrow books, listen and record music, and use computer programs. The transformation of the copyright law as described by the working group have affected the everyday legality of our actions in relation to intellectual property.

REACTIONARY LAWS

Congress has not taken a wait-and-see approach to copyright protection in the information age. As mentioned above, there are a variety of bills introduced each year debating the extent to which copyright on the Internet should be controlled. These bills range from highly restrictive to relatively balanced. Some of the more restrictive legislation includes the No Electronic Theft (NET) Act, discussed at greater length in the next chapter, which became law in 1997 and allows for stronger criminal sanctions for copyright infringers.[82] Due to the immanent loss of copyright protection for Walt Disney's beloved Mickey Mouse, which will enter the public domain without Congressional action in 5 years, Congress has introduced the Copyright Term Extension Act.[83] This act would extend copyright protection for an additional 20 years and clearly represents a sovereignty move. At a time when technology practically forces new innovations every year in the software industry (negating the need for lengthy protection), Congress is considering extending the number of years protection of copyrighted works is awarded.

Two of the more balanced bills recently introduced are The Digital Copyright Clarification Act (S. 1146) and The Digital Era Copyright Enhancement Act (H.R. 3048). The Digital Future Coalition (DFC), a group which represents the rights of consumers, researchers, and those who use the Internet, endorses both these bills. They suggest that this legislation balances the needs of users and owners while still providing for fair use.[84]

The clash between sovereignty and exchange will continue as Congress hammers out the rules that will govern the Internet. Current legislation is reactionary at best. There has been little time to accurately assess the many dimensions of copyright on the Internet. The response has tended to be to legislate quickly without thinking through the consequences.

CONCLUSION: EXPANDING COPYRIGHTS

The NII narrative is a complex interpretive act of the present engaged in designing sovereign boundaries for the future. The recommendations by the U.S. government task force on the NII and intellectual property make clear how the traditional story of copyright leads us into deeper control of ideas, expressions, and information and further away from sharing and exchange.

The software industry is engaged in a fight to control the ownership of software. Publishers, record labels, and the movie industry are engaged in a fight to control ownership of creative texts and information. Authors, too, are fighting to protect their interests in the emerging NII. The prevailing tendency is toward increasing emphasis of control of information. This control goes so far as to assert ownership in the ideas a person carries in his or her head. Increasingly, if one works for a company, one's ideas remain the property of that company.[85]

This chapter discussed the extension of the traditional copyright story as a mechanism to control intellectual property in the technological age through the government task forces. This discourse establishes authors and publishers as victims and intellectual work as the "crown jewels."

The NII provides a mechanism for circumventing the traditional controlling structures of the culture industry. Additionally, new technologies provide the technical support to "liberate" texts from their bounded form. The impact of new technologies are multiple and the possibility of new myths very real. Because we are standing at a gateway to the future, it is important to understand how that future is interpretively constructed, and who benefits most from that construction.

NOTES

1. Office of Technology Assessment, *Intellectual property rights in an age of electronics and information, summary* (OTA-CIT-303) (Washington, DC: U.S. Government Printing Office, April 1986), 78.
2. "Porn on the Internet," *Time* (3 July 1995): 38.
3. OTA, *Intellectual property in an age of electronics*, 190.
4. National Writers Union, *Electronic publishing issues, a working paper* [On-Line], Available: University of Maryland Gopher <anon@info.umd.edu> (30 June 1993).
5. M. J. Shapiro, *Reading "Adam Smith": Desire, history and value*, Newbury Park, CA, London, & New Delhi: Sage (1993), 37.
6. The National Information Infrastructure Protection Act of 1995 was reintroduced in 1996 as the National Information Infrastructure Protection Act of 1996. At this reading, the bill has passed in the Senate and has been referred to the House Committee on the Judiciary. To find current legislative information and to track bills go to: http://thomas.loc.gov.
7. See the statements of Representative Burman in No Electronic Theft (NET) Act, (1997, November 4), *Congressional Record, Vol. 143, 152*, p. H9887.
8. OTA, *Intellectual property in an age of electronics*, 23.
9. Ibid., 24.
10. Ibid., 40–53.
11. Ibid., 55–56.
12. Ibid., 69–70.
13. Ibid., 21.
14. Ibid., 97.
15. Ibid., 209.
16. Ibid., 191.
17. Ibid., 192.
18. *OTA report on intellectual property rights in an age of electronics and information: Joint hearing of the subcommittee on patents, copyrights, and trademarks of the senate committee on the judiciary and the subcommittee on courts, civil liberties, and the administration of justice of the house committee on the judiciary*. 99th Cong., 2nd Session (16 April 1986).
19. From the prepared statement of D. Linda Garcia, *OTA Report*, Joint Hearing, p. 12.
20. Ibid., 12.
21. Ibid., 13. In another speech given by D. Linda Garcia to the Library of Congress Network Advisory Committee Meeting, some light is shed on why

OTA concluded their report in such a radical manner. She described the beginnings of OTA as a research arm of Congress designed to look at the long-term impacts of technology on society. Given this mandate, and the fact OTA emerged at the end of the 1960s when institutional disillusionment was high and the negative aspects of technology were widely known, the OTA looks at technological issues from the larger perspective of their impact on society. Thus, the special interests of any given industry are less likely to play a role in the final outcome than in some other settings. She stated, "OTA, then, was created to do technology assessment: to look at the long-term impact of technology on society. This does not mean that we take a position on technology—that we are either for or against it. Rather, we try to plan for technology. We try to anticipate its unintended consequences so that we can plan ahead, so that we can try to avoid, or at least ameliorate, the negative consequences and take full advantage of the benefits that new technologies afford." See: D. L. Garcia, *The OTA report on intellectual property rights. Intellectual property rights in an electronic age: Proceedings of the Library of Congress network advisory committee meeting* (22–24 April 1987), 10–11.

22. Statement of Paul Goldstein, *OTA Report*, 30.

23. J. M. Gaines, *Contested culture: The image, the voice, and the law* (Chapel Hill & London: The University of North Carolina Press, 1991), 47.

24. Garcia, *OTA Report*, 13.

25. Ibid., 11.

26. Ibid., 38.

27. Ibid.

28. Garcia, *Proceedings of the Library of Congress*, 11–12.

29. Ibid.

30. http://iitf.doc.gov/

31. P. Samuelson, "The NII intellectual property report: National Information Infrastructure," *Communications of the ACM, 37* [Lexis-Nexis] (December 1994): 21.

32. Information Infrastructure Task Force, *Intellectual property and the National Information Infrastructure: The report of the working group on intellectual property rights* (September 1995), 4–5.

33. Executive summary and recommendations from intellectual property and the national information infrastructure, The report of the working group on intellectual property rights, *Daily Report for Executives* [Lexis-Nexis] (6 September 1995).

34. *Intellectual property and the national information infrastructure*, 212.

35. Ibid., 213–218.

36. D. Goldberg, & R. J. Bernstein, "The white paper's proposed amendments to the act," *New York Law Journal* [Lexis-Nexis] (17 November 1995): 3.

37. Ibid.

38. *Intellectual property and the national information infrastructure*, 72.

39. Samuelson's critique of the initial green report regarding "browsing" applies to the final recommendations as well. She explained:

> But rather than explicitly recommending that copyright law be amended to make all browsing, reading, and uses of copyrighted works in digital form into acts of infringement—a recommendation likely to be highly controver-

> sial—the Report takes advantage of an incidental property of digital works (that they need to be copied in order to be browsed or otherwise used) to assert that existing law already allows publishers to control all uses of works in digital form. This lucky happenstance makes it unnecessary for the drafters of the Report to mention that they are advocating a vast expansion of copyright scope.

See: Samuelson, "NII intellectual property report."

40. In the 1976 Copyright Act the owner of a copyrighted work can dispose of it without the copyright owner's permission. See: 17 U.S.C.A. 109(a).

41. Information Infrastructure Task Force, Working group on intellectual property rights, *Intellectual property and the National Information Infrastructure: A preliminary draft of the report of the working group on intellectual property rights* (July 1994).

42. Copyright Act of 1976, 17 U.S.C.A. §107.

43.

> It would be inaccurate to say that the NII Report recommends abolishing fair use law. And yet, it takes such a narrow view of existing fair use law and predicts such a dim future for fair use law when works are distributed via the NII that the Report might as well recommend its abolition. Since the fair use doctrine has been one of the historically important ways in which the law has promoted public access to copyrighted works, the virtual abolition of fair use law for which the Report argues would represent another vast expansion of copyright law in favor of publishers.

See: Samuelson, "NII intellectual property report" [Lexis-Nexis].

44. *Intellectual property and the National Information Infrastructure*, 4.

45. Goldberg & Bernstein, "The white paper's proposed amendments."

46. *Will we need fair use in the 21st century?* [On-Line], Available: http://www.utsystem.edu/OGC/intellectualproperty/confu.htm, [visited 2/13/98].

47. Ibid.

48. P. Miller, "Final meeting on the conference on fair use," *NCC Washington Update, 4,* #19 (May 20, 1998). H-Net Distribution List for NCC Reports. H-NCC@h-net.msu.edu.

49. C. Reid, "Free speech or piracy?: Copyright ruling favors Scientologists," *Publishers Weekly* (15 April 1996): 14.

50. *Intellectual property and the National Information Infrastructure*, 122.

51. "Scientology finds refuge in white paper," *Information Law Alert: A Voorhees Report* [Lexis-Nexis] (25 September 1995).

52. P. Miller, "Senate passes digital copyright law 99–0," *NCC Washington Update, 4,* # 19 (May 20, 1998). H-Net Distribution List for NCC Reports. H-NCC@h-net.msu.edu.

53. Copyright Bills, Joint hearing of the courts and intellectual property subcommittee of the House judiciary committee and Senate judiciary committee, *Federal News Service* [Lexis-Nexis] (15 November 1995).

54. Ibid.

55. "PTO, copyright office praise bill to direct traffic on the information highway," *BNA Washington Insider* [Lexis-Nexis], 16 November 1995.

56. "Copyrights, PTO, Copyright office praise bill to direct traffic on information superhighway," *Daily Report for Executives* [Lexis-Nexis], 15 November 1995, 221.

57. C. J. Moorhead, "Protect copyright holders and the internet will grow," *The Washington Times*, 3 December 1995, B2.

58. J. J. Marke, "Proposed legislation on digital copyright," *Law Journal Extra!*, May 18, 1998. http://www.ljextra.com:80/copyright/0519digcplegis.html.

None of this legislation has become law (to date), but its very existence speaks to the importance of intellectual property and the need to legislate control over how intellectual property is exchanged. The "rules of the road" may still be under construction, but it is generally recognized that these rules need to be created and a distinct tension exists between the narratives of sovereignty and exchange.

59. *Intellectual property and the National Information Infrastructure*, 10.

60. Ibid., 16.

61. Ibid., 14.

62. "Copyrights, PTO," *Daily Report*, 2.

63. *Intellectual property and the National Information Infrastructure*, 206.

64. Samuelson, "The NII Intellectual Property Report."

65. Ibid.

66. A. Johnson-Laird, "Copyright owners' rights and users' privileges on the internet: The anatomy of the internet meets the body of the law," *University of Dayton Law Review* (Spring 1997): 470.

67. Shapiro, *Reading Adam Smith*, 6.

68. Ibid., 46.

69. Ibid., 34–35.

70. *Intellectual property and the National Information Infrastructure*, 15.

71. M. E. Tigar, "The right of property and the law of theft," *Texas Law Review, 62* (1984): 1443–1475.

72. There is also current legislation entitled "Digital Copyright Clarification and Technology Education Act of 1997" that is under discussion in the Senate. This type of legislation emphasizes the importance education will play in getting people to adhere to copyright law. See: http://fairuse.stanford.edu/current_legislation/. (Visited 2/11/98.)

73. *Intellectual property and the National Information Infrastructure*, 201.

74. Ibid., 201–202.

75. Ibid., 202.

76. Ibid., 204.

77. Ibid., 205.

78. Ibid.

79. Ibid., 205–206.

80. Ibid., 208.

81. D. W. Stowe, "Just do it," *Lingua Franca* (November/December 1995): 32–42.

82. This act is discussed in more detail in the next chapter. "No Electronic Theft (NET) Act," *Congressional Record*, H9883.

83. J. Horn, "Mickey in middle of copyright fight," *Columbus Dispatch*, 19 February 1998, 8E. For a full text copy of this legislation see: http://thomas.loc.gov.

84. Marke, http://www.ljextra.com:80/copyright/0519digcplegis.html.

85. J. Bennet, "Who owns ideas and papers, is issue in company lawsuits," *New York Times*, 30 May 1993, 27.

3

Controlling Technology: Legal Narratives of Copyright

The Congressional reports and laws described in chapter 2 illustrate how the constantly negotiated boundary between sovereignty and exchange has moved in larger circles to limit exchange. In this extension of boundaries there has been a strong relation between the courts and Congressional action. Step by step, the applicability of copyright has been expanded by those who might benefit from possible new property interpretations to include virtually all uses of a creative work. Over the years, the Copyright Act has been amended to include music, photographs, films, and most recently computer programs, in the definition of a literary work.[1] The expansion of copyright protection has occurred primarily as a mechanism for increasing profits and more tightly controlling possible uses. As we move further into an information economy, ownership claims grow fiercer. The courts serve as an excellent window through which to view the climate of copyright interpretation. As intellectual property becomes a more important commodity, proprietary rights are taken more seriously. This translates into heightened litigation to reaffirm a sovereignty system that uses copyright to stake out territory. As software activist Mitchell Kapor noted, "too many companies seem to have decided it is easier to sue their rivals than compete with them."[2]

As information becomes increasingly vital to economic security it is important to ask, along with Pamela Samuelson, "Have we outgrown the Enlightenment tradition which viewed information sharing as the best means of increasing wealth and stimulating innovation?"[3] Despite the fact that copyright law provided a temporary monopoly, it did so in order to facilitate greater exchange of information. As discussed in chapter 1, the original copyright was a very limited grant. The slow expansion of copyright has provided new protections and stronger versions of older protections. The ultimate question remains unanswered: "What level of sharing is appropriate and how do we balance public and private interests?"

Balancing public and private interests, especially in how much protection will be afforded computer software, is left for the courts to decide. As copyright is technologically challenged, the courts become the arbiters of how copyright will be interpreted. The courts are not a place from which a significant challenge to the status quo has emerged on the copyright issue. It is worth discussing how they have helped establish the boundaries of copyright law in the information age, and how intellectual property-related industries use the courts to police their property.

It is no longer argued that information sharing is an activity that enhances wealth. Copyright industries claim the free flow of information is detrimental to their businesses and is a disincentive to future creation, research, and development. The fact that products can be so easily replicated and exchanged outside of the owner's economic control, many companies argue, is the greatest threat to industry growth. Under these conditions, instead of providing an incentive to share, copyright is being asserted as a doctrine that absolutely privileges ownership.

What makes these sovereignty maintenance tactics interesting is that they highlight the effect new technology is having on our old ways of constructing property rights. When the Internet makes the exchange of information easy and uncontrollable, those benefiting from the old copyright sovereignty system have much to fear. The free flow of information, I argue, is critical when power and information ownership coalesce as they do in the computer age. There is an important reason for the free exchange of information—human freedom and cultural exchange in the face of increasing information ownership. However, the trend that repeatedly becomes clear in the realm of intellectual property is the drawing of larger and larger boundaries around protected materials. The vast majority of recent court cases dealing with intellectual property move us further from the free exchange of information.[4] The drama occurring in the courtrooms has been an important thread in the intellectual property discourse underway in the United States.

Computer programs can serve as a site for understanding how the discourse of copyright is used to enhance the boundaries of property. Case law is an excellent place to turn for insight into how the copyright story is constructed and resisted because the oppositional nature of the legal system gives voice to many different perspectives. For example, if strict control over "look and feel" is granted, new innovation is virtually halted.[5] However, it can also be argued that lax control results in a lack of incentive to innovate because software designers will be unwilling to support research and development. We can watch how the courts arbitrate these issues and more importantly gain insight into the types of property claims made by intellectual property owners as they attempt to gain legal protection for what they see as their property. Computer software pushes the limits of copyright law because it is a technology that requires sharing in order to remain efficient. Additionally, because software is a utilitarian product in many ways, it is difficult to know how much protection it should be given. In this chapter, I look at how technology and litigation have interacted in two areas: computer software (which exemplifies the problems of using copyright in the information age) and the way in which the courts are used to police copyrights on the Internet.

COMPUTER PROGRAMS AND THE EXTENSION OF COPYRIGHT

CONTU recommended that computer programs be included as copyrightable works in 1979, and Congress then passed the Computer Software Act of 1980. In doing so, Congress initiated a protection regime that ultimately favors ownership over exchange. By accepting the general assumptions of copyright, the groundwork was established for fitting computer software into traditional copyright instead of delving into possible alternatives for software development. The task of the courts was to ask if infringement of copyright in computer programs occurred, not to ask if copyright was the appropriate form of protection for computer programs. The legal discourse on computer software thus owes its character to the statutes that define copyright and the inclusion of computer programs under copyright.

Including computer software in the Copyright Act and defining it as a literary work, as proposed by CONTU, brought software within the intellectual property tradition. The courts found property rights in the fundamental aspects of computer programs soon after the 1980 Computer Software Protection Act was signed.[6] This included protection for operating programs,[7] embodiment of computer programs in ROM (Read Only Memory),[8] and the equal protection of object and source code.[9] These first steps were logical conclusions because computer programs were defined as literary works and many of the first copyright cases dealt with this issue.[10]

In developing software as a literary work it was important to understand the act of writing software as creative and the result of original authorship. Strong protection of computer software began with arguments that extended authorship and original genius to the creation of computer software. In order to establish a justification for allowing computer software to be copyrighted, those seeking strong protection needed to use the tropes of the traditional copyright story to make the analogy between traditional literary works and computer programs as close as possible.

Anthony Lawrence Clapes, assistant general counsel at IBM, in his book *Softwars: The Legal Battles for Control of the Global Software Industry* clearly illustrated how the argument for strong protection begins. He relies heavily on the romantic notion of the original genius in order to explain why software deserved protection as a literary work. Claples collected quotations from a variety of computer scientists and software programmers to make this point. For example, Professor Frederick T. Brooks stated that, "The programmer, like the poet, works only slightly removed from pure thought-stuff. He builds his castles in the air, from air, creating by exertion of the imagination. Few media of creation are so flexible, so easy to polish and rework, so readily capable of realizing grand conceptual structures."[11]

Clapes summed up the creative aspect of software as follows: "*Almost pure thought-stuff. Castles in air. Gratifies creative longings. The ultimate creative medium. A tangible form of dreams and imagination. Magic and mystery. Simplicity and elegance. So beautiful you could hang it on the wall. Trying to create a perceptual impression. A combination of both art and science. A lot of subconscious activity. The best software comes from the realm of intuition*. That is the kind of property we call computer programs."[12] In the space of a few short pages, Clapes likened computer software writing to the essence of the creative process. He then proceeded to depict the type of person who creates such beautiful things.

> Noting that good programmers are often compared to artists and musicians, Patricia Keefe of *Computerworld* describes the task of managing these "often unconventional or egocentric types" as posing unique challenges. She quotes one software manager as saying that "People program because they love the intellectual challenge," and another manager as observing that because programming is a creative process, people tend to be more possessive of their work. A third suggested that programmers need a greater degree of freedom than other employees in order to "look around and explore different ideas." "A good programmer," the president of a small software company told Keefe, "is definitely a prima donna."[13]

When described in this manner, it is obvious that the creative act of computer software writing is as deserving of copyright protection as any other literary creation.[14]

Clapes ignored two important points in emphasizing the admittedly creative aspect of computer programming. First, he constructed a narrative that centers the creative aspect of the individual programmer and neglects the utilitarian function of the program, which necessitates the re-use of efficient code. When the computer industry was in its infancy, and computer programming was done for fun, programs were a freely shared asset.[15] Typically, a computer programmer would add his or her own personal touch and continued to use it, share it, and improve it. Computer code authors kept efficient code and rewrote inefficient code. Thus, sharing written code was an important (and remains an important) aspect of software writing. As the industry developed, a great effort was made to move computer programs under the clear protection of copyright law and out of the realm of collective innovation. The introduction of profits into the software world transformed the way computer programs were written by making computer code proprietary and unavailable for sharing. However, new legal protections did not replace the utilitarian need to use code efficiently. The exchange of code disrupted the traditional boundary of copyright that relies on carefully delineated boundaries between owners of property.

Second, Clapes obscured the role huge companies like IBM, his employer, play in the ownership of copyright. Ownership of copyright usually rests with the company for which a programmer works. The myth of the romantic author conceals the political economy of software production and design. When huge companies own the rights to all aspects of a computer program and can set a market standard that then makes competition virtually impossible it is important to recognize that copyright battles are less about creative authorship and more about economic monopoly.

Despite the creative aspect of computer software, it is important to remember that it serves a utilitarian function and is different from books, poetry, or movies. The economic dimension of computer software affects how computer software is legally defined and politically protected. Computer software is awarded copyright protection because of its economic value and its kinship to other literary work. Computer software is likened to the "crown jewels" of the information age because it provides the backbone for the burgeoning information industry.[16] It is no longer controversial to claim that the important commodities in today's market are information based; information is compiled in databases, information is codified as computer software, and information is collected on most Americans about their buying habits, credit rating, medical condition, and much more.[17] The economic importance of software drives litigation over copyright infringement. The rhetoric of copyright merges author's rights and economic protectionism nicely. As Professor Paul Goldstein noted, in a different context but one appropriate here, these arguments have "a moral surface and an economic core."[18]

As the United States moves toward a service economy, the perception of needing to provide protection to the software industry has grown. Wendy Gordon noted, "As the economic hopes of a less confident, service-oriented economy have become increasingly dependent on the nation's intangible assets, legislatures and courts seem willing to extend intellectual property protections on the questionable, and surely often unconscious, assumption that protection means prosperity."[19] The tension this creates between control and exchange is important for everyone involved in the software industry, and as later chapters illustrate, to U.S. citizens more generally.

Generally, the trend is toward increased protection of copyrightable technology.[20] The most radical protections have already been unproblematically accepted—the transformation of computer programs from exchangeable, free tools, to economically important creative products. Treating computer programs as commodities is made legitimate through legal battles that reinforce the traditional copyright story. Even exchange-oriented decisions operate under the assumption that computer programs are property.[21] The Supreme Court, in its opportunity to return a decisive opinion on the issue, merely reaffirmed the lower court ruling without writing a decision.[22]

There are two important components of software protection that are discussed, the protection of literal and nonliteral aspects of the program. The first question deals with the protection given to literal code. The literal elements of a program is the programming code. Cases dealing with literal elements of computer code were decided in the early to mid-1980s when the proprietary nature of computer software began to emerge as an important issue.[23] It was easy to protect the literal elements because they were the most easily analogized to print. If you copy a book, you plagiarize the book. If you copy the code of a computer program you have "plagiarized" the computer code.

The second, and by far the more difficult question the courts have had to deal with was how far does protection of the nonliteral aspects of a program extend? Nonliteral elements include the user interface, icons (like trash cans), and the general "look and feel" of the program. Nonliteral elements are the part of the software we see when using the program.[24] Many software companies have claimed all aspects of a computer program are copyrighted and argue that other companies making similar products are infringing their copyrights. The response is that creating compatible products is necessary to be competitive, especially when a specific program has created a market standard. The court is used to resolve the conflicts that erupt over where the property line should be drawn.

There are other important aspects of computer programs that also challenge property boundaries; specifically, what is considered original in the eyes of the court and the role reverse engineering should play in understanding a computer program. These issues are taken up in order to more fully explore the manner in which copyright is used and challenged in the information age.

PROGRAMS AS LITERARY CREATIONS

Apple Computer, Inc. v. Franklin Computer Corp. provides a view of how computer programs were first incorporated under copyright protection.[25] In *Apple,* Franklin Computer Corp., a small computer company that manufactured "Macintosh-compatible" computers, was charged with violating copyright on 14 different programs written by Apple. Franklin's computers, Apple argued, used exact copies of Apple software, with only minor changes such as the elimination of the copyright warnings and author's names. Apple claimed, and Franklin never denied, that their software was copied. Apple said they could prove authorship because the software writer's name was embedded in the programs in question and had not been removed by Franklin.

Franklin argued it was necessary to copy the code from Apple in order to build a 100% compatible machine. Unless 100% compatibility was achieved, the Franklin product would not be marketable. Franklin's argument hinged on the notion that there was only one way of expressing the desired idea. The court reversed a lower court's decision in favor of Franklin and extended "copyright protection to all forms of software."[26] The court affirmed that computer programs are "literary works" under the Copyright Act of 1976.[27] This case illustrated the underlying tension between a large company with a virtual monopoly over a certain expression of an idea and a smaller company wishing to produce a similar product.

Literal code is protected according to the *Apple v. Franklin* decision. Because Franklin admitted copying the code directly, issues of nonliteral characteristics of computer programs were not discussed. Franklin claimed a need to copy the programs to ensure compatibility. Apple argued programs aimed at performing the same function could have been written by Franklin, but they found copying easier. Because the issue of a limited number of ways to arrange computer operating systems was considered irrelevant, Franklin lost. The best way to deal with computer code and authorship will have to be addressed at some point, however, because as many software writers know, the utilitarian function of computer code is such that it is inefficient to rewrite code simply because a certain "phrase" has already been used. In the computer world, if a line of code works and is better than any other way of expressing the same idea it will be reused, not rewritten. Copying is at the base of programming.

Apple allowed first creators to monopolize the code they created. Although copying an entire operating system line by line seems fairly illegitimate, the question does arise—"At what point has too much copying occurred?" What is a legitimate amount of exchange? Controlling code too tightly halts the exchange process that has played a significant role in the development of the software industry. Too much exchange makes it difficult for the software companies to maintain a competitive edge.

MOVING BEYOND THE LITERAL TO THE NONLITERAL ELEMENTS

In order to understand how the courts have interpreted the nonliteral aspects of computer programs it is first necessary to clarify how the courts deal with any copyright infringement. In determining if the particular expression has been infringed, the courts must first determine where the idea ends and the individual expression begins. Copyright law prohibits ownership of ideas (which many people may have simultaneously),[28] but protects a person's expression of that idea. The question then becomes one of where the idea ends and the expression begins.

Justice Learned Hand in *Nichols v. Universal Pictures Corp.*, (1930)[29] makes perhaps the most famous comments on the idea–expression dichotomy. He stated the following:

> Upon any work, and especially upon a play, a great number of patterns of increasing generality will fit equally well, as more and more of the incident is left out. The last may perhaps be no more than the most general statement of what the play is about, and at times might consist only of its title; *but there is a point in this series of abstractions where they are no longer protected, since otherwise the playwright could prevent the use of his "ideas," to which, apart from their expression, his property is never extended. Nobody has ever been able to fix that boundary, and nobody ever can.* (italics added)[30]

The result of the *Nichols* decision was the "series of abstraction" test that can be used for computer programs as well as literary works.

Although recognizing that the arbitrary distinction between ideas and expression was prone to collapsing on itself, Learned Hand suggested the court look at levels of abstraction. At certain levels, such as specific dialogue between characters, infringement would be obvious. Less protection is granted at each new level of abstraction until the expression merged with the general idea. Thus, there is less protection given to a story line than to the actual play that may emerge from that story line. Learned Hand recognized the ambiguous nature of the boundary between ideas and expression. He recognized the court was engaged in a balancing act between two powerful tensions. The idea–expression dichotomy is an important concept that must be carefully watched as it is applied to computer programs.[31]

Prior to the *Apple v. Franklin* decision, where literal code was protected, the courts in *Synercom Technology, Inc. v. University Computing Co* (1978) held that the structure, sequence, or organization of a computer program was not copyrightable.[32] Structure, sequence, and organization are nonliteral elements dealing with how the program appears visibly to the user. Since *Synercom,* the courts have tended to protect the structure, sequence, and organization of computer programs as well as the literal code. In *Whelan v. Jaslow Dental Laboratory, Inc.* (1986)[33] the Third Circuit Court declined to follow *Synercom* and was the first to hold that structure, sequence, and organization (which the court used as interchangeable terms) of a computer program may be copyrighted.[34] *Whelan* extended copyright protection far beyond the literal elements of a computer program into the higher levels of abstraction—the user interface—arguing that "by far the larger portion of the expense and difficulty in creating computer programs is attributable to the development of the structure and logic of the program, and to debugging, documentation and maintenance, rather than to the coding."[35]

In *Whelan v. Jaslow,* Rand Jaslow decided that the records for his dental business would be better ordered if computerized. Because he lacked the programming experience to write a program himself, he hired Elaine Whelan who worked for Strohl Systems Group, Inc.[36] Whelan wrote the program for Jaslow and then entered into her own business to market Dentalab, the resulting product.[37] Whelan and Jaslow entered into a business relationship to market and improve Dentalab. However, as Jaslow became more proficient at programming, he realized there were additional markets that would require a new program. Jaslow hired a new programmer to write the program and sent a letter to Whelan Associates terminating their agreement.[38] Jaslow began marketing Dentcom, his new product, as an improved version of Dentalab. Although Jaslow had told Whelan they could no longer market the product, Whelan continued to do so and Jaslow sued for copyright violation.[39]

In *Whelan,* once it was decided that Whelan owned the copyright, it became important to understand if the program written by Jaslow was substantially similar to that written by Whelan. On appeal, Jaslow argued that because there were no substantial similarities in the "literal" aspects of the computer code, the newer program was not a copyright violation.[40] However, it was the second, nonliteral aspect of the programs where the real decision needed to be made.

In reaching its decision, the court argued that the non literal elements of the computer program were indeed protected and thus Jaslow had violated Whelan's copyright. The court made several logical moves to reach this decision. First, it needed to create a rule for distinguishing idea from expression in a computer program.[41] The court decided that the structure of the program was part of the expression, not part of the idea. The court argued that the largest economic costs are invested in developing the structure and logic of the program and thus protection should extend beyond the literal computer code.[42] Because it was possible to organize this information in different ways, Jaslow violated Whelan's copyright when he created a substantially similar program.

The *Whelan* decision strongly protected computer programs. As David Ladd and Bruce Joseph noted, "Under *Whelan*'s broad rule, it may be impermissible to take anything (short of the same function) from another work. As a result, special caution is necessary to ensure that employees who have left competitors are not using program expression gained from their prior employer's work."[43] *Whelan* broadly extended copyright protection over computer programs.

Whelan clearly provided the justification for Lotus Development Corp. to pursue its own copyright cases. Lotus filed suit against Paperback Software International over the Lotus 1–2-3 spreadsheet program the same day the Supreme Court denied certiorari in *Whelan v. Jaslow*.[44] The court in *Lotus Development Corp. v. Paperback Software International* (1990) agreed with *Whelan* when it ruled the user interface (i.e., the way a computer user relates to the screen) of Lotus 1–2-3 was copyrightable. The court protected the user interface as the "most unique element" that made Lotus 1-2-3 so popular.[45] Thus, it seemed that protection of nonliteral elements of computer programs was fairly well established. However, *Computer Associates International Inc., v. Altai, Inc.* (1991)[46] changed the rules for protection of the nonliteral elements of computer programs.

Computer Associates International, Inc., v. Altai, Inc. also addressed the nonliteral aspects of a computer program. In late 1983, Claude F. Arney, III, an employee of Computer Associates (CA), was approached by James P. Williams (president of Altai) about working at Altai. When Arney accepted, he brought with him (unbeknownst to Williams) information about computer programs under development and marketed by CA. These included a program called CA-SCHEDULER and ADAPTER. CA-SCHEDULER scheduled tasks running on a large mainframe. ADAPTER was a subprogram that acted as a translator for different operating systems.

In 1982, Altai had begun marketing its own scheduler titled ZEKE. Shortly after coming to work for Altai, Arney discussed with Williams the possibility of writing an adapter program for ZEKE. Arney went to work on a program called OSCAR, using the code from CA, unbeknownst to Williams or other Altai employees. On hearing its code was used in creating OSCAR, CA obtained copyrights of the code and filed suit against Altai.

Once Altai learned OSCAR was the product of copied code from CA, they began to rewrite it. Altai put together a team of programmers with no prior knowledge of OSCAR or the CA program, and had them rewrite OSCAR from the ground up, something called the *clean room* technique. Altai then marketed this new program as an updated version and sent free upgrades to all customers already owning the first version.

The court decided, and Altai did not contest, that the company's first program infringed on CA's copyright. However, the rewritten version of OSCAR, Altai argued, was not subject to infringement because it was a completely new program. The court agreed. The court's argument about the idea–expression dichotomy departed quite drastically from the *Whelan* decision. The court agreed that protection of ideas under *Whelan* was overbroad.[47] Thus, even though the second computer program created by Altai would violate *Whelan*, it was considered a legitimate program under *Computer Associates*.

The court recognized that copyright is not "ideally suited to deal with the highly dynamic technology of computer science."[48] The court took issue with the idea–expression dichotomy created in the *Whelan* decision arguing that it was inadequate and inaccurate.[49] Thus, the court concluded that "even assuming that Altai had access to ADAPTER's source code—after the rewrite, OSCAR 3.5 was not substantially similar to ADAPTER, and therefore did not infringe CA's copyright."[50] *Computer Associates* left room for substantial maneuverability and market competition. It was "violently opposed by a lot of the larger companies who are interested in broadly extending copyright protection to limit competition."[51] The decision in this case indicated that the courts might be willing to maintain a lower level of copyright protection than many companies believe was adequate. The Ninth Circuit ruled in *Ashton-Tate Corp. v. Ross* (1990)[52] that the command structure of a spreadsheet was not expressive enough to be protected. Subsequent copyright litigation between Microsoft, Apple, and Hewlett-Packard was an excellent example of the importance larger companies placed on their intellectual property.

Although copyright owners do not always win their arguments, the more recent battles between computer giants Microsoft, Apple, and Hewlett-Packard indicated that enough money is on the line to make pursuing litigation worthwhile. The Apple litigation exemplified the continuation of the sovereignty impulse. Apple accused Microsoft and Hewlett-Packard of copying the "look and feel" of the Macintosh interface when creating their own graphical interfaces (Microsoft's windows, and Hewlett-Packard's "New Wave Office"). Apple documented more than 150 alleged similarities between the products, concluding that the "look and feel" of its user interface was infringed.[53] Xerox then accused Apple of copying the idea from Xerox in the first place.[54]

Of the 150 infringing items outlined by Apple, the court narrowed the possible infringing items down to 5 falling under the "virtually identical" standard and another 4 falling under the "substantially similar" standard.[55] The ruling was less than definitive. Although lawyers for Apple attempted to argue this case was about more than the similarity of the garbage can icon on the screen, the approach taken (an item-by-item evaluation) lent itself to this type of analysis. Indeed, this case was about more than individual icons (which the court found to be insignificant to the ultimate copyrightability of the program). This case was about defining ownership of intangible intellectual property, especially a user interface that is the manifestation of literal code, not the written code itself. Ultimately, the court found some items infringed and others did not.

Strictly construed, all aspects of the computer program would be protected—the literal code and the more general "look and feel." As Apple's defense noted,

> I don't want to end up with this case saying, "Oh, well, all we have to do is change a trash can or change this or that." That isn't what this case is involving. We didn't bring a small case; we brought a case of tremendous significance to the client and to the industry. It's virtually the most important—certainly the most important case I have ever tried—but it's important because of the impact, the importance of this intellectual property asset of Apple's that they created and they owned and the totality of that expression.[56]

Apple v. Microsoft illustrated how even large computer companies build on what others have done. The commodification of application programs, however, apparently has led these same companies to quickly forget the roots of their own programs in favor of tightly protecting their ownership rights. Still, as mentioned earlier, the courts do not always protect the tightly controlled ownership rights of the large computer companies.[57]

The *Apple* litigation, it has been argued, marked a turning point in the copyright protection granted to user interfaces.[58] Although protection had expanded up to 1994,[59] since that time the trend seems to be toward less protection. It does not help that different circuits have adopted different methods for dealing with computer software cases.[60]

The trend toward less protection of the "look and feel" of a program was reinforced by the Supreme Court's affirmation of the First Circuit's decision in *Lotus Development Corporation v. Borland International Inc.*[61] The Supreme Court agreed to hear *Lotus* but did not write a decision.[62] By upholding the First Circuit decision, the court tacitly agreed with a less restrictive standard for dealing with the nonliteral elements of computer programs. In evaluating the amicus curaie briefs for *Lotus v. Borland* it becomes obvious that those favoring the rejection of the First Circuit decision belong to major U.S. computer companies.[63] In contrast, computer scientists, programmers, law professors, and user's groups all favored the less restrictive standard upheld by the First Circuit decision. One possible interpretation of these briefs is that the large computer companies were interested in protecting their economic advantages, and copyright was a useful tool for such protection. Additionally, those groups who clearly understood the manner in which software is written and used realized that exchange was a necessary component of future development. Although the Supreme Court decision itself was not clear as to how the courts might deal with copyright in the future, the briefs clearly illustrate the oppositional approaches being taken to this issue premised on either ownership and control or exchange.[64]

REVERSE ENGINEERING AND THE FREEDOM OF IDEAS

If ideas are not protected and expressions are protected, should a person be able to take a computer program and find out how it was written? This process is called *reverse engineering* and has become quite controversial. Because the object code of a computer program is not immediately visible or understandable, reverse engineering sometimes has been used to understand how a computer program works. Usually a licensing agreement prohibits the buyer from reverse engineering the software to discover the source and object code.[65] Because object code, the machine language, is not readable by human beings (at least not very many), devices known as *decompilers* translate object code into source code, which can be read by humans. Companies do not want others to be able to read their object or source codes. The legal question has been to determine to what extent reverse engineering should be allowed. It was argued in *Sega Enterprises v. Accolade, Inc.* (1992) that reverse engineering via an intermediate copy did not fall under the fair use doctrine.[66] However, this opinion on appeal was affirmed in part, reversed in part, and remanded. The modification dealt with fair use and concluded that, "where disassembly is the only way to gain access to the ideas and functional elements embodied in a copyrighted computer program and where there is a legitimate reason for seeking such access, disassembly is a fair use of the copyrighted work, as a matter of law. Our conclusion does not, of course, insulate Accolade from a claim of copyright infringement with respect to its finished products."[67]

Although the appeals court seemed willing to let this matter work itself out, this issue remains problematic. Jessica Litman stated that decompiling a program is equivalent to translating a book from Japanese to English.[68] However, others argue the source code is a trade secret and thus protectable.[69]

Decompilation of a program does not result in a duplicate of the original program. However, it does allow the new programmer to investigate the ideas, processes, and logic of the first program—items that are not copyrightable.[70] It can also result, as *Sega* showed, in a compatible program or game.[71]

Computer companies want to tightly control what they see as their property. Because computer code is unreadable, this property extends past the expression to the ideas, processes, and logic itself (traditionally public goods). It is easy to maintain control over these ideas without a decompiler. Some assert a trade secret right to computer code. Once another company decompiles the code, a second product can be built using the same ideas and logic of the first. The second product can be written with different source and object code, but will rely on the first product for its idea.

Another cause for concern from the software industry is the fact that computer software is so easily loaned and transferred without losing the original copy. Unlike a book, which can be legally resold or given away, computer software can be given away *and* remain with the original buyer. Because all software is a copy, it is virtually impossible to protect the sovereignty of the product. Computer companies market software under "shrinkwrap" agreements that prohibit the buyer from loaning, leasing, or transferring the software. However, there is nothing stopping a customer from violating this agreement because it is practically impossible to enforce it.

What is at stake is both market competition and the process of creativity. Without the ability to compete at the same level with similar products, there is no competition in the computer program market. It is ironic that companies dedicated to a free market system so willingly embrace monopoly when they can benefit from it. Industry compatibility remains an important goal stifled by overly strict rules of copyright and regulations against reverse engineering.

Gary R. Ignatin wrote, "Copyright law, while protecting the rights of authors, allows others freely to study and analyze their works, so that further advances can be made in their field."[72] In opposition to this perspective, Clapes, the lawyer for IBM, stated:

> Their (people who support reverse engineering) assertion is that the purpose of copyright is to cause dissemination of ideas, and that if programs are published only as unreadable object code and translation is prohibited, the ideas in the program are not disseminated. That assertion is fundamentally wrong on all counts. The purpose of copyright is to encourage publication of original work. More specifically, in the United States, the purpose of copyright is to promote progress in science and the useful arts.[73]

Although Thomas Jefferson might have disagreed with IBM's lawyer, those with control of the industry have favored strong protection despite the original intent of copyright law. Clapes noted that there are numerous methods for evaluating a program that do not infringe on copyright protection. Reverse engineering is not one of them.

These positions illustrate an important point. The economics of the situation cannot be separated from the politics. Clapes refused to endorse sharing, arguing that the market system is about competition, not cooperation. Ignatin endorsed reverse engineering because he understood the hardships of creating compatible software and the need to provide a useful product for the public. Ignatin explained, "It would be ridiculous for an author to stipulate that his book could not be studied, or for a painter to stipulate that his painting could not be analyzed. Software manufacturers, however, routinely use 'shrink-wrap' licenses to contractually prevent any unauthorized study or decompilation of their programs."[74] Ignatin worried that commercial advantage had taken precedence over progress in ideas.

The focus on computer software as a work of authorship and creative genius has obscured that software is a technology. As Ignatin noted:

> While overprotecting a novella will likely have little effect upon the field of literature as a whole, overprotecting a crucial advancement in technology could seriously hamper future innovation in the industry. . . . Restricting innovation in the software industry is especially troubling because software is used so extensively in the development of technology in other industries. Computers have been essential to recent advances in biotechnology, communications, transportation, manufacturing, and virtually every other field of study. Improperly protecting computer programs will thus have ramifications far beyond the perimeters of the software industry.[75]

Computer software has offered compelling evidence that exchange, although representing a dissolution of strictly controlled property, can benefit the public good in ways that private property cannot.

One final case illustrates the tensions between sovereignty and exchange in relation to computer software. The controversy over quoting unpublished material has become a clear example of an increasing desire to assert ownership over information and computer code. In 1991, the U.S. Court of Appeals in New York ruled that nonfiction authors could no longer quote extracts from unpublished sources (even small extracts).[76] Although most historians were appalled, there was strong support from the computer industry. The computer industry saw the ability to quote limited amounts of unpublished material as a threat to its ability to control software:

> When the authors say they want legislation to provide them once again with limited access to unpublished works "in order to clarify or demonstrate the validity of their own assertions," the computer people shudder. "That means they can use snippets," says Mr. Lehman. A "snippet" may be "fair use" of unpublished material to an author, but a snippet taken from an unpublished software program under fair-use doctrine could be enough to "decompile" the entire program. "They are talking about our crown jewels," says Mr. Lehman. "We take this very seriously."[77]

As Ingrid Voorhees, chief lobbyist for the Computer and Business Manufacturers Association, said, "We like the current law, and we are concerned that we could be damaged by legislation aimed at protecting the authors."[78] Of course, Voorhees was referring to literary authors, not program authors. Program authors are appropriately invisible and unprotected because most proprietary computer software is made on a "work made for hire" basis.

ORIGINALITY IN DATABASES

Originality has been a defining principle of copyright law since its inception. Originality is what makes a literary work unique from others, it is what defines it as an independent creation. Although originality is the goal, other works that involve a significant amount of labor have also received copyright protection. Thus, two standards for copyright are possible. The first is an original creation, the second is a work that is produced by the "sweat of the brow." Both involve authorial rights, the strongest of which are given to the original work. The decision of *Feist Publications, Inc. v. Rural Telephone Service Co., Inc.*, (1991)[79] brought the discourse on originality into the technological age. This decision touched on the possibility of copyright in databases and illuminates how important originality continues to be in our society.

Databases have been a growth industry since the computer made it easy and efficient to store and retrieve information. Typically, database information is a reproduction of available "facts," such as names, addresses, and phone numbers. Databases are used to organize these facts into useful categories. Although copyright explicitly rejects ownership of "facts," an original presentation of the facts can be copyrighted, thus making computer databases protected by copyright law. Because databases can be a source of immense revenue, one might expect them to be strictly controlled. However, in a recent court case dealing with the copyrightability of the white pages, the Supreme Court ruled that there was not sufficient originality for the white pages to constitute a creative work. In this case, Rural Telephone Service accused Feist Publications of copying its white page listings without permission. Feist's actions could be proven because its phone book included dummy numbers that Rural added to protect itself from just such a case. Even though Rural could prove Feist copied the numbers instead of researching its own, the Supreme Court ruled there was no copyright infringement. Justice Sandra Day O'Connor delivered the opinion in which the court found that Rural's white pages were not sufficiently original to be copyrightable. Thus, copying the phone numbers directly from Rural's phone book was not a violation of copyright. By allowing this action to be legitimate, *Feist* redefined the "sweat of the brow" standard for copyright.[80]

On the surface, the *Feist* decision appears to allow for substantial exchange of information. This would include consumer information databases that take hard work to compile, but are low on creativity. Although the computer industry was concerned about this decision, *Feist* will most likely not affect computer-related data. As Robert Gorman noted, computer databases like Westlaw or Lexis meet the minimum requirement of creativity and are eligible for copyright protection. To ensure copyright protection of primarily database information, one must include "value-added" material such as commentary and rankings.[81]

This case turns on the degree to which a compilation of facts can be copyrighted. In doing so, the court applied an originality test to the arrangement of the material. The court defined originality as: "To qualify for copyright protection, a work must be original to the author. Original, as the term is used in copyright, means only that the work was independently created by the author (as opposed to copied from other works), and that it possesses at least some minimal degree of creativity. To be sure, the requisite level of creativity is extremely low; even a slight amount will suffice. . . ."[82] In this case, the court relied on a standard of creativity that compared differences between works. A new work must be substantially different from the previous one to avoid infringement. This concept is called *legal originality*.[83] Legal originality, combined with the standard that an original work must be derived from the creative expression of an author, is crucial in establishing the distinction between cultural works. Making distinctions is crucial to owning creative work. Thus, the sovereignty impulse also works through this notion of legal originality.

The *Feist* story does not end with the Supreme Court decision. Congress reacted to what it perceived as threats to intellectual property. In response to *Feist v. Rural Telephone*, Congress proposed the Database Investment and Intellectual Property Antipiracy Act of 1996.[84] Because *Feist* only provided thin copyright protection to databases and allowed other people to lift the facts out of a database to use in a competitive product, Congress proposed legislation that would provide additional protection.[85] This law was modeled after the NII Copyright Protection Act of

1995. If passed, it could provide additional incentives to keep U.S. producers of databases competitive both domestically and internationally. Thus, the sovereignty impulse continues to extend property protection despite the potential lack of originality exhibited by databases.

The language of copyright has implications for the way we think and relate to all forms of creative work. It is to an example of copyright infringement of a written work and the problems that arise when copyrighted works are uploaded to the Internet that I now turn. The multiple lawsuits introduced by L. Ron Hubbard's Church of Scientology posed an excellent example of the tension between sovereignty and exchange when published and unpublished documents become the subject of electronic exchange.

COPYRIGHT AND THE INTERNET

How copyright will be protected in an environment that facilitates the unregulated distribution and sharing of information is yet to be seen. Some groups post copyright notes at the bottom of their copyrighted works and offer rewards for those who turn in violators. Others consider the distribution of their work over the Internet to be appropriate as long as the material is not used for monetary advantage.[86] Still other groups actively seek out copyright violators. Perhaps one of the most vociferous copyright protectors has been the Church of Scientology.

The Church of Scientology has taken great care to ensure that the writings of L. Ron Hubbard are kept secret from everyone but those ready to hear what they have to impart. As one moves higher in the church organization, more of the writings are revealed. These secret texts, which are, according to scientologists, copyrighted and trademarked, made their way onto the Internet through the work of several scientologists-turned-critics. Once on the Internet, these documents became impossible to control. The information moved freely from one site to another. The Scientologists did not desire this type of uncontrolled exchange of private church documents. In fact, when one of their private documents became part of the public record, known as the Fishman affidavit, the Church sent members to the U.S. District Court for the Central District of California to check out the document each day to ensure no one other than church members could read it.[87] In order to further control the boundaries of its proprietary work, the Church had someone scan the Internet watching for potential violations of its copyrights.[88] Once a potential infringer was identified, he or she was asked to delete the infringing documents. The Church also illustrated its readiness to use the courts to protect its copyrighted work by filing copyright and trade secret suits against potential infringers.

Not only has the Church's practice of rigidly defending proprietary work become interesting as an example of how copyright can be used to halt exchange (and possibly chill speech), it is also interesting because of who the Scientologists argue have infringed their copyrights. The Religious Technology Center (RTC), or Scientology, cases included the Internet service provider in their litigation net as well as specific individuals accused of copyright violation.

There was some level of precedent for the operators of bulletin boards to be held liable for the information on their server. In *Playboy v. Frena* (1993),[89] it was found that a bulletin board operator may be directly liable for distributing or displaying public copies of protected works. In *Sega Enterprises Ltd. v. Maphia* (1994),[90] it was established that an unauthorized copy is made when it is uploaded to a bulletin board. Although it would seem that a precedent of sorts had been established for copyrighted work displayed over the Internet, both of these cases differ from the RTC case in that the bulletin board operators were involved either directly or indirectly[91] in soliciting the copyrighted materials. In the RTC litigation, the material in question was merely added to a discussion list as part of thousands of other notes. The Scientologists took their copyright claim very seriously and also sued *The Washington Post* for writing an article on the controversy and quoting from what they claimed were copyrighted works.[92] Fortunately, the court found *The Washington Post* was within the scope of fair use when it quoted from what was then a publicly available document.[93]

The court found that the information service providers were not direct infringers for allowing copyrighted information to exist on their computers, but the defendants went to trial to decide the issue of contributory infringement.[94] If RTC had succeeded on the claim of direct infringement, it could have been interpreted to mean online companies would always have to err on the side of copyright claims (even where one may not exist) in order to ensure they were not brought to court as copyright infringers. This would have meant a more guarded level of discussion due to fear of violating the proprietary rights of others.

This litigation should not, however, be understood as a victory by copyright owners over critical debate and discussion, or even as a decision that could solidify a strong version of copyright into the 21st century. The court, in *RTC v. Netcom* (1995), introduced two standards of liability. If the bulletin board (BBS) owner directly encouraged the uploading of copyrighted information (as in *Sega*) it is a case of strict liability. If the uploading happened on a BBS in the course of a dialogue, the BBS owner cannot be held liable.[95] As the court explained, "The court does not find workable a theory of infringement that would hold the entire Internet liable for activities that cannot reasonably be deterred.

Billions of bits of data flow through the Internet and are necessarily stored on servers throughout the network and it is thus practically impossible to screen out infringing bits from noninfringing bits."[96]

Although the RTC cases leave room for exchange, especially when it can be linked to criticism and fair use, other cases have set strict liability standards for individuals uploading proprietary information to a bulletin board. In fact, Playboy successfully argued that Frena's bulletin board constituted "unfair competition" by providing copyrighted adult photos for free. The court reasoned that if this activity were to be reproduced all over the Internet, Playboy would lose money.[97] Frena's activities were indicative of the horror felt by traditional copyright owners in the face of virtually unlimited duplication and exchange. There is little to stop rampant copying because, of course, the Internet is designed to produce copies. As a result, solidifying copyright boundaries against "unfair" competition through the legal system is all the copyright owner can do.

Much of this litigation is about making examples of infringers in order to control how proprietary work is used. Playboy, an enormous multimillion dollar company, would be hard pressed to show any real harm. Instead, it quickly turned to litigation in an attempt to get future infringers to think twice before exchanging proprietary photos. The potential for a lawsuit is a strong incentive to be careful of what is uploaded or downloaded from one's server.

The Internet has added a new dimension to the struggle between sovereignty and exchange, as illustrated by copyright. Once a copyrighted work is uploaded to the Internet, the ability to control it is reduced to almost zero. The case of David LaMacchia is one final example of the extension of property rights to the Internet. The software industry has done its best to go after "software pirates" who exchange copyrighted works via the Internet. David LaMacchia is one such "pirate." He was arrested for making available copyrighted software over the Internet.[98] The Massachusetts courts found LaMacchia not guilty of wire fraud or copyright violations because he had not sold the software he pirated, but gave it away.

In response to the LaMacchia case, Congress has proposed the NET Act. This act is a logical extension of the NII Copyright Act of 1995, which was discussed in chapter 2. Where the NII Act was concerned with plugging the holes in copyright law as it relates to published work on the Internet, the NET Act is concerned with plugging the loopholes in the criminal code for punishing copyright theft on the Internet. The NET Act redefined financial gain to mean the "receipt, or expectation of receipt, of anything of value, including the receipt of other copyrighted works."[99] Thus, to even receive a software program became a financial gain. The act went further to redefine criminal infringement to mean not only commercial advantage, but also the reproduction or distribution of one or more copies worth $1,000.

LaMacchia was acquitted because he had not taken commercial advantage of the programs he shared. The new law makes the reproduction or distribution of copyrighted products without any financial gain also subject to criminal penalties.[100] Criminal liability continues to require evidence of *willfulness*, which is defined as more than the mere reproduction and distribution.[101] The NET Act passed in December 1997.

The Internet makes it possible to share works outside the legal framework of copyright law and publisher's control. Many authors, publishers, and copyright owners have been unhappy with this newfound ability to exchange information. Publishers of books and unpublished documents have not wished their works to become part of the Internet public where they are uncontrollable. Copyright law as interpreted by the courts and extended by Congress has helped solidify property boundaries in the information age.

The courts have provided an important stage where these dramas are enacted and result in judgments that, although leaving room for flexibility, always respect copyright law and punish copyright infringers. These cases are made more complex by their interactions with censorship of obscene materials, First Amendment claims, and the desire to exchange information. As technology intersects with the products of the publication industry, these stories will become more numerous. Generally, copyright infringers should beware—the courts will protect publishers and authors from unauthorized use. Of course, although the initial upload can often be traced, the paths of copyrighted material, once it enters the Internet, is another matter. Despite the threat of litigation, exchange of information will most likely continue unabated.

CONCLUSION: LEGAL NARRATIVES IN THE INFORMATION AGE

Martin Gardiner Reiffen is a millionaire who, in December 1997, was granted a patent over a process called *preemptive multithreading*. After receiving this patent, Reiffen initiated a lawsuit against Microsoft. He argued that virtually all software on the market uses this process and because Microsoft represents a significant chunk of the software market it was the most likely target for a big lawsuit. When asked why he was suing Microsoft, he replied, "They asked Willie Sulton: 'Why do you rob a bank?' And he answered, 'Because that's where the money is.' "[102] Reiffen illustrated the type of property claim we can expect to see more of in the future.

I share the legal story because it depicts an approach by which the software industry and other copyright owners attempt to extend sovereignty over the new realm of exchange—electronic information. The outcome is a clear understanding of computer programs as intellectual property, the emergence of "legitimate" and "illegitimate" ownership of intellectual property, and ultimately the construction of villains who prey on "helpless" owners of copyrights.

The legal discourse helps reconstruct the traditional copyright story for use on the Internet and incorporate computer software under the rubric of ownership. What is packaged for the American people is a notion of intellectual property rights that is solid and permanent. Court cases help provide that solidity by establishing precedents that can be followed. As this chapter shows, the courts have appeared willing to balance competing property claims. However, these claims are balanced within an already existing set of property assumptions that are extended to cover new types of creative work and new methods for exchanging information. The courts have not questioned the applicability of copyright or property law. Copyright has become a commonly accepted myth legitimized through the legal system.[103] Yet, our current copyright paradigm is breaking down as it is stretched to make illegal the exchange that is practiced on the Internet and through the process of creation. Because copyright litigation is about protecting market share, the romantic notion of exchange it was meant to foster is dying. As we move further into the information age, the discourse on copyright is being used to develop the lines between appropriate and inappropriate actions. In the next two chapters, I look more closely at the production of villains. These villains help define the manner in which information should be shared.

NOTES

1. *Literary works* are works, other than audiovisual works, expressed in words, numbers, or other verbal or numerical symbols or indicia, regardless of the nature of the material objects, such as books, periodicals, manuscripts, phonorecords, film, tapes, disks, or cards, in which they are embodied. Copyright Act of 1976, 17 U.S.C. § 101. The National Commission on New Technological Uses of Copyrighted Works (CONTU) recommended in 1979 that computer programs be recognized as copyrighted works. Congress complied and codified this recommendation in 17 U.S.C. §§ 101, 117.

2. Statement of Mitchell D. Kapor. *Computers and intellectual property: Hearings before the subcommittee on courts, intellectual property and the administration of justice of the committee on the judiciary, House of Representatives*, 101st Cong., 1st, & 2nd Session (1989), 242.

3. P. Samuelson, "Information as property: Do *Ruckelshaus* and *Carpenter* signal a changing direction in intellectual property law?" *Catholic University Law Review* (Winter 1989): 367.

4. Samuelson cited two cases: *Ruckelshaus v. Monsanto Co.*, and *Carpenter v.*

United States in which a property right in information was found. Wendy Gordon also viewed *Feist* as leaving a backdoor open for states to find a property right in information and facts. *Feist* only states that Congress does not have copyright power over facts. "The opinion, therefore, can be read as hinting that state protection for facts might not be preempted." W. J. Gordon, "On owning information: Intellectual property and the restitutionary impulse," *Virginia Law Review, 78* (February 1992): 154 fn. 21.

5. "Look and feel" is a way of describing in fuzzy terms what may be protectable about a program outside its literal code. The look and feel would include the visual display and the general "feel" of the program. If these elements are copied there may be an infringement.

6. This information comes from the prepared statement of Ralph Oman, register of Copyrights and Associate Librarian for Copyright Services before the joint hearing on *Computers and intellectual property*, 259–324.

7. The definitive court case for this issue is *Apple Computer, Inc. v. Franklin Computer Corp.*, 714 F.2d 1240 (3rd Cir. 1983). See: Oman, *Computers and intellectual property*, 267.

8. The precedent is *Tandy Corp. v. Personal Micro Computers, Inc.*, "which concerned protection of an operating program establishing an 'input–output routine.' The district court ruled that 'a silicon chip is a tangible medium of expression within the meaning of the statute, such as to make the program fixed in that form subject to the copyright laws.' " See: *Computers and intellectual property*, 269.

9. *Source code* is the code written by the programmer in something close to a readable language. *Object code* is the compiled source code that is machine readable. Arguments have been made that object code should be unprotected because it is usually unreadable by humans. These arguments have failed in the courts. See: *Computers and intellectual property* 270.

10. Object code was found copyrightable in: *Williams Electronics Inc., v. Arctic International, Inc.*, 685 F.2d 870, 876–77 (3d Cir. 1982); and *Hubco Data Products, Corp. v. Management Assistance Inc.*, 219 U.S.P.Q. (BNA) 450, 454 (D. Id. 1983). Source and object code were found copyrightable in: *Apple Computer, Inc. v. Franklin Computer Corp.*, 714 F.2d 1240, 1243 (3d Cir. 1983), cert. dismissed, 464 U.S. 1033, 104 S. Ct. 690, 79 L. Ed. 2d 158 (1984); *GCA Corp. v. Chance*, 217 U.S.P.Q. (BNA) 718, 720 (N.D. Cal. 1982); *Midway Manufacturing Co. v. Strohon*, 564 F. Supp. 741, 750 (N.D. Ill. 1983); and *Digital Communications Associates, Inc. v. Softklone Distributing Corp.*, 659 F. Supp. 449, 2 U.S.P.Q.2D (BNA) 1385 (N.D. Ga. 1987).

11. A. L. Clapes, *Softwars: The legal battles for control of the global software industry* (Westport, CT, & London: Quorum Books, 1993), 11.

12. Ibid.

13. Ibid., 11–12. The image of a prima donna software programmer is developed in Steven Levy's book on hackers as well. Levy pointed out that as the software industry developed, *prima donnas* were replaced with programmers who would work in a manner more appropriate for the corporate world. See: S. Levy, *Hackers: Heroes of the computer revolution* (Garden City, NY: Anchor Press, 1984).

14. Clapes' opinion was used to provide support for strong copyright pro-

tection in *Lotus Development Corp. v. Paperback Software Intl.*, 740 F. Supp. 37, June 28, 1990.

15. Levy, *Hackers*.

16. A. W. Branscomb, "Computer software: Protecting the crown jewels of the information economy" in *Intellectual property rights in science, technology, and economic performance*, eds. F. W. Rushing & C. G. Brown (Boulder, San Francisco, & London: Westview Press, 1990).

The economic value of computer software was also repeatedly emphasized in the Congressional Hearings on Computers and Intellectual Property.

17. A. W. Branscomb, *Who owns information? From privacy to public access* (New York: Basic Books, 1994).

18. *OTA report on intellectual property rights in an age of electronics and information: Joint hearing of the subcommittee on patents, copyrights, and trademarks of the senate committee on the judiciary and the subcommittee on courts, civil liberties, and the administration of justice of the house committee on the judiciary*, 99th Cong., 2nd Session (16 April 1986), 34.

19. Gordon, "On owning information," 157.

20. A. Mody, New International environment for intellectual property rights, in *Intellectual property rights in science, technology, and economic performance*, eds. F. W. Rushing & C. G. Brown, (Boulder, San Francisco, & London: Westview Press, 1990). "The U.S. has also seen the development of case law in the area of information technology (software and databases) which has proved particularly difficult to protect. Although case law has evolved in an uncoordinated manner, the general direction of change has been towards substantially increased protection" (p. 214). See also: Gordon, "On owning information," 156; Samuelson, "Information as property," 365–400.

21. This is certainly true for *Computer Associates International, Inc., v. Altai, Inc.*, 775 F.Supp. 544 (E.D.N.Y. 1991) where, even though a certain leniency was allowed, everything remained under the copyright law.

22. *Lotus Development Corp. v. Borland International Inc.*, 516 U.S. 1167.

23. Cases, besides *Apple v. Franklin*, dealing with literal code include: *Stern Electronics, Inc. v. Kaufman*, 669 F.2d 852 (2d Cir. 1982); and *Williams Electronics, Inc. v. Arctic International, Inc.*, 685 F.2d 870 (3d Cir. 1982).

24. For example, Apple has been involved with litigation over its user interface with Microsoft and Hewlett-Packard since 1989. They have been relatively unsuccessful and were denied cert. on February 21, 1995. 115 S.Ct. 1176. Apple had claimed that both Microsoft and Hewlett-Packard violated their license with Apple and copied Apple's user interface too closely.

25. *Apple v. Franklin*, 714 F.2d. 1240 (3d. Cir 1983) cert. dismissed per stipulation, 464 U.S. 1033 (1984).

26. A. G. Rodau, "Protecting computer software: After *Apple Computer Inc. v. Franklin Computer Corp.*, 714 F.2d 1248 (3rd Cir. 1983), does copyright provide the best protection?" *Intellectual Property Law Review* (1986): 414.

27. The Court cites the legislative history as evidence of Congressional intent to protect computer programs as literary works. Additionally, the Commission on New Technological Uses (CONTU) recommended that copyright be extended to computer programs, defining them as literary works "that . . . embody an author's original creation." *Apple v. Franklin*, 714 F.2d at 1247.

28. 17 U.S.C.A. 102(a).

29. *Nichols v. Universal Pictures Corp.*, 45 F.2d 119, 121 (2d Cir. 1930). In P. Goldstein, *Copyright, patent, trademark and related state doctrines: Cases and materials on the law of intellectual property*, (3rd ed. (Westbury, NY: The Foundation Press, 1993), 733.

30. *Nichols v. Universal Picture Corp.*, Quoted in Goldstein, *Cases and materials* 736.

31. For an analysis of the idea/expression dichotomy as it relates to computer languages see S. Posner, "Can a computer language be copyrighted? The state of confusion in computer copyright law," *Intellectual Property Law Review, 25* (1993): 485–518.

32. *Synercom Technology, Inc. v. University Computing Co.*, 462 F. Supp 1003 (N.D. Tex. 1978).

33. *Whelan v. Jaslow Dental Laboratory, Inc.*, 797 F.2d 1222 (3d Cir. 1986), cert. denied, 479 U.S. 1031 (1986).

34. Ibid., at 1248.

35. Ibid., at 1231.

36. Ibid., at 1225.

37. Ibid., at 1226.

38. Ibid.

39. Ibid., at 1227.

40. Ibid., at 1233.

41. Ibid., at 1235.

42. Ibid., at 1237.

43. D. Ladd, & B. G. Joseph, "Expanding computer software protection by limiting the idea," *The Journal of Law and Technology, 2* (1987): 15.

44. P. Samuelson, "Computer programs, user interfaces, and section 102(b) of the Copyright Act of 1976: A critique of *Lotus v. Paperback*," *Law and Contemporary Problems*, (Spring 1992): 316.

45. *Lotus v. Paperback*, 740 F.Supp. at 68.

46. *Computer Associates International, Inc., v. Altai, Inc.*, 775 F.Supp. 544 (E.D.N.Y. 1991).

47. "In *Whelan*, the court adopted an extremely broad view of copyrightability for a computer program. . . . The *Whelan* test is inadequate and inaccurate. Professor Nimmer pointed out one of its pitfalls: "The crucial flaw in this reasoning is that it assumes that only one 'idea,' in copyright law terms, underlies any computer program, and that once a separable idea can be identified, everything else must be expression" Ibid., at 558–559.

48. Goldstein, *Cases and materials*, 803.

49. *Computer Associates International, v. Altai, Inc.*, 775 F.Supp. 544 at 559.

50. Ibid., at 561.

51. J. Markoff, "Ruling restricts software copyright protection," *The New York Times*, 24 June 1992, D1 (L).

52. *Ashton-Tate Corporation v. Richard Ross*, 916 F.2d 516 (17 July 1990).

53. *Apple Computer v. Microsoft Corporation*, 821 F.Supp. 616 (N.D. Cal. 1993) at 619.

54. *Xerox Corp. v. Apple Computer Inc.*, 717 F. Supp. 1428; 1989 U.S. Dist. LEXIS 8622.

55. Ibid., at 619.

56. Ibid., at 624.

57. Cert. was denied *Apple* in February 1995. Reported at: 1995 U.S. Lexis 1535. Apple will have to live with the decision of the lower courts.

58. N. P. Terry, "GUI wars: The windows litigation and the continuing decline of look and feel," *Arkansas Law Review*, (1994): 98.

59. F. J. Macchiarola, "Copyright protection: Has look and feel crashed?" *Cardozo Arts and Entertainment Law Journal* (1993): 724.

60. Terry, "GUI wars," 113.

61. *Lotus Development Corporation v. Borland International Inc.*, 116 S. Ct. 804 (1996).

62. Ibid.

63. Briefs for the Lotus were filed by Digital Equipment Corporation, The Gates Rubber Company, Intel Corporation, Xerox Corporation, IBM, Hewlett-Packard, and Apple.

64. There is additional evidence to suggest that copyright and unfair competition claims are closely associated as big companies attempt to control their copyrights and their control over the market. See: D. M. Maiorana, "Privileged use: Has Judge Boudin suggested a viable means of copyright protection for the nonliteral aspects of computer software in *Lotus Development Corp. v. Borland International*?" *The American University Law Review*, (October 1996): 149–188.

65. J. Litman, "Copyright and information policy," *Law and Contemporary Problems*, (Spring 1992): 200.

66. *Sega Enterprises v. Accolade, Inc.*, 785 F. Supp. 1392.

67. Ibid.

68. Litman, "Copyright and information policy," 200. Strictly speaking translation is a violation of copyright law as well.

69. *Vault Corp. v. Quaid Software Ltd.*, 655 F. Supp. 750.

70. Litman, "Copyright and information policy," 198.

71. Accolade reverse engineered Sega's Genesis game cartridges so it could develop Genesis-compatible video games. Additionally, Accolade copied the code that would make its programs run on the Genesis III machine. In so doing, Accolade copied the code that made the Sega Message (produced by or under license from Sega Enterprises) appear. See: *Sega Enterprises v. Accolade, Inc.*, 785 F. Supp. 1392.

72. G. R. Ignatin, "Let the hackers hack: Allowing the reverse engineering of copyrighted computer programs to achieve compatibility," *University of Pennsylvania Law Review*, (1992): 2008.

73. Clapes, *Softwars*, 146.

74. Ignatin, *Hackers hack*, 2015.

75. Ibid., 2021–2022.

76. J. M. Perry, "What publishers call quoting, computer firms call piracy as industries face off on Capitol Hill," *Wall Street Journal*, 23 April 1991, A24.

77. Ibid.

78. Ibid.

79. *Feist Publications, Inc. v. Rural Telephone Service Co., Inc.*, 111 S.Ct. 1282 (1991).

80. Jane Ginsburg attributed the lack of protection for sweat of the brow items to the overreliance on an authorial personality. Copyrightable works break into

two categories—high authorship and low authorship. Within such a framework, concepts of original authorship obscure the importance of labor-intensive work. She argued, copyright would do much better if it let go of its surface coherence and instead adopted a form of protection more compatible with the variety of works out there. See: J. C. Ginsburg, "Creation and commercial value: Copyright protection of works of information," *Columbia Law Review, 90* (1990): 1865–1936.

81. R. A. Gorman, "The *Feist* case: Reflections on a pathbreaking copyright decision," *Intellectual Property Law Review, 25* (1993): 395–396.

82. *Feist Publications, Inc. v. Rural Telephone Service Co.,* at 1287.

83. Legal originality supposedly exists to "assure a sufficiently gross *difference* between the underlying and the derivative work to avoid entangling subsequent artists depicting the underlying work in copyright problems." R. H. Rotstein, "Beyond metaphor: Copyright infringement and the fiction of the work," *Chicago-Kent Law Review, 68* (1993): 748.

84. "The database investment and Intellectual Property Antipiracy Act of 1996," *Congressional Record*, 23 May 1996, vol. 142, #74, p. E890.

85. Antipiracy Act, p. E890.

86. This approach has been termed *copyleft* and is the idea of Richard Stallman, one of the original hackers and a strong advocate for the free exchange of information. See: R. U. Sirius & St. Jude, *How to mutate and take over the world* (New York: Ballantine Books, 1996), 233.

87. *Religious Technology Center v. Lerma,* Civil Action No. 95–1107-A, 1995 U.S. Dist. Lexis 17833. Memorandum Opinion.

88. Ibid.

89. *Playboy Enterprises, Inc. v. George Frena,* 839 F.Supp. 1552, 1554 (M.D. Fla. 1993).

90. *Sega Enterprises Ltd. v. Maphia,* 857 F.Supp. 679, 683 (N.D. Cal. 1994).

91. Part of Frena's defense was that he was unaware of the copyright violations taking place on his bulletin board and once he was informed he immediately halted this activity. The court found this argument unpersuasive. In the case of Maphia, there was significant evidence that he and his codefendants had solicited copyrighted work. They unsuccessfully claimed fair use as their defense.

92. *Religious Technology Center v. Lerma,* 897 F. Supp. 260.

93. Ibid.

94. *Religious Technology Center and Bridge Publications Inc. v. Netcom On-Line Communication Services, Inc., Dennis Erlich, Tom Klemesrud, Clearwood Data Services,* NO. C-95–20091 RMW; 1995 U.S. Dist. Lexis 18173.

95. Contributory liability was found in the RTC litigation because after being warned that there was unauthorized copyrighted information on their servers the companies did nothing to eliminate it.

96. *RTC v. Netcom,* at 20 (Lexis).

97. *Playboy v. Frena.*

98. *United States of America v. David LaMacchia,* 871 F.Supp. 535.

99. "No Electronic Theft (NET) Act," *Congressional Record*, 4 November 1997, Vol. 143, 152, H9887.

100. Ibid., H9883.

101. Ibid., H9884.

102. R. Court, "Inventor stakes claim to MS fortunes," *Wired News* [On-line],

Available: http://www.wired.com/news/news/business/story/10251.html. (12 February 1998).

103. As noted in chapter 1, Barthes argued the "very principle of myth" is that it "transforms history into nature." See: R. Barthes, *Mythologies*, trans. A. Lavers (New York: Hill and Wang, 1972). 129. This naturalizing of history is exactly what has occurred with copyright law to the extent that natural rights theory is often times used to justify the copyright system.

4

International Piracy: Finding External Intellectual Property Threats

As long as there has been a concept of property there has been piracy.[1] In fact, it can be argued that the notion of the proprietary author developed on the backs of pirates. Law does not emerge fully formed to address the injustices of the world. Rather, law is created in response to stories that manufacture injustice. The law is used to label unwanted behavior as illegal. It is impossible to separate the construction of intellectual property deviants from the construction of intellectual property rights. Thus, focusing on intellectual property pirates lends insight into how the law of copyright is narratively constructed. Although the primary narrative construction of intellectual property pirates occurred more than a century ago, we are witnessing the expansion of this label to include new forms of piracy today.

As intellectual property becomes one of the United States' most important commodities, both at home and abroad, there is a corresponding increase in entertainment and computer software piracy. Because new technology produces products prone to perfect duplication, and thus open to rampant (and oftentimes free) exchange, the traditional notion of copyright is experiencing an unparalleled threat. Given the threat posed by a new era of technology that enhances the sharing of information, copyright owners are finding it necessary to utilize their narrative abilities to render the activities of the pirate illegal. The internationalism of this particular threat amplifies the potential damage and gives rise to a variety of fascinating narratives.

The United States has been able to impose the U.S. copyright story on the rest of the world through international treaties and agreements. When the United States exports cultural products via intellectual property industries, it exports intellectual property laws and a certain notion of authorship and originality as well. However, the expansion of property rights is also a narrative process used to justify U.S. actions against pirates and to construct piracy as an enormous threat to U.S. industries.

The expansion of property rights is a complex and multifaceted process. Passing laws and asserting property rights via court cases are blatant methods for expanding property rights and applying the copyright narrative to new areas. The manner in which deviant behavior is produced is a somewhat more subtle method for inscribing property boundaries. This chapter, as well as chapter 5, deal specifically with how deviants are used to construct property boundaries.

The law is needed to encourage people to respect the property rights of intellectual property owners. It becomes more difficult, however, to convince other countries, countries that do not operate on the same intellectual property premises as our own, that they should follow our laws. In order to protect what should be considered a relatively abstract notion of property, some aspect of law must be involved. Thus, the narrative of the pirate emerges as the threat to hard-working folks whose livelihoods depend on their intellectual property. Narrating specific activities as illegal helps establish definitions of normalcy for U.S. citizens and provides justification for aggressive international action to stop foreign pirates.

The narrative constructed goes like this: The hard-working intellectual property company spends money and time creating a product. The company's hard work and ingenuity should be rewarded so it gets to own the product exclusively. Anyone caught with unauthorized copies is a pirate. These pirates are engaged in illegal and immoral activities, which deprive the rightful owners of their profits. Pirates are lazy because they steal instead of create. They should be punished for their actions. In this case, the narrative process is about staking out property lines in new technology. The piracy narrative is one of many that is currently operating to construct new expanded intellectual property boundaries. However, by analyzing the piracy narrative, and by understanding law as a narrative process, it is possible to begin uncovering the hegemonic processes at work.[2]

HISTORY OF PIRACY

For hundreds of years, there has existed a theory of intellectual property based on the assumption that creation is facilitated by the provision of a temporary monopoly, which ensures the author will benefit monetarily from his or her work (and I use this language deliberately).[3] Among the most powerful metaphors used to explain this intangible right was the Lockean concept of landed property. This metaphor was used to justify the extension of proprietary rights in intellectual property. The metaphor of a landed estate has helped individuals become accustomed to the ownership of ideas for centuries.[4]

Intellectual property has been the subject of international conventions and agreements for more than 100 years and piracy has been an issue from the beginning.[5] Until 1891 the United States would not recognize foreign copyrights,[6] meaning foreign literary work could be freely published in the United States without royalties returning to the copyright owner. The United States had strong copyright laws protecting citizens and residents, however, foreigners and foreign products were explicitly excluded from protection by U.S. law.[7] During this period, U.S. citizens legally pirated British work.[8] As one commentator on copyright said, "as long as the work of a foreign author was not legally protected it was common property; it was no more piratical for a publisher to print it than for a peasant to graze his pigs on common land."[9] The fact that Americans did not consider their actions piratical did not stop the British from viewing them that way. Although some foreigners found ways around the law (such as co-authoring a work for copyright reasons with an American), most British work was blatantly pirated in the United States and sold for less than the British could ask.[10]

Finally, in 1891, the United States passed the Chace Act, which provided protection for foreign authors. Even then, U.S. copyrights were not considered profitable. As one publisher of the time noted, Americans were used to books sold at significantly reduced prices. In order for British publishers to print copyrighted works in the United States, they would have to raise prices or forego profits. Raising prices would depress potential sales. Thus, even with copyright available in the United States, it was not in the publisher's best interest to procure a U.S. copyright when the volume could be sold in Britain at a profit.[11]

Between 1891 and 1988, the United States made the transition from pirate to police and consequently underwent a significant change in the way it viewed intellectual property.[12] So much has changed, in fact, that the United States has become the leading advocate of strong international intellectual property protection. This advocacy has been the motivating force behind the inclusion of intellectual property rights in the GATT, the United States–Canada Free Trade Agreement, NAFTA, and numerous other treaties.[13] It is ironic that the United States should be the world enforcer of intellectual property rights when not so long ago it was among the world's worst pirates.

The emergence of intellectual property as a critical international issue to the United States occurred in the mid-1980s when intellectual property leapt from obscurity to a central place on the national agenda. Congress made the protection of intellectual property a principle negotiating objective of the Trade and Tariff Act of 1984 and defined intellectual property inadequacies as unfair trade practices.[14] These goals were reaffirmed in the 1988 Act.[15] Section 301 of the Trade and Tariff Act allows the United States to sanction countries that violate its intellectual property laws (regardless of the intellectual property laws in the country where the violation occurs).

The report of the President's Commission on Industrial Competitiveness in January 1985 argued that "strengthening of intellectual property rights at home and abroad should be a priority item on the nation's policy agenda."[16] Intellectual property rights were made a priority by President Ronald Reagan in his trade statement of September 23, 1985.[17]

Why is it that intellectual property became an issue in the mid-1980s? In the mid-1980s the United States was undergoing a transformation from an industrial to an information economy. Waning industrial competitiveness was hurting U.S. companies and U.S. international trade. The United States began searching for new areas of commerce that would maintain U.S. competitiveness. Intellectual property came to be viewed as "a new basis of comparative advantage."[18]

There were several intellectual property-dependent industries that were becoming extremely important contributors to the U.S. economy, namely the entertainment industry (records, movies, and books), pharmaceutical companies, and the computer industry. Computer technology, for example, emerged as a huge growth industry during the mid-1980s as personal computers hit the market, computer games became hot items, and computer software proved itself as a commercial product with a high level of economic return.[19] As the computer began to assert its muscles nationally, issues such as copyright of computer code hit the courts.[20] Copyright owners and new businesses dealing in technological products were finding they traded and marketed products that could be easily copied or replicated. Because a significant portion of foreign trade was in countries with little or no intellectual property laws, U.S. companies became frustrated with international piracy that kept them from maximizing potential profit. As new technologies helped subvert traditional methods of proprietary control, concerns emerged among the intellectual property industries.

The trade problems of the United States created the perfect justification for putting intellectual property rights at the top of the national trade agenda. Professor William P. Alford noted:

> The realization that trade and intellectual property concerns were linked did not spring full blown from the head of Ronald Reagan in the 1980s (as if much of anything did). . . . But what did occur in the 1980s that brought these issues together in a politically powerful fash-

> ion was a conjunction of interest between industry and government. American exporters heavily reliant upon intellectual property—such as the computer, entertainment and pharmaceutical industries—were growing ever more frustrated with both legitimate competition and proliferating piracy, while the White House found itself casting about for a politically painless way to address the growing trade deficit.[21]

The emergence of intellectual property as a trade issue for the United States during the mid-1980s coincided with the growing trade deficit, the transformation of the economy, and the increasing ability to pirate intellectual works made possible by new technologies. With these problems knocking on the U.S. foreign policy door, international piracy provided a clear answer to why the United States was having difficulties in the world market. The piracy narrative provided Americans with a villain who could be fought, unlike the murky domestic and economic factors at the root of the problem.

Today, the protection of intellectual property has become a primary motivating factor behind the U.S. position on international trade, and it informs treaties at both a bilateral and multilateral level. Implicit in the focus on intellectual property has been an increased concern over enforcement of intellectual property rights and a focus on piracy. The pirate emerges as a threat against which the United States finds itself competing in a new environment where legal and illegal competition are infringing on its ability to maintain market share. The pirate is especially threatening within countries lacking a legal framework that provides incentives for creating intellectual property and punishments for violating these "rights."

The general economic conditions of the United States continued to affect intellectual property relations throughout the 1990s. Perhaps most dramatic was the ongoing U.S. aggressiveness toward the Chinese government and its approach to intellectual property piracy. The Chinese drama illustrates how copyright has become a set of principles that the United States believes the entire world should embrace. Through its link with international trade and piracy, the U.S. version of the intellectual property story moved beyond U.S. borders and was forced on the developing (and some developed) nations of the world, including the world's most populated nation.

CHINA AND PIRACY

Pirates have emerged as a significant problem for U.S. companies attempting to do business internationally, especially in Asia and the developing world. The International Intellectual Property Alliance noted that in 1993 the United States lost $110 million in computer program revenue to China alone, and the figures are similar for other Asian countries including Japan, Taiwan, Indonesia, Philippines, and Thailand.[22]

It was not until the May 1989 occupation of Tiananmen Square that the eyes of the world were brought to China. Even as the Bush Administration expressed concern about interfering with China's internal affairs in regard to Tiananmen Square, they were threatening the Pacific Rim with "massive and unprecedented trade sanctions if China did not promise to devise legal protection for computer software to America's liking."[23] As Alford said:

> The decisions that led the U.S. government to pay insufficient heed to the epochal events culminating on June 4, 1989, and instead to devote a goodly portion of its available leverage to securing promises about software, were neither inadvertent nor passing tactical errors. On the contrary, they exemplify the high priority that intellectual property protection has assumed in American foreign policy with respect to the Chinese world and beyond since the mid 1980's, and the concomitant conviction that the key to securing such protection is the passage of new legislation, through pressure if need be.[24]

Although 1989 was not the first time pressure had been put on China to improve its intellectual property laws,[25] this new pressure illustrated the importance of intellectual property in international policymaking. Additionally, it showed how important software as an exchangeable commodity had become to the United States. The 1989 negotiations were not to be the last.

On April 26, 1991, the U.S. government used Section 301 of the 1988 Trade Act to place China on the priority list of countries having problematic intellectual property laws.[26] The United States gave China a November 26, 1991 deadline to comply with U.S. demands or face trade sanctions. Secretary of State James Baker visited China in November 1991 and "informed the Chinese that the misuse of American intellectual property stood with the sales of weapons of mass destruction to international outlaws such as Iran and abuses of fundamental human rights as one of three issues impeding better bilateral relations."[27] One month later, the United States Trade Representative (USTR) gave China its ultimatum—either "rewrite its Intellectual Property laws to the satisfaction of Washington or face the imposition of hundreds of millions of dollars of punitive tariffs."[28]

China, for its part, was already improving its intellectual property laws. In 1991, it implemented its own copyright code, in part because of Section 301 threats in 1990.[29] The 1991 threat ended when China agreed to outlaw theft of computer software and protect patents of agricultural chemicals and pharmaceuticals if the United States agreed to take China from the "priority list."[30] Chinese officials were less than happy, however, at what they saw as a violation of their sovereignty.

It was predicted that China's new stance against piracy would create a climate more amenable to U.S. investment. After the Section 301 investigation in 1991 and 1992, China agreed to sign a Memorandum of Understanding with the United States to address piracy concerns.[31] China even executed a man caught selling fake *Maotai*, a brand name liquor, in 1992 during an antipiracy campaign. This strong stance against piracy made companies like Walt Disney feel safe enough to reinvest in China. In 1993, Walt Disney granted 20 licenses to manufacturers in China to produce Walt Disney products.[32]

However, the issue of intellectual property piracy soon reared its ugly head again. In 1995, China and the United States were on the brink of another trade war following accusations by the United States that China was not meeting its end of the agreement due to its failure to protect products as far ranging as Disney's *The Lion King* to Microsoft's computer programs. At issue was enforcement of the intellectual property laws China had already put on the books. The United States felt China had not tried hard enough to eliminate piracy. Again, the Clinton Administration used its Section 301 weapon to "investigate" China's intellectual property record and possibly impose sanctions if China did not comply. China listed its retaliatory measures if the United States imposed sanctions and in January 1995 a trade war looked immanent.[33]

Faced with $1.1 billion of sanctions if it did not agree to U.S. demands, China capitulated to the United States, making "the China market safer for American computer programmers and pop stars."[34] Although the United States emerged victorious again, the price was high. China may have given in to U.S. pressure on intellectual property, but it retained its diplomatic dignity by rejecting an attempt to ban nuclear weapons testing and by publishing a report, "timed to coincide with the copyright accord, that China has no political or religious prisoners."[35] The possible $1 billion returned to U.S. companies due to decreased piracy made an "enormous impact" on the $30 billion trade deficit the United States had with China.[36] However, as one diplomat stated: "When you add up the costs and benefits of the intellectual property accord, I wonder if it's really worth it."[37]

The United States had been threatening trade war with China over intellectual property for many years. There is evidence to suggest that this hard-line attitude toward China was really about trade barriers and untapped markets, as pointed out by Awanohara and Kaye: "Outclassed by Japan in consumer products and unable to vie with the easy-credit terms of European capital-manufacturers, the US' only hope of narrowing its growing trade deficit with China—US $10 billion last year and projected at nearly US $15 billion this year—must lie in technology exports."[38] Because technology was protected by intellectual property law, the United States used intellectual property to open China's markets.

The link between open markets and intellectual property was made clear in the statements of Representative Nancy Pelosi who in an effort to introduce new sanctions against the Chinese stated, "Despite all these efforts by United States officials, the Chinese Government is not abiding by the agreement, piracy is increasing, and market access to United States products is being denied."[39] America's increasing trade deficit with China, Pelosi added, did not include the millions lost because of China's violations of intellectual property rights.[40] Obviously, to those making the laws, the easiest way to address trade barriers and trade deficits was to focus on and attack a clearly defined enemy. In this case, intellectual property piracy made a clear scapegoat that could help, it was hoped, to force China's markets open and decrease the U.S. trade deficit. U.S. pressure was justified with the argument that piracy is an illegal practice that must be halted.

The rocky intellectual property relation between China and the United States could in part be attributed to the very notion of intellectual property itself. The United States possessed a well-defined intellectual property system with a long European history. The United States, now that it was a leading exporter of intellectual property, was interested in having other nations of the world understand intellectual property as U.S. citizens understood it. However, China was still in the process of developing a legal system based on notions of legal rights and the rule of law.[41] China wrote its first intellectual property laws in the beginning of the 20th century under pressure by foreign governments.[42] In the 1980s, China still had little concept of intellectual property law. China, with a strong history of government censorship and control over ideas, and its different approach to private property rights, looked on intellectual property as a collective good, if it thought about intellectual property at all. China added and "improved" these laws only at the pressure of foreign governments. It was perhaps inevitable that significant problems would erupt given the opposing viewpoints held by China and the United States. The United States invited an adversarial relation with China by impatiently and aggressively expecting immediate compliance with its notion of property. A clearer example of exporting a specific narrative of property could not be found.

PIRATES AS THE ENEMY

Technology has made possible more sophisticated piracy. Not only are computer programs, movies, compact disks, and videos easily pirated and sold, but technology also makes it possible to rapidly reproduce and distribute books. The computer industry is especially threatened because its products are so easily replicated and sold. Software companies have highlighted their plight in China and other Asian countries. They estimate, for example, that 99% of the software used in Vietnam is pirated, while the numbers are around 96% in China.[43] The possibilities created by technology are responsible for making intellectual property piracy a threat.

It is worth outlining the important aspects of the pirate as enemy narrative. The first thing that must be done is to illustrate that significant harm is created by the act of piracy. Businesses and Congress use statistics of money lost to piracy in order to define the problem. Critical to the piracy narrative was a survey completed by the U.S. International Trade Commission (ITC) to discover the extent of piracy. The ITC pursued the study for the USTR by asking U.S. businesses to estimate the amounts they lost per year to piracy. The ITC reported that the 431 companies responding to the questionnaire suffered losses of more than $23.8 billion in 1986 due to piracy.[44] From these numbers, the ITC estimated that, overall, the United States lost between $43 billion and $61 billion from piracy each year.[45] Although there are serious questions about the methodology used in the ITC study,[46] these numbers were picked up and used uncritically by politicians and special interests.

The ITC survey proved that piracy was costing U.S. industries millions, if not billions, per year. However, it was not clear what the numbers actually represented. For example, in Congressional testimony in 1997, Representative Howard Coble of North Carolina asserted that intellectual property piracy, according to industry groups, cost $11 billion in 1996 with some claiming it to be as high as $20 billion.[47] If these numbers are accurate then piracy might actually be decreasing.[48]

Numbers specific to China have shown an even greater disparity in facts. Representative Pelosi, for example, argued that in 1995 Chinese piracy cost U.S. companies $2.5 billion.[49] However, 4 days earlier, numbers by former Deputy USTR Charlene Barshefsky were entered into the Congressional Record that stated that in 1995 U.S. industries lost $866 million to piracy in China.[50] If anything, the lack of consistency in how much piracy actually occurs is not important. As long as the numbers are sufficiently high the vilification of pirates can continue. Additionally, the veracity of the numbers is unimportant. It is the assertion of harm that is necessary for this narrative. The numbers are supplemented by an important step in which the deviants are identified and the victims produced.

The identifiable evil involved corrupt pirates (both domestic and foreign) and even more important, the lax intellectual property laws found around the world but found especially in Asian countries. As a study by the Annenberg School reported: "Though piracy occurs in every country, it is most concentrated in nations like Taiwan—developing countries with active commercial sectors."[51] Using Taiwan as exemplary of piracy was not an accident. It centered piracy in a very specific geographical spot—Asia. The Intellectual Property Alliance helped the USTR identify other "problem" countries. Although these countries varied from year to year, the following have all been considered "priority-watch" countries: Korea, Taiwan, Thailand, Saudi Arabia, Philippines, India, People's Republic of China, Malaysia, Indonesia, Egypt, Brazil, and Nigeria.[52] Although piracy occurs everywhere, a disproportionate number of countries singled out for action are developing countries or, as this list makes clear, Asian countries. It is on these numbers and places that the story of piracy has been developed. It has become a story that clearly draws north–south distinctions. Additionally, the problem has been conceptualized as possessing two distinct ingredients: blatant disrespect for the law and the lack of law altogether. Thus, in the emerging piracy narrative the most obvious solutions include more law for foreign countries and tougher restrictions at home.

In 1986, as the enemy was first beginning to be defined, the problem was established as one that pit hard-working U.S. citizens against lazy foreigners, ultimately costing U.S. jobs and creating trade deficits.[53] Pirates, in the U.S. narrative, were stealing from hard-working Americans.[54] Honest (U.S.) people work hard. Pirates steal this hard work and profit because they do not have to invest anything in the project. The image of lazy foreigners and hard-working U.S. citizens has continued to provide important narrative support for the greater protection of intellectual property rights.

Perpetual problem countries have been the Philippines, Indonesia, Malaysia, Singapore, Thailand, Korea, Taiwan, India, Brazil, and Mexico. The generalization from pirates to entire states occurs with the identification of problem countries. The narrative transforms the entire country into the pirate instead of focusing on piracy within specific countries. The result has been a targetable agent for retaliation—the government of each problem state. The converse is also true—a relatively small group of intellectual property industries are generalized into the United States.

In order to clearly justify intervention, the story needs to explain why economic retaliation is the best solution. Senator Pete Wilson conceptualized the problem as one that cannot be solved through diplomatic channels. He has been especially clear about his belief that Asian governments are incapable of responding to negotiation and only understand force. Wilson stated:

> I think the only way we're going to convince them that it is in their interest—and in the short rather than in the long term, because we can't afford to allow the problem to continue—is by taking very severe

> retaliatory measures against them, of the kind that you have outlined here with respect to the possible denial of continued preferences, to Korea. . . . Mr. Good, I think as we have all learned the hard way, they regard rhetoric as cheap and, frankly, not at all persuasive. I think they will be persuaded only by a clear determination to see reform or else to bring about retaliation in order to compel it. That's not the way we like to do business. It's unfortunately apparently the only way that we're going to secure their attention and cooperation.[55]

Senator Wilson provided insight into how the problem of piracy is constructed. First, the United States identifies piracy as a problem that it can understand in terms of U.S. interests. Second, a villain is identified without asking what may motivate the villain's actions. Indeed, many economists and developing countries argue that strict intellectual property laws are not in the best interest of developing economies.[56] There is also evidence to suggest that once a country develops its own technological industries, it will move to eliminate piracy on its own.[57]

Attempting to understand the problem from the perspective of the enemy has not been part of the U.S. narrative.[58] Although the United States was able to negotiate with European and Canadian pirates (both of whom posed threats to the United States), force was the only understandable method for dealing with piracy in Asia. Finally, in a feat that defies most political economy analysis, multimillion dollar industries have become victims. Turning billion-dollar industries into victims is perhaps the most remarkable aspect of the intellectual property narrative. Despite the fact that these companies were reporting millions in profits each year, the piracy narrative placed them in the role of victim and alluded to the rapid demise of these industries if swift action was not taken.[59]

As Jack Valenti, president of the Motion Picture Association of America said, the result of such piracy is "heartbreaking." He stated, "Pirates are skimming the cream off of the American hit pictures and some who 'almost' hit. They are devastating the theatrical release of these films, abusing the flow of revenues that would come in the post-theatrical marketplaces."[60] The lack of an intellectual property "shield" makes the movie industry "easy prey for pirates, for unscrupulous businessmen," and moreover, added Valenti, the United States is "prey for legitimate businessmen who, if they break no law in their country by taking that which belongs to us, using it without our authorization, and without giving us any compensation for what they use, they do it."[61]

Charles Morgan, senior vice president of Universal City Studios also testified regarding U.S. victimization. His story was one of cable piracy by a Panamanian company called Rexsa. Rexsa had been selling television programming it pirated from U.S. broadcasts. Universal City Studios tried to get the Panamanian government to help them stop the illegal piracy, but 10% of Rexsa was owned by two former Panamanian presidents and a former foreign minister. In addition to its political connections, Rexsa was making up to $400,000 per month from pirated products while Universal City Studios relied on external sources for litigation funding. This meant Rexsa was in a better position to protect itself. As Morgan stated, "Our opponent is rich, influential, and adept in using that system to his advantage. We have seen Rexsa transform its losses into delays, and those delays into victories, for each month of transmission is another $400,000."[62] Again, the U.S. motion picture industry was placed in this narrative as a victim, while a developing nation became the victimizer.

The testimony of Valenti and Morgan led Senator Wilson to conclude that we: "[C]annot rely upon the moral probity of the people that we're dealing with to suddenly persuade them to do the right thing. I think it is in the nature of things that they are going to have to see that it is in their economic interest only by being persuaded that there is going to be a tremendous cost to them for failing to operate as they should."[63] The problem has been conceptualized as a moral one where innocent U.S. victims are deprived of their rightful property by pirates who not only have no sense of morality, but have government support for their actions. Making foreign piracy a moral issue instead of a legal one was an important step in distinguishing the good actors from the bad. As U.S. history indicates, a country develops intellectual property laws as its own intellectual property industries develop. It is not an issue of morality but one of development. Piracy as a moral issue, however, gave the United States a justification for interference. Of course, the way these countries "should" act was in a manner dictated by the United States.

The morality play is further substantiated by the fact that the original creators, who are both innovative and creative, are deprived of royalties from piracy. One cannot have a story about intellectual property without the original author making an appearance, however brief. Intellectual property rests on the assumption that monopoly protection provides the incentive to create. The creator is the person most hurt by piracy (at least that is a part of the story). As Valenti said, "Producers, distributors and most importantly creative artists are cheated of their rightful royalties in the process and so is American trade."[64] Stanley M. Gortikov, president of the Recording Industry Association of America, agreed. He stated, "But despite that universal popularity, the American creators and copyright owners and performers realize virtually no revenue from the sales of their property and their creativity. They are literally robbed every day almost everywhere and seemingly most of the governments in their foreign territories condone the thefts and really just don't give a damn."[65]

In such a situation, the pirates benefit and the creators of such uniqueness and innovation end up as "total losers."[66]

Finally, Frank G. Wells, president of Walt Disney Co., widely known for its aggressive stance on intellectual property, stated:

> At Disney, story people and artists spend hour upon hour of work in developing a number of character concepts, most of which are discarded for a variety of reasons. Once a concept is preliminarily accepted by our people, stories are created to provide personality and a setting in which the characters can be perceived. . . . As you can see, all of this activity takes enormous dedication and inspiration, as well as large investments of risk capital and the hard work of many Disney employees.[67]

Wells wished us to empathize with those hard-working Disney employees by asking us to "imagine, then, how our Consumer Products division feels when, after having spent all that time, effort, and money, they see 'Chinese' or counterfeit copies of their characters on the marketplace."[68]

Of course, the president of Walt Disney did not want Congress to hear that the very artists and story designers to which he referred work for hire. Work for hire means they receive an hourly wage for their creative labor, while Disney reaps the millions of dollars in profits from their creativity. Such a division of labor is obscured in the testimony that placed the Walt Disney Co. in the place of the victim. The Chinese slur helped switch the emphasis away from the millions in profits Disney made each year to the victimization of Disney by immoral foreigners.

Although there was mention of the original creator in the testimony provided to Congress, the larger picture was hidden. Each storyteller was careful to include "copyright owner" as well as producers and other workers in their victimization scheme. Although the moral ground may rest with the protection of creative and innovative work, the reality is that the creators are not the primary benefactors of the intellectual property system. Creation as discussed by these businessmen occurs within a fully developed industry where those who make the money are rarely those who create. The division of original author from copyright is rarely addressed, yet the author is pulled out of the bag when a defense of intellectual property rights and the incentive they provide for creation is needed. Again, the economics of the culture industry is obscured, masking the fact that artists and authors are robbed daily by the industry that siphons off the lions' share of royalties from the creative folks that make the industry possible.

The testimony describing victims contains tragic stories where hard-working Americans are deprived of their property by immoral foreigners. Although the numbers used to support the story may have been inaccurate, the story has the capacity to stick with the committee members in detail and could be recalled at a later date to provide evidence of international piracy. This is the power of a political narrative that can now be used as fact and presented to the nation.

The proposed solution to the problem of piracy was aggressive trade policies. Euphemistically called *suggestions* for improvements,[69] the United States was able to extend its notion of intellectual property on the developing countries in Asia. The fact that Asian and other developing countries began heeding U.S. "suggestions" about how to improve their intellectual property laws only fulfills the narrative that makes U.S. industries the victims, immoral foreigners the villains, and the U.S. government the hero.

PIRACY AND FAIR TRADE

In April 1991, the USTR used Section 301 of the 1988 Trade Act to identify China, India, and Thailand as priority foreign countries.[70] Interestingly, trade deficits existed within all three nations.[71] The testimony of Carla Hills, along with numerous other "experts," continued to perpetuate the story that Asia and other developing countries were the bad guys. The focus of government and business leaders has continued to be the threat to the United States posed by Asian pirates. It was even argued that Asians were stealing the very soul of America—its ideas.[72] Valenti put a masculine tone on the story when he claimed that pirates deliberately intend to "impede us, to shrink us, to exile us."[73]

There are people who voiced doubt about the U.S. intellectual property story. Even though Ralph Oman, the registrar of copyrights, favored strong protection, he also suggested the United States needed to open its markets to foreign intellectual property in order to show that protection was not a one-way street.[74] A more assertive voice of disagreement came from Stanley M. Besen, a senior economist at the Rand Corporation. He pointed out that the U.S. position on intellectual property was shortsighted because it assumed the United States would be a technological creditor indefinitely. He feared that if the United States lost the upper hand, it could be disadvantaged by the very intellectual property laws it designed.[75]

Besen also suggested that the exchange of knowledge was more important, or should be more important, than immediate payback. Of course, the outcome of GATT, where all countries agreed to "harmonize" their laws with the United States, proved Besen's voice was not successful. Besen's conservative approach, although rational, did not comply with the intellectual property story that U.S. policymakers wanted to tell.

By protecting intellectual property, according to the U.S. story, the United States ensured its continued hegemony because it stopped the only possible avenue through which its dominant position could be challenged. Of course, the United States' continued technological superiority remains to be seen.

Placing confidence in an ability to remain the best at creating intellectual property is an important part of the U.S. narrative. It was important not to question U.S. superiority at creating new ideas, especially because our superiority at providing the best manufactured goods had long since vanished. Representative Pelosi illustrated why protection of intellectual property is so important for hard-working Americans. "This comes at a time that we are telling the workers of America that we live in a global economy, that many products which are labor intensive must be made in areas where labor is less costly, but that the comparative advantage of the United States is our intellectual property, our ideas, information, our software."[76] Pelosi's statement reflected a more dominant U.S. theme—that the United States is number one.[77] The United States may not be able to compete with Asian countries in terms of wages, but its comparative advantage is better ideas. If Asian countries take away the United States' competitive advantage in the production of ideas, it is not "fair" trade.

By the end of the 1980s, piracy and intellectual property were firmly established as important trade issues. The story that emerged was complete with plot, villains, innocent victims, and a hero. In this case, an organized effort by foreign countries, especially those located in Asia, to systematically usurp U.S. creativity and technological knowledge emerged as a threat. The innocent victims were U.S. companies, such as Microsoft or Walt Disney, whose products were stolen without any recourse. The U.S. government stepped in to save the day. Armed with Section 301 of the 1988 Trade Act and an insistence that intellectual property be protected via the GATT, the United States coerced virtually all Asian countries (and developing countries) to comply with U.S. standards for intellectual property protection.[78] With some grumbling because protection and enforcement would not meet U.S. business standards immediately, the United States claimed a trade negotiating victory due to U.S. efforts both bilaterally and multilaterally.

It was repeatedly asserted that U.S. companies could not do business without strong intellectual property protection. It was repeatedly said that intellectual property provided the incentive to create and do research. It was repeatedly argued that foreign piracy was in part responsible for the U.S. trade deficit, for the high prices of intellectual property-related products, and for unsafe products entering the market. It was also repeatedly said that the lack of strong international intellectual property laws hindered international trade (even though most intellectual property-related fields were certainly already active in all the markets they complained about).

Besides strong negotiating tactics by the United States, software companies were doing their own work to protect intellectual property. For example, the state of copyright enforcement in Taiwan led computer companies such as Apple, Ashton-Tate, IBM, Lotus Development Corp., and Microsoft to engage in surprise "SWAT" type raids against potential pirates.[79] Pirates in Thailand saw periodic raids by police as part of business.[80] Software companies were developing new protective strategies as well. In Hong Kong, it is now possible to call a toll-free hotline to report piracy and receive a reward.[81] The hotline is part of a new pirate campaign aimed at end-user piracy more than at retail piracy, much like the U.S. war on drugs.[82] Perhaps the most radical suggestion has been the discounted price regime. Although the U.S. government toils to make other countries pay attention to intellectual property law, some businesses have decided to try to compete with pirates. Thus, companies like Microsoft are offering their products at a 40% to 80% discount.[83] The hope is that these types of programs can have a more positive impact than the legislative efforts. Ultimately, as Asian markets develop there will probably be a decrease in piracy.

The U.S. story obscures the political economy of developed and developing nations in which typically the developing nations are considered victims and special considerations are taken to remedy their problems.[84] In the U.S. version, the roles are reversed. The United States is a victim and the developing countries are the hostile aggressors that threaten the very foundation of America—its creativity and ideas. This switch represents a significant departure from what traditionally transpired with international trade negotiations where "most favored nation" status provides protection for developing countries in order to facilitate development. However, it fits well with conventional U.S. development policy toward developing countries.[85]

Developing countries, especially Asia, are allowed to participate in world trade only if they follow the rules established by the United States. These rules include the U.S. version of intellectual property to which the developing world must "harmonize." The extension of the U.S. intellectual property story to developing countries around the world shows how the dependency of developing countries is perpetuated through presumably "neutral" trade laws. The intellectual property story developed in the United States was literally forced on other countries, regardless of these countries' interests and philosophies.

There is another, even more threatening phenomenon emerging today. The battle of the future will be over economic espionage. This type of espionage has long been a part of doing business. What makes economic espionage unique today is the high cost to intellectual property and the widespread nature of its use. It is estimated that intellectual property losses from foreign and domestic espionage may have exceeded $300 billion in 1997.[86] At least 23 countries from Germany to China target U.S. companies.[87] What makes this form of espionage even worse is that it is practiced by countries that are considered political allies. France is among the worst offenders.[88] In response to the threat of economic espionage, Congress passed the 1996 Economic Espionage Act, which makes economic spying and theft a felony punishable by $10 million in fines and up to 15 years in prison.[89] Additionally, President Clinton has ordered the CIA to step up its "friendly spying" operations, which has resulted in some embarrassment for the United States.[90] Despite some embarrassing fumbling, we can expect to see economic espionage become one of the justifications for increased security in the future.[91] Any future role for the CIA in global politics will rely quite heavily on economic espionage.

CONCLUSION: THE FUNCTION OF PIRACY IN THE INFORMATION AGE

Pirates serve a function in the narrative the United States is constructing on intellectual property and the way it should be protected internationally. Conceptual fences are being built around intangible property and pirates serve as justification for tough laws and harsh penalties. Norms and practices for dealing with intellectual property in an information age are still in flux. Additionally, the nature of technology makes copying and exchanging information easier than controlling it. The division of intellectual rights from tangible property are not fully appreciated by the average citizen who feels he or she owns something if he or she buys it. In the world of intellectual property, ownership is not straightforward. Ownership of the tangible item does not confer ownership of the intellectual property rights. Pirates are used to articulate the boundary between ownership and exchange internationally. Identifying pirates for punishment helps average citizens understand the difference between legitimate and illegitimate uses of new technology. In the process, the pirate becomes a scapegoat for economic insecurity and is elevated to the level of a national "threat." In the 1990s, pirates have become threatening criminals.

I am not applauding the actions of pirates. Rather, I wish to point out that they serve a function in the U.S. intellectual property story. They are the designated villains, the aggressors, and the evil ones that must be fought in order for upstanding and innocent Americans to practice business. This story has winners and losers and, if it is accepted uncritically, the power relation it inscribes on us will pass unchallenged. Such a conversation leaves no room to critically assess the world's political economy, the role of multinationals in that economy, the way in which the push for stronger intellectual property laws has specific benefits for a few U.S. corporations at the expense of the developing world, and the long-term interests of the United States.

The construction of pirates as criminals has not occurred in a vacuum. There are very specific beneficiaries of such a story. The beneficiaries are those companies engaged in new forms of business reliant on technology that is easily copied, reproduced, and "pirated." It is because of their interest to maximize profits, and the fact that their products are easily reproduced by pirates, that a dilemma has risen, thus necessitating the construction of pirates.

At the heart of the U.S. government's interest in intellectual property, lies the fact that despite its efforts to control the exchange of intellectual goods, this control will only come at the expense of extremely aggressive laws. We have entered a stage when the very definition of "author" is under question. As computer technology begins to influence the way we create, communicate, and exchange information, new ways of thinking about intellectual property can be created. The U.S. response to date merely reflects a desire to control for the short-term benefit of a few industries. It also reflects outdated assumptions about ownership of knowledge and authorship.

Although the stories written by the U.S. government may be politically persuasive, they may not last in the face of the larger transformation of how knowledge is produced and owned unless there is increasing amounts of pressure, legal action, and "education." It remains to be seen whether the United States will critically reflect on the future instead of playing the international bully and creating rules that ultimately may be detrimental, even to itself.

NOTES

1. An earlier version of this chapter appeared as: D. Halbert, "Intellectual property piracy: The narrative construction of deviance," *International Journal for the Semiotics of Law, 10* (1997): 55–78.

2. Sara Cobb and Janet Rifkin outlined this hegemonic process in their article. See: S. Cobb, & J. Rifkin, "Neutrality as a discursive practice," *Politics and Society* (1991): 69–91.

3. This language is used in almost every analysis of copyright. For example: "Intellectual property rights are society's attempt to achieve a balance in this fundamental tension among information providers and users. Patents, trademarks, and copyrights allow creative interests to extract a return to their investments in exchange for making available new technologies, products, and artistic efforts." See: K. E. Maskus, "Normative concerns in the international protection of intellectual property rights," *World Economy* (September 1990): 387.

4. For a closer look at these original metaphors see: M. Rose, *Authors and owners: The invention of copyright* (London & Cambridge, MA: Harvard University Press, 1993).

5. The Berne Convention, an international agreement on copyright, has existed since 1886. 17 U.S.C.A. provides the amendment to include the Berne Convention in U.S. Copyright statutes. The World Intellectual Property Organization (WIPO) was created in 1967 and the Universal Copyright Convention (UCC) was created and administered by UNESCO in 1952. See: R. P. Benko, *Protecting intellectual property rights: Issues and controversies* (Washington, DC: American Enterprise Institute for Public Policy Research, 1987) 1–8. Also, for a look at intellectual property rights as they relate to international organizations and north–south politics see: S. Sell, *Power and ideas: North–south politics of intellectual property and antitrust* (Albany: State University of New York Press, 1998).

6. Benko, *Protecting intellectual property rights*, 6.

7. S. Nowell-Smith, *International copyright law and the publisher in the reign of Queen Victoria* (Oxford: Clarendon Press, 1968).

8. W. P. Alford, "Intellectual property, trade and Taiwan: A GATT-fly's view," *Columbia Business Law Review* (1992): 107.

9. Nowell-Smith, *International copyright law*, p. 15. Quoting Mr. Graham Pollard.

10. Ibid., 64–84.

11. Ibid., 77.

12. To highlight this transition, it is interesting to note that the United States did not join the Berne Convention on the protection of copyright until 1988, 100 years after it was written and signed by most major participants. Even after signing the Berne Convention, the United States continued to reject one of its major components—moral rights. Moral rights give certain rights to the author, even after the copyright has been sold. Because the Berne Convention requires all signatories to harmonize their laws in concordance with the convention, the moral rights posed a problem for U.S. compliance. Finally, it was decided that the United States met the moral rights requirement through a combination of federal and state laws. See: P. Goldstein, *Copyright, patent, trademark and related state doctrines: Cases and materials on the law of intellectual property*, 3rd ed. (Westbury, NY: The Foundation Press, 1993), 771.

13. S. W. Waller, & N. J. Byrne, "Changing view of intellectual property and competition law in the European community and the United States of America," *Brooklyn Journal of International Law, 20* (1993): 8. An online version of the GATT, specifically the Trade Related Aspects of Intellectual Property Rights (TRIPS), agreement can be found at: http://itl.irv.uit.no/trade_law.

14. *Intellectual property and international issues. Subcommittee on intellectual property and judicial administration of the House Judiciary Committee.* 102nd Cong., (1991, May 15 and 16), 199.

15. Ibid., 199.

16. Benko, *Protecting intellectual property rights*, 1. Quoting President's Commission on Industrial Competitiveness, *Global Competition, the New Reality* (Washington, DC, 1985), 52.

17. Ibid., 1.

18. A. Subramanian, "The international economics of intellectual property

right protection: A welfare-theoretic trade policy analysis," *World Development*, 19 (1991): 945.

19. Bill Gates claimed that software is the country's sixth largest manufacturing business, having grown nine times faster than the rest of the U.S. economy between 1982 and 1993. A. R. Edge, "Preventing piracy through regional trade agreements: The Mexican example," *North Carolina Journal of International Law and Commercial Regulation, 20* (Fall, 1994): 175. See also: Steven Levy for a review of the beginning of the computer industry. S. Levy, *Hackers: Heroes of the computer revolution* (Garden City, NY: Anchor Press, 1984).

20. *Apple Computer Inc. v. Franklin Computer Corp.*, 714 F.2d 1240 (3d Cir. 1983). The court decided that Franklin's Macintosh compatible operating system infringed on Apple's copyright by directly copying the code. Franklin claimed there was no protection of computer code under copyright.

21. Alford, "GATT-Fly's view," 99.

22. D. Smith, "News: Corporate losses due to international copyright piracy," *Cu Digest, 6.57*, file 1 (26 June 1994).

23. W. P. Alford, *To steal a book is an elegant offense: Intellectual property law in Chinese civilizations* (Stanford: Stanford University Press, 1995), 112.

24. Ibid., 113.

25. Alford did an excellent job of illustrating the pressure put on China since the early 1900s to pass intellectual property laws that favored Western countries. Ibid., 30–55.

26. India and Thailand were also placed on the priority list, but made moves toward stronger protection quickly. Even though Thailand continues to be closely watched, both countries were taken off the priority watch list in 1994.

27. Alford, *To steal a book*, 113.

28. Ibid.

29. S. Awanohara, & K. Lincoln, "Patently hostile: Washington set to impose sanctions on China," *Far Eastern Economic Review* (5 September 1991): 69–70.

30. P. Engardio, "Yankee traders breathe a sigh of relief," *International Business* (3 February 1992): 39, 42.

31. For a succinct description of U.S./China negotiations on intellectual property see: "The China IPR agreement," *Congressional Record*, 3 May 1996, Vol. 142, 60, pp. S4672–S4675.

32. "Mickey Mouse back in China," *Far Eastern Economic Review* (4 November 1993): 46.

33. K. Huus, "Back to normal: US–China trade war looms closer," *Far Eastern Economic Review* (19 January 1995): 52.

34. L. Kaye, "Trading rights: Beijing exacts a high price for copyright accord," *Far Eastern Economic Review* (9 March 1995): 16.

35. Ibid.

36. Ibid.

37. Ibid.

38. Awanohara and Kaye, "Patently hostile," 69.

39. Statement of Representative Nancy Pelosi, China's violations of United States intellectual property rights, *Congressional Record*, 7 May 1996, Vol. 142, 62, p. H4435.

40. Ibid.

41. S. Lubman, "There's no rushing China's slow march to a rule of law," *Los Angeles Times* (19 October 1997): M2.

42. Alford's book provides valuable insights into the Chinese understanding of intellectual property.

43. Y. Cohen, "Software pirates pile up profits in afflicted Asia," *Christian Science Monitor* (27 December 1997): 1.

44. G. M. Hoffman, "Curbing national piracy of intellectual property," *The report of the international piracy project, The Annenberg Washington Program* (1989): 9.

45. Ibid.

46. Members of the Annenberg Antipiracy Project felt these numbers were insufficiently valid for policy recommendations. See: Ibid., 25. In the words of Alford, "A GATT-fly's view," 99. "The USTR not only asked companies to estimate themselves, but used the full price of the object to calculate the amount lost to piracy. This method ignores the fact that many people who can afford the pirated version of an item would be unable to afford the 'real' version and thus refrain from buying it (this would be true even if U.S. goods are sold for less than their U.S. rate in foreign countries)." See also: E. Helpman, "Innovation, imitation, and intellectual property rights," *Econometrica, 16* (16 November 1993): 1248.

Additionally, and on a slightly different note, a link between trade and strong IP laws (meaning that the presence of strong IP laws influences a company's decision to do business in any particular country) is ambiguous at best. See: K. E. Maskus & M. Penubarti, *How trade-related are intellectual property rights?* Unpublished paper (September 1990).

47. No Electronic Theft (NET) Act, *Congressional Record*, 4 November 1997, Vol. 143, 152, p. H9887.

48. In 1995, the Business Software Alliance (BSA) and the Software Publishers Association (SPA) estimated that $13.1 billion was lost worldwide to piracy. Given these numbers, the 1996 numbers also represent a decrease in piracy. See: C. Blizzard, "Pirates in cyberspace: The internet is creating a generation of software thieves," *The Toronto Sun*, 3 January 1998, p. 17.

49. "China's violations of United States intellectual property rights," H4435.

50. "The China IPR agreement," S4672.

51. Hoffman, *Curbing national piracy*, 11.

52. Ibid., 29–31.

53. "The focus of our hearing this morning is piracy. We are going to stop piracy of intellectual property rights. The copyright industries in this Nation provide jobs, they provide entertainment, they contribute significantly to what would be a favorable balance of trade, or at least a far more favorable one were it not for the fact that this piracy goes on." *International piracy involving intellectual property. Hearing before the subcommittee on trade, productivity, and economic growth of the joint economic committee.* 99th Cong., (1986, March 31), Statement of Pete Wilson, p. 1.

54. Ibid., 1–2. Statement of Pete Wilson.

55. Ibid., 21–23. Statement of Pete Wilson.

56. See: "Intellectual property . . . is theft," *The Economist, 330* (22 January 1994): 72–73; K. Gopinath, "Computer software and intellectual property rights: Issues at stake for developing countries," *Economic and Political Weekly, 27* (29

August 1992): m101–m104; T. A. Oyejide, "The participation of developing countries in the Uruguay round: An African perspective," *World Economy* (September 1990): 427–444.

57. Taiwan, for example, used to be a problem country. However, as the country's own technological industries have grown, there has been a move from piracy to innovation. See: A. Huang, "Made in Taiwan: A high-tech revolution pirates' paradise goes legit to become formidable competitor," *The Ottawa Citizen*, 8 September 1997, C4.

58. There is some indication that at least some members of Congress understand that China has done a phenomenal job in the past 15 years of implementing intellectual property laws and beginning to enforce them. However, according to the United States, China's efforts are not good enough. "They should have known when they signed the agreement if they were capable of living up to the standards set. They had better do it." "The China IPR Agreement," S4675.

59. See: P. E. Ross, "Cops versus robbers in cyberspace," *Forbes* (9 September 1996): 134–139.

60. *International piracy*, 26. Statement of Jack Valenti.

61. Ibid., 27–28. Statement of Jack Valenti.

62. Ibid., 46. Statement of Charles Morgan.

63. Ibid., 50. Statement of Senator Pete Wilson.

64. Ibid., 31. Statement of Jack Valenti.

65. Ibid., 54. Statement of Stanley Gortikov.

66. Ibid.

67. Ibid., 86. Statement of Frank G. Wells.

68. Ibid., 87. Statement of Frank G. Wells.

69. "I am somewhat cheered to report that with some well-conceived, and I think carefully implemented suggestions from the United States, the Governments of Taiwan, Singapore, Malaysia, South Korea, and the Philippines have enacted, or have pledged they will enact, laws which will be protective of material that's copyrighted. Ibid., 28. Statement of Jack Valenti.

70. *Intellectual property and international issues*, 9. Statement of Carla A. Hills.

71. Ibid., 43. Statement of Carla A. Hills.

72. The link between who we consider piracy threats and the countries to which we want to increase market access cannot be left unconsidered. U.S. companies not only wanted access to two markets that represented enormous profit potential—China and India—but also to the newly industrialized countries in south and east Asia. These markets remained relatively untapped by U.S. products, but represented the fastest growing markets for exports. These countries also had few, if any, intellectual property laws, meaning that U.S. law had to be introduced to make the climate safe for U.S. products.

73. *Intellectual property and international issues*, 123. Statement of Jack Valenti.

74. Ibid., 137. Statement of Ralph Oman.

75. Ibid., 202. Statement of Stanley M. Besen.

76. "China's violations of United States intellectual property rights" H4436.

77. "The United States is the world's leader in creativity, both artistic and industrial." *Intellectual property and international issues*, 2. Statement of William J. Hughes.

78. For a breakdown of what each ASEAN country did to comply see: S. J. La

Croix, *Intellectual property rights in ASEAN and the United States; Harmonization and controversy, private investment and trade opportunities (PITO) economic brief* (Honolulu: East-West Center, December 1994).

79. M. Foster, "U.S. firms battle the pirates of Taiwan," *Electronic Business* (3 April 1989): 83–84.

80. Cohen, "Software pirates pile up profits in afflicted Asia," 1.

81. A. Chetham, "Rewards to catch pirates," *South China Morning Post*, 11 December 1997, p. 2.

82. E. Lai, "Leading the war to end software piracy," *South China Morning Post*, 2 December 1997, p. 10.

83. "Solutions emerge as U.S. sanctions loom," *South China Morning Post*, 23 May 1996, 6.

84. According to Alex Mercer, an Australian marketing executive with the BSA, there is a link between struggling economies and increased piracy. Thus, we could expect to see piracy decrease as these economies become stronger. Cohen, "Software pirates pile up profits," 1.

85. William Preston Jr. outlined our perspective on the position of the third world in international development. He stated:

> [the United States] offered [the Third World] orderly economic growth, stability, technical assistance, and political reform; [the Third World] in turn had to fit into the world economy on [United States] terms, follow the [United States] model of development regardless of their indigenous culture, and stop short of choosing radical political alternatives. Order took the precedence over democracy, and containment against fundamental change in the world system remained a dominant priority. Dollar diplomacy, loan embargoes, and financial sanctions against international agencies offending United States interests served to enhance the latter's pervasive influence.

See: W. Preston Jr., *Hope and folly* (Minneapolis: University of Minnesota, 1988), 20.

86. R. Kilborn, & C. Hanson, "News in brief," *Christian Science Monitor* (13 January 1998): 2; J. Nelson, "More spies targeting U.S. firms," *The Dallas Morning News*, 12 January 1998, p. 1D.

87. "Foreign spies hurt American business," *Newsday*, 13 January 1998, p. A43.

88. Ibid., A43.

89. "FBI links 23 countries to economic espionage," *The Buffalo News*, 12 January 1988, p. 5A.

90. J. Dettmer, "Clinton friendly spying scandal," *Scotland on Sunday*, 5 October 1997, p. 21 [Lexis–Nexis]; H. Gurdon, "Humiliations tarnish CIA's reputation," *The Ottawa Citizen*, 29 March 1997, p. A16.

91. "Neither the end of the Cold War, nor the economic recession, has dampened enthusiasm for the CIA. The future, RIT students say, is in economic espionage, helping U.S. corporations get the edge on foreign competition." See: L. Doyle, "Majoring in the arts and crafts of spying," *The Independent*, 2 July 1991, p. 10.

5

Hackers: The Construction of Deviance in the Information Age

The preceding chapters introduced the historical context and modern manifestations of the traditional copyright story.[1] This copyright story has a large number of adherents, mostly lawmakers and copyright owners who oppose the tendency toward exchange displayed by the general public. Having legitimate definitional control, and thus control over the copyright story, is important if the general public is to be convinced of the boundaries imposed. Because the government intervenes on the part of copyright owners and provides an illusion of fairness to the process, a sense of legitimacy is imparted through governmental authority. The power to define the villains and heroes, appropriate and inappropriate, ethical and unethical behavior, constitutes control over the story. By changing the terminology used to describe computer-related actions, copyright owners control the discourse. Thus, sharing becomes stealing. Creative work becomes private property. Corporations become victims of piracy.

This chapter is about another villain in the copyright story—the computer hacker. This chapter is about more than the crime of hacking, it is a story about the construction of the hacker identity in the United States. The threat, because it transcends national boundaries, is a threat to national security, as well as to economic well-being. This chapter deals primarily with the hacker story, its transformation from harmless teenager to dangerous computer criminal, and the implications for defining intellectual property. Computer viruses, associated closely to hackers, also play a role in controlling the intellectual property discourse. The villains (the hacker, the computer virus, and the pirate) are united through the function they serve in helping extend property boundaries in the information age.

On May 8 and 9, 1990, the U.S. Secret Service executed 27 search warrants in 14 different states to confiscate computers used in illegal activities. The press reported the existence of a nationwide computer conspiracy with hackers working in tandem to commit computer credit card fraud, "computer tampering," and "computer trespass."[2] This Secret Service sting, *Operation Sundevil,* is the largest computer crackdown attempted to date in the United States. The Secret Service targeted a "close-knit" group of hackers suspected of using and selling stolen credit card numbers, telephone access codes,[3] and other illegally obtained information from Bell South. Several hackers pled guilty and received 14-month sentences and $233,000 in fines for the value of the "access devices."

The Secret Service asserted hackers imperiled the health and welfare of individuals, corporations, and government agencies. However, there was little evidence that "stolen" information was critical or expensive. The Electronic Frontier Foundation even questioned how a value could be assessed without a demonstrable loss.[4]

If measured in terms of indictments, the raid failed. However, *Operation Sundevil* did more than provide indictments, it helped launch what Bruce Sterling called the "Hacker Crackdown."[5] *Operation Sundevil* can be understood as a Secret Service sting concerned with catching criminals, but it can also be interpreted as an effort to publicly depict hackers in negative terms. Garry M. Jenkins, when commenting on *Operation Sundevil* and the hackers who had been caught, described hackers as: "no longer misguided teenagers, now high tech computer operators using computers to engage in unlawful conduct."[6] *Operation Sundevil* helped provide an image for hackers that emphasized the criminal element.

Operation Sundevil set the stage, but it wasn't until recently, with the popularization of the World Wide Web, discussion surrounding the NII, the commercialization of the Internet, and a heightened awareness of the potential for information warfare, that a concern about the hacker threat became widespread. For example, the Pentagon recently announced its computers had been "probed" more than 250,000 times in 1996, with only a portion of these infractions being detected. This announcement sparked much discussion.[7] Although arrested hackers are few, they are remarkably visible as harbingers of a possible future where computer crime and terrorism run rampant.

Hackers and law enforcement have opposing views of what constitutes a hacker. It is in each group's best interest to control this image.[8] How the hacker is portrayed in the media is a contest over an image. This image is created through stories about hackers. This narrative is important not only to the hackers involved, but to the larger U.S. population. As Kai Erikson pointed out:

> The only material found in a society for marking boundaries is the behavior of its members—or rather, the networks of interaction which link these members together in regular social relations. And the interactions which do the most effective job of locating and publicizing the group's outer edges would seem to be those which take place between deviant persons on the one side and official agents of the community on the other.[9]

It is the role of the deviant to mark the boundaries of legitimate behavior. Hackers, constructed as deviants, help define appropriate behavior and appropriate identities for all U.S. citizens, especially in a computer age where ethical guidelines are still ambiguous.

As we go further into the information age it becomes more important to understand what citizenship means without the clearly marked boundaries of the nation state. Thus, the type of deviance that needs to be distinguished here is that which is constructed in order to provide what David Campbell called a "discourse of danger." The hacker defines the border between private ownership of information and public control. *Operation Sundevil*, and the arrest of Kevin Mitnick, highlight the way hacker identities are used to draw lines between freedom of information and private ownership; between a secure state and anarchy; and between normal U.S. citizens and abnormal ones.

This chapter argues that the hacker is constructed as an information deviant and that this image is helpful in providing rules for appropriate behavior in an information society. The hacker accounts in this chapter are designed to give the reader an understanding of the types of things being said about hackers. What is more important, however, is how these narratives are used to support a specific notion of property ownership and government secrecy. In making this argument, I trace the development of the narrative about the hacker from harmless computer nerd to terrorist.

EARLY HACKERS AND THE "GOLDEN AGE"

Hackers were not always portrayed as computer criminals. During the "Golden Age," before personal computers and the development of a computer industry, when there were minimal proprietary interests in computer software, hacking was relatively nonproblematic.[10] The word *hack* was first used at the Massachusetts Institute of Technology to refer to a feat "imbued with innovation, style, and technical virtuosity."[11] As early as 1958, computers were influencing young minds. Students would stay up all night to get time on the big university mainframes. These people were fascinated with computers and spent hours writing programs to see what could be accomplished. Golden Age hackers were interested in the "pure hack," not the monetary value of their work.

During the mid-1980s, computer technology became available on a mass scale and movies such as *War Games* romanticized hacking. Many young adults realized that computers were empowering tools.[12] As awareness of similarities between hackers emerged, hacking developed its own ethical guidelines. This ethic involved several tenets outlined in Steven Levy's book *Hackers: Heroes of the Computer Revolution*. Hacker ethics are based on the bedrock of freedom of information. As Gareth Branwyn quoted in *Mondo 2000*, "As every reality hacker knows: 'Information wants to be free' and 'plagiarism saves time.' "[13] The lifeblood of the hacker ethic is freedom of information.

Steven Levy outlined the hacker ethic as follows:

1. Access to computers—and anything that might teach you something about the way the world works—should be unlimited and total. Always yield to the hands-on imperative!
2. All information should be free.
3. Mistrust authority—promote decentralization.
4. Hackers should be judged by their hacking, not bogus criteria such as degrees, age, race, or position.
5. You can create art and beauty on a computer.[14]

These criteria put hackers in opposition to mainstream economics. As Anne Wells Branscomb noted, scientists and computer hackers "are frustrated to discover that their electronic playgrounds have been invaded by avaricious and enterprising entrepreneurs who prefer dollars to the joy of the 'great hack' or the reward of the Nobel Prize."[15]

The belief in freedom of information makes certain behaviors conceivable that are defined as theft in the mainstream legal discourse. As Emmanuel Goldstein, editor and publisher of *2600*, a hacker journal, stated, "If I want to access a credit [tracking] company like TRW and access my credit file, is that an invasion of TRW's privacy? What about my privacy—all that information they've gathered on me?"[16] Hackers prioritize freedom of information and are suspicious of centralized control. Private ownership of information is considered illegitimate. Hackers question why a few corporations can own information about others and control information that might be helpful to the public at large. This view puts hackers on a collision course with the more powerful conglomerate of technology owners and the government itself. Hackers' willingness and ability to go anywhere does not sit well with corporate America.

Generally speaking, hackers tend to emphasize the positive aspects of their subculture, whereas the mainstream media emphasizes the negative.[17] It is important to look at the characteristics of hackers because mainstream media consciously and consistently wrests control of the hacker public image out of hacker hands. Hackers construct the image of a creative innovator who "takes on" the institutions controlling information in order to engage in a knowledge-expanding and creative process.[18] Hackers tend to hack for the thrill of seeing if it can be done. Hackers enjoy seeing how far they can push themselves and the computer.[19] Levy defined a *hacker* as "a person whose devotion to something, in this case computers, is near total and who has a deep-seated desire to do what's impossible to do. I think the great thing about hackers is that quite often they achieve what is considered impossible, because they refuse to accept limits."[20] Hackers are labeled *misfits,* but tend to embrace their difference as setting them apart from others.[21] They tend to be avid readers with good intellectual abilities. Hackers are predominately male and white, but consider themselves gender-and colorblind due to the textual relationships they hold (in which personal attributes mean less). It is agreed that hackers dress informally, relate better to computers than to people, and can absorb large amounts of information.

Hackers perceive themselves to be mostly harmless, highly intelligent people. They view their hacking as a game and the Internet as a playground.[22] Sociologists Gordon Meyer and Jim Thomson put an academic spin on hacker culture. They wrote:

> Our data reveal the computer underground as an invisible community with a complex and interconnected lifestyle, an inchoate anti-authoritarian political consciousness, and dependent on norms of reciprocity, sophisticated socialization, rituals, networks of information sharing, and an explicit value system. We interpret the CU (computer underground) culture as a challenge to and a parody of conventional culture, as a playful attempt to reject the seriousness of technocracy, and an ironic substitution of rational technological control of the present for an anarchic and playful future.[23]

Hackers come in many forms, shapes, and sizes. This section can do little but provide some insights into the hacker personality. I examine mainstream stories of hackers in more detail, pointing out the emerging image of deviance applied to hackers and the impact of this image.

THE HACKER AS THREAT

A great deal has been made of the "dark side" of the computer.[24] Many articles equivocate hacking with computer crime, glossing over the minor detail that most computer-related crimes are committed by employees (or former employees). Hackers are singled out, whereas disgruntled employees are ignored or, occasionally, called hackers.[25]

Beginning with *Operation Sundevil*, mainstream media has contributed to the removal of normalcy from the hacker image. The way hackers are characterized by the media is important because it helps define the improper hacker and the normal U.S. citizen. As officials offer their opinions on hacker behavior, and these opinions are sifted through the media to our ears, images of normalcy and deviance are produced.

A variety of articles written in the late 1980s and early 1990s outlined the abnormality of hackers. Hackers are socially awkward nerds who do not fit in. They are more comfortable with computers than with people. The "hacker-as-nerd" narrative, which remains strong in the late 1990s, helped provide insight into the hacker psychology.[26] These articles are about labeling and name calling. James Aho, who has done work on northwest hate groups, noted, naming, or labeling is a crucial step in creating an enemy.[27] Most early attempts at labeling hackers included calling them names such as: "yuppie vandals,"[28] nerds,[29] nosy showoffs lacking any sense of shame,[30] and hoods from broken homes with psychological problems.[31] These articles are supplemented by longer pieces on specific hackers such as Kevin Poulsen or Kevin Mitnick. Additionally, *Operation Sundevil* highlighted the name-calling process by providing a clear starting point for identifying hackers as a serious threat.

Labeling hackers as *victimizers* also helps create the enemy. The term *victim* is used repeatedly in articles dealing with hacking, viruses, and computer piracy.[32] In the victim–victimizer narrative, companies are afraid to disclose their victim status for fear of embarrassment, loss of confidence in their company, and fear that making their vulnerability public will only increase the chances of invasion—all images that help align the hacker with a rapist. One programmer, tired of hackers entering his system, made the victim status of his company explicit:

> We seem to be totally defenseless against these people. We have repeatedly rebuilt system after system and finally management has told the system support group to ignore the problem. As a good network citizen, I want to make sure someone at network security knows that we are being raped in broad daylight. These people freely walk into our systems and are taking restricted, confidential and proprietary information.[33]

Treating hacking as rape helps establish what "a good network citizen" should not do as well as offer a strong negative label for anyone interested in hacking. Additionally, it is a powerful label to attach to the computer hacker that helps people understand the hacker as enemy.

Establishing abnormality is a first step in demonizing the hacker. Popular magazines running stories on hackers and hacker-related issues reveal the extent to which the hacker is depicted as threatening. An effort is made to link hacking to crime, to taint this crime with the most dangerous elements possible, and to show ill will toward those who would embrace the ideology of hacker.

Initial hacker threats were vague. Computer security dangers were becoming a greater issue, but were still considered a future problem. The possible futures that hackers would bring included terrorist attacks,[34] computer viruses as dangerous as chemical or nuclear weapons,[35] and more general hacker-induced deaths.[36] All these possible scenarios are part of a labeling process that helped define the deviance of the hacker. As Aho stated, "The point is that defamatory language rarely, if ever, simply describes things; it also rhetorically 'accomplishes' them. And what it accomplishes is an enemy, ready for violation."[37] Although many articles about hackers may seem ineffectual at best, they initiate a naming process crucial to constructing an enemy who can then be fought.

These initial forays into naming an enemy were not greatly successful because the potential threat of the hacker had not been fully realized. A few individuals, like Gail Thackery who had been involved in *Operation Sundevil,* foresaw the threat and warned that for every hacker caught, many others remained freely engaged in potentially dangerous activities.[38] Additionally, there were some who linked hackers and theft of information to organized crime in an attempt to escalate the threat.[39]

Aho identified additional steps in creating enemies that are also instructive. Naming is typically followed by validation of the threat. *Validation* can take the form of public trials, hearings, or other ceremonies.[40] A second method for validating labels is through a process Aho described as *mythmaking*. Mythmaking "refers to the biographical or historical accounts of defamed persons showing why it is inevitable, necessary, and predictable that they act as they do—namely, as evil ones."[41]

A recent case made headlines because a 19-year-old hacker "was deemed so cunning that he was released under house arrest Thursday with orders not to even talk about computers."[42] Federal authorities said "he's capable of controlling virtually any computer."[43] This mythologizing helps shape the hacker into an enemy worth fighting. Additionally, such rhetoric helps provide the image of an evil wizard manipulating the computer in almost magical ways.

The mythologizing effect, or explaining why it is inevitable that the hacker acts as he or she does, is further supported by the assertion that hackers are addicted to hacking. [44] One hacker in England was acquitted because he convincingly argued he was a hacking junkie who "couldn't help himself."[45] Understanding hacking as addictive behavior helps categorize hackers as pathological. David Campbell made this apparent: "What animates the careers of social problems like drug consumption or drunk driving are moral concerns about what constitutes 'normal' behavior in contradistinction to 'pathological' behavior. In other words, the interpretation of some problems as social dangers subject to intense concern and punitive sanctions is integral to the inscription of the ethical boundaries of identity."[46] It is obvious from the manner in which hackers are portrayed that their behavior is not normal. If one can validate the hacker as an addict, a pathological person, and someone capable of activities bordering on mythical then the substance of the enemy will be more clearly understood.[47] Hackers make good scapegoats because their actions are difficult to understand, have overtones of adventure and action, and make for good publicity.[48]

Good scapegoats do not necessarily make for good indictments, however. Craig Neidorf's case was thrown out when it was discovered that the stolen Bell South document worth an estimated $79,449 was publicly available for $13.[49] The well-publicized Morris case, which prosecutors wanted to use to send a clear message to hackers, had little impact.[50] Most publicized cases have not had a noticeable impact on hacking, or have failed to bring in significant convictions.[51] Additionally, because many hackers are adolescents or first-time offenders (like Morris), convictions are not as severe as some prosecutors would like. The highly publicized manhunt resulting in the capture of hacker Kevin Mitnick[52] will probably be anticlimactic. In April 1996, Mitnick plead guilty to one federal charge and to violating his probation.[53]

The authorities are struggling to contain the crimes, or at least to slow their rapid growth."[54] One recent article warned that small companies "are the perfect place for a new hacker to try out his or her skills."[55] If a site proves easy to hack, it could be labeled a "penetration test site" and become a training ground for hackers. Additionally, if a website is well secured, it is bound to attract hacker attention.[56] It is generally understood that no place is safe from hackers. If they wish to, they will crack any system.

Computer extortion by hackers has also been documented. A hacker will send e-mail asking for money, or the account will be *bombed*. A bombing means thousands of messages will be sent to clog the address and make it unusable.[57] In 1996, the General Accounting Office (GAO) reported there had been an enormous number of attempted break-ins to Pentagon computers. The GAO report directly links the threat of hackers to national security and argues that "the potential for catastrophic damage is great."[58] The potential for "electronic warfare" has become a newsworthy possibility. All these efforts help support another criterion for the creation of an enemy outlined by Aho, that of *sedimentation*, when "legends come to have lives of their own."[59] It does not matter that most economic loss can be attributed to disgruntled or dishonest employees, or that our national security has not been significantly affected, the potential threat posed by hackers is enough to warrant even tougher legislation and penalties. What might be possible, now that the hacker identity is fully established, is enough to warrant tougher sanctions.

One computer on the Internet is broken into every 20 seconds.[60] Kehoe and Stephens also claimed that hackers are rising to the challenge of even more sophisticated security systems.[61] Although some companies are challenging hackers to break their codes,[62] other hackers are going to prison for such behavior.[63] In 1996, a hacker brought the King County Library system to a standstill, [64] which sparked new claims that the hackers caught were just the tip of the iceberg.[65]

Computer fraud and telecommunications crime is on the rise. It is estimated that U.S. losses from hackers is between $150 billion and $300 billion a year. This is assumed to be a low assessment because many companies do not report computer theft.[66] Hackers also can victimize corporations by engaging in other types of deviant behavior: "But hackers don't have to steal anything to inflict damage and financial loss on corporate victims. In a nefarious practice known as 'pinging,' hackers can render an Internet IP address virtually inoperative by bombarding it with thousands of mail messages or postings, using automatic remailer tools."[67] In response to the potential rise in hacker-related crimes, the FBI has opened new offices to deal with computer crime.[68]

The hacker is both a foreign and domestic threat. There is mounting evidence that encryption and security technology can be broken, illustrating the threat of hackers, both domestic and foreign, who can break encryption.[69] In 1996, a French hacker proved it was possible to find the key to Netscape.[70]

There are numerous foreign hacker incidents that help cement the danger of the hacker. There is the case of the German hacker, Kim Schmitz, who sold access codes from the U.S. phone system.[71] There was a British hacker arrested for infiltrating the U.S. defense department, NASA, and other computers.[72] An Israeli hacker was arrested for infiltrating the Pentagon and taking classified information about the Patriot missile and other secrets during the Gulf War.[73] There have been crackdowns on hackers in the Netherlands and Mexico through legal reform and raids.[74] An assault on a jet propulsion lab (JPL) in 1988 was thought to have been conducted by a West German group called the Chaos Computer Club.[75] The JPL case is an excellent example of creating an international danger from only a few threads of evidence. The infiltration of the JPL was actually accomplished by Kevin Mitnick and Lenny DiCicca. Australian hackers arrested for breaking into U.S. and Australian computer systems "raise troubling questions about the vulnerability of technology to intruders operating beyond American borders and laws."[76]

Finally, a recent foreign hacker to threaten U.S. computers is 21-year-old Argentinean, Julio Cesar Ardita, who gained access to the Pentagon, NASA, and Navy computers and retrieved information about nuclear installations and defense programs.[77] This case is important because of the government response to the hacker. Ardita's case is the first in which the government obtained a court order to tap private electronic communications.[78] Such monitoring could become the wave of the future as the government as the "good guy" takes action to control the evil hacker both abroad and at home.

The threat posed by hackers translates into fear of crime. Fear of computer crime is on the rise.[79] As Flanagan and McMenamin said, "serious computer crime is beginning to reach epidemic proportions. How the government deals with this crime is important. There is now a climate in which victims must be protected and victimizers attacked, resulting in the final criteria for Aho's enemy construction paradigm—*ritual*, when the 'good guys' respond 'appropriately' to the threat."[80] In the United States this means additional arrests and more attention paid to hacker-related acts.

Hackers within the United States are linked to espionage to clarify the threat as external and "other." As Wilder and Miolino reported, all the security people left over from the Cold War are turning into "information brokers" and are using the Internet to advertise their abilities to attain confidential information. "In late 1993 or early 1994, a service called 'BlackNet,' which publicly advertised the brokering of illegal information, was posted on an Internet Usenet group and then widely disseminated. BlackNet turned out to be a hacker's hoax, but it nonetheless indicates the seriousness of the problem."[81] Although their example turned out to be a practical joke, it did not deter the authors from inferring that information brokerage is a serious threat to be watched.

As the United States relies more heavily on technology for everything from high-tech weapons to security systems, the real threat hackers pose becomes greater. From automobiles to airlines to toaster ovens, our interaction with objects is increasingly mediated by computer technology. This technology is anything but perfect. Indeed, most computer scientists and security agents will point out that computers are inherently insecure, unreliable, and unpredictable.[82] Despite the vulnerability caused by overreliance on computer technology, we continue to entrust vital aspects of our economic and political systems to technological care. As people become more familiar with the Internet and more dependent on computer technology, it is easier to use the hacker as a threatening figure. The media, law, and government offer different perspectives on the hacker, but when taken as a whole, a sinister character emerges—an enemy.[83]

IDENTITY AND DISCOURSES OF DANGER

Campbell used the concept of a *discourse of danger* (a discourse used to create insecurity from real and imagined threats within and without the United States) to describe how foreign policy and U.S. identity have been shaped.[84] It is a discourse reliant on a sufficiently dangerous "other." Campbell argued, "Central to the process of imagination has been the operation of discourses of danger which, by virtue of telling us what to fear, have been able to fix who 'we' are."[85] It is important for the state to write discourses of danger because this danger provides a mechanism through which to understand who "we" are, as well as a justification for defense against the "other."

During the Cold War, the Soviet Union operated as the "other" and explained defense spending and government secrecy. Today, with no clear enemy, one would expect our fears to subside. Instead, we have found new threats to our national security. The hacker-as-threat is a relatively new development and marks another step in outlining enemies for the future. Recent government hearings held that information warfare is one of the largest threats to U.S. security and must be immediately acted on, thus justifying the need for greater security in an unstable world.

Campbell argued that the end of the Cold War has created a globalization of contingency. There is no longer a single all-encompassing threat (communism), the threat is dispersed throughout the world.[86] This contingency can no longer be explained through a worldview premised on a strong Soviet threat and the spread of communism. "Danger, in short, is no longer capable of just being written as 'out there.' Security is not to be found 'within'."[87] The eruption of contingency calls into question all conventional boundary markers. Because the state is not a stable, bounded space, it has been necessary to constitute identity "through the negation of difference and the temptation of otherness."[88]

The hacker is the perfect threat to highlight this transformation of danger. The hacker is a highly decentralized threat, both within and outside of the United States. The hacker is the best possible threat in a world defined by contingency because the hacker so clearly highlights the meaninglessness of national boarders. With computers networked globally, the necessity for geographical proximity to a target is no longer necessary. The hacker is the model for a new security threat and illustrates the dangers of electronic warfare and terrorism.

Issues of security and insecurity take the foreground within a discourse of danger because "the state grounds its legitimacy by offering the promise of security to its citizens who, it says, would otherwise face manifold dangers."[89] The state externalizes contingency in order to maintain control over boundaries. Populations are mobilized through a common identity and members who can be counted as the enemy are denounced.[90] As Campbell said, "For some, feminism, homosexuality, and support for social ownership of the relations of production are threats to be considered as on a par with a foreign enemy."[91] The hacker becomes an internal "other" used as a scapegoat for national insecurity in a technological age.[92] The justification for state defense can in part be laid at the door of the hacker threat. Because Campbell argued that U.S. identity is the result of these security postures and the clear sense of us versus them, hackers play a role in the subplot of U.S. identity construction, a plot that grows thicker as information ownership becomes more important.

Thus, the impact of the hacker threat is not only the real risk a hacker might pose. Rather, the hacker is a pawn used to construct normalcy in the information age. It is not just society that needs deviants in order to understand social rules, but governments also need to legitimize their actions by developing enemies. As Campbell pointed out, "the establishment of certain standards against which attitudes and behavior can be proscribed as legitimate or illegitimate."[93] Describing hackers as illegitimate helps entrench a certain orientation toward ownership of information and leaves untouched the hacker position that challenges the legitimacy behind vast databases collected on virtually all U.S. individuals. The hacker poses a threat at two levels: the private industry/intellectual property level and the national government/national security level. In both areas, the hacker can be used to help define the proper boundaries of U.S. citizens. The hacker can also be used as an example to justify further police and government enforcement and surveillance of U.S. citizens.

CONCLUSION: THE FUNCTION OF HACKERS IN THE INFORMATION AGE

John Perry Barlow is a well-known advocate of cyber-rights and the transformative potential of computer networks. In May 1990 he was visited by FBI agents, who questioned him about a group called the nu-Prometheus League. During this interview, Barlow said he "realized right away before I could demonstrate my innocence, I would first have to explain to him what guilt might be."[94] Additionally, it became clear that the approach taken by the government toward hackers was changing. As Bromberg said,

> Suddenly, the high-school and college students who had only recently been tolerated as joy riders on the nation's information networks didn't seem so innocent. They were electronic swindlers. Criminals. Possibly even spies. . . . Computer crime, the United States Government decided, wasn't just costing the country billions of dollars and endangering the very basis of intellectual property in the electronic age; it was becoming a potential threat to national security.[95]

We find ourselves now understanding the hacker as a national security threat and a threat to intellectual property. As privatization slowly strangles the electronic commons, behavior once considered normal and legal becomes abnormal and dangerous, hence the demonization of hackers. The time is long past when hackers are harmless computer geeks. Today, hackers have a new image tainted with a criminal element. The youthful hacker depicted in the mid-1980s movie *War Games* is now a credit card thief, technological addict, trespasser, and possibly a spy or terrorist. This approach redraws the victim–victimizer dichotomy in an era of corporate ownership of information. Thus, the 18-year-old hacker becomes a victimizer and the corporate entity of AT&T, for example, becomes the victim. This definition of victims and victimizers obscures the larger economic critique about who owns technology, information, and ability to communicate in the United States (and globally). The question of who is victimized by telephone companies is never asked. In our modern economic system, the important property is intangible, even though this type of property is extremely difficult to control.[96]

Marie Christine-Leps, writing on the development of the criminal in the 19th century, argued police were needed by industrial and commercial entities because they lacked the time and resources to protect themselves directly. Positioning the police between the industrial elite and the lower classes helped render invisible the social and economic dominance of the elite behind the rule of law.[97] A similar process is at work in the approach the United States is taking toward hackers. By labeling the hacker a criminal, and an abnormal member of society, then drawing law enforcement agencies into the drama to clean up the newly emergent problem, powerful economic interests in the computer industry are obscured. Additionally, by labeling the hacker as a national security threat, and a threat not easily controlled, further justification for the national security state becomes available.

What will the future hold in the arena of information technology? If hackers have their way, we will see the opening of databases and a significant decrease in secrecy. However, if trends continue in the present direction, we can expect to see the national government increasingly attempt to patrol its information borders. We will see companies seeking harsher penalties for data theft. We will see insecurity mount as it becomes increasingly obvious that computers are prone to information sharing instead of information secrecy. We will see hackers going to jail for longer periods of time. We will see the boundaries of what is legitimate computer behavior clearly defined by example. Hackers will become more like criminals and less like the next-door neighbor. The threat will be both foreign and domestic. We will label this threat the "war against hackers." In the process, civil liberties will be threatened as the government seeks to make an example out of someone. This is beginning today. It is not simply the fate of hackers that hangs in the balance. How freedom of information, property, and privacy are defined are central to this discussion. The hacker has become a symbol of danger, a symbol necessary for protecting information, and producing a U.S. identity.

NOTES

1. An earlier version of this chapter appeared as: D. Halbert, "Discourses of danger and the computer hacker," *The Information Society, 13* (1997): 361–374.

2. P. Elmer-Dewitt, "Cyberpunks and the Constitution," *Time, 137* (8 April 1991): 81; M. Lewyn, & E. I. Schwartz, "Why the legion of doom has little to fear of the feds," *Business Week,* 15 April 1991, 31; "United States v. Zod," *The Economist, 316* (1 September 1990): 23–24.

3. "Computer hacker ring with a Bay area link," *San Francisco Chronicle,* 9 May 1990, A30; "Probe focuses on entry, theft by computers," *Chicago Tribune* [Lexis-Nexis], 10 May 1990.

4. "A. Beam, Free the Sun Devil 6! (Why?)," *The Boston Globe,* 1 August 1990, 55; P. Mungo, & B. Clough, *Approaching zero: The extraordinary underworld of hackers, phreakers, virus writers, and keyboard criminals* (New York: Random House, 1992).

5. B. Sterling, *Hacker crackdown: Law and disorder on the electronic frontier* (New York: Bantam Books, 1992).

6. J. Aldrich, "Push button felonies," *The Epic Project* [On-line], Available: jefrich@well.sf.ca.us (1990); W. Schatz, "The terminal men: Crackdown on the legion of doom ends an era for computer hackers," *Washington Post,* 24 June 1990, pp. H1, H6.

7. "Attacking the pentagon," *The Commercial Appeal* (24 May 1996), 12a.

8. M. Alexander, "Hackers promote better image," *Computerworld, 25* (24 June 1991): 124; J. Daly, "Hackers switch sides, offer security package," *Computerworld, 27* (1 March 1993): 6.

9. K. Erikson, *Wayward puritans: A study in the sociology of deviance* (New York, London, & Sydney: Wiley, 1966), 10–11.

10. Although these early hackers are important in the general understanding of hacker identity, this is not the place to detail their experience. An excellent book on the subject is Steven Levy's. See: S. Levy, *Hackers: Heroes of the computer revolution* (Garden City, NY: Anchor Press, 1984).

11. Ibid., 10.

12. "For the first time in recent history you *could* reach out and change reality,

you could *do stuff* that affected *everything* and everyone, and you were suddenly living this life that was like something out of a comic book or adventure story . . ." P. Kroupa, "Memoirs of a cybernaut," *Wired, 1* (November 1993): 59.

13. G. Branwyn, "Street noise," *Mondo 2000* (1992): 30.

14. Levy, *Hackers*, 27–31.

15. A. W. Branscomb, "Computer software: Protecting the crown jewels of the information economy," in *Intellectual property rights in science, technology, and economic performance*, eds. F. W. Rushing & C. G. Brown (Boulder, San Francisco, & London: Westview Press, 1990), 48.

16. T. Kiely, "Cyberspace Cadets," *CIO* (February 1992): 70.

17. Except for a few fairly neutral articles, and one or two pro-hacker editorials, most mainstream press either condemns hackers or publishes articles about convictions and arrests.

18. "You can create art and beauty on a computer." Levy, *Hackers*, 30.

19. It should be remembered that hackers come in all shapes and sizes. Of course, not all hackers push the limits to see what they can accomplish. There are many varieties of hackers and in part the arguments over images of hackers can be understood as definitional. Those who wish to portray hackers in a negative light lump all hackers, crackers, and general thieves who use computers into the same categories. Hackers wish to maintain definitional distinctions between their objectives and those of the more criminal element.

20. J. Kelleher, "The hacker as scapegoat," *Computerworld, 23* (23 October 1989): 80.

21. I am using the "Portrait of J. Random Hacker" from Eric Raymond's *The New Hacker's Dictionary*. G. L. Steele Jr., "Confessions of a happy hacker," In *The new hacker's dictionary*, ed. R. Eric (Cambridge, England & London: MET Press, 1991), 413–420. In Appendix B, Raymond detailed characteristics of a hacker. These characteristics stem from comments he received from posting a version of his portrait onto USENET with about 100 replies.

22. Levy, *Hackers*; Mungo and Clough, *Approaching zero*.

23. G. Meyer, & J. Thomson, *The baudy world of the byte bandit: A postmodern interpretation of the computer underground* [On-line], Available: http://www.eff.org/pub/Net_info/Net_culture/Cyberpunks_hackers/Publications/Papers/ (10 June 1990).

24. Katie Hafner and John Markoff's book *Cyberpunk: Outlaws and Hackers on the Computer Frontier*, details the exploits of several hackers, most prominently Kevin Mitnik whose actions are narrated in the first 137 pages. See: K. Hafner, & J. Markoff, *Cyberpunk: Outlaws and hackers on the computer frontier* (New York & London: Simon & Schuster, 1991).

25. This equivocation is clearly done in an article by Michael Alexander entitled "Hacker Stereotypes Changing." In this article, a study by the National Center for Computer Crime Data (NCCCD) is quoted saying women and minorities are equally likely to engage in computer crime as are white males. Nowhere does the NCCCD mention computer hackers. Instead, it points to former and current employees as the single greatest threat to companies. However, Alexander, who writes virtually all the articles on hackers for *Computerworld* tends to blend hackers with computer criminals. M. Alexander, "Prison term for first U.S. hacker-law convict," *Computerworld, 23* (20 February 1989): 1, 12.

26. Kevin Poulsen was one such hacker whose torrid career Jonathan Littman narrated for *Los Angeles Times* readers. Poulsen, depicted by Littman as an awkward teenager, was an obsessed hacker. His abnormality, inferred from reading about his inability to interact well with others and a poor family life, is emphasized at the expense of the friendships he was able to cultivate. See: J. Littman, "The last hacker," *Los Angeles Times*, 12 September 1993, pp. 18–23, 64–65.

27. J. Aho, *This thing of darkness: A sociology of the enemy* (Seattle & London: University of Washington Press, 1994), 28.

28. Alexander, "Prison term," 12.

29. D. H. Freedman, "The goods on hacker hoods," *Forbes ASAP, 152* (3 September 1993): 32–40.

30. P. Keefe, "Portrait of hackers as young adventurers not convincing," *Computerworld, 26* (22 June 1992): 33.

31. R. Behar, "Surfing off the edge," *Time, 141* (8 February 1993): 62–63.

32. For use of the term *victim* to describe corporate and government agencies and for articles that position these groups as victims see: Freedman, "Goods on hacker hoods"; J. Bird, "Inside track on hackers," *Management Today* (June 1992): 78–82; M. Alexander, "Computer crime: Ugly secrete for business," *Computerworld, 24,* (12 March 1990): 1,104; M. Alexander, "Hacker victims heartened by convictions," *Computerworld, 23,* (20 February 1989): 1,12.

33. Hafner and Markoff, *Cyberpunk*, 120.

34. O. Johnston, "Experts call for better computer security," *Los Angeles Times*, 6 December 1990, A29.

35. J. Peterzell, "Spying and sabotage by computers," *Time, 133* (20 March 1989): 25–26.

36. Alexander, "Computer crime" 1.

37. Aho, "This thing of darkness," 28.

38. M. Alexander, "Complex crimes stall enforcers," *Computerworld, 24* (19 March 1990): 4.

39. W. G. Flanagan, & B. McMenamin, "The playground bullies are learning how to type," *Forbes, 150* (21 December 1992): 184–189.

40. Aho, "This thing of darkness," 29–30.

41. Ibid., 30.

42. "Alleged hacker is ordered not to talk about computers," *The Orlando Sentinel*, 5 April 1996, p. A12.

43. Ibid.

44. One example is a quote from Leonard Rose, Jr. who called his computer habit an "obsession." W. Schatz, "The terminal men: Crackdown on the legion of doom ends an era for computer hackers," *Washington Post*, 24 June 1990, pp. H1, H6.

45. "Supra-national response to networked world," *Computer Weekly*, 2 March 1995.

46. D. Campbell, *Writing security* (Minneapolis: University of Minnesota Press, 1992), 204.

47. Katie Hafner's article on Kevin Mitnick in *Esquire* is an excellent example of providing an account of deviance stemming from hacking addiction and a bad family life. See: K. Hafner, "Kevin Mitnick, unplugged. Computer hacker," *Esquire*, August 1995, p. 80 [Lexis-Nexis]. Additionally, Jonathan Littman's book *The*

Fugitive Game enhances the myth of Kevin Mitnick by including a photographic insert of "The Many Faces of Kevin Mitnick." See: J. Littman, *The fugitive game: The inside story of the great cyberchase* (Boston, New York, Toronto, & London: Little, Brown, 1996).

48. Clifford Stoll's book *The Cuckoo's Egg*, is an example of romanticizing the chase for hackers as well as providing another cite from which to draw negative images of the hacker. If a leftist astronomer sees the actions of the hacker as illegal then who could possibly support the hacker? C. Stoll, *The cuckoo's egg: Tracking a spy through the maze of computer espionage* (New York & London: Doubleday, 1989).

49. R. Karpinski, "Charges dropped against alleged Bell South hacker," *Telephony, 219* (6 August 1990): 12–13.

50. Morris was found guilty of letting loose on the Internet a worm that caused as many as 6,000 computers to crash. M. Alexander, "Morris case impact slight," *Computerworld*, 25 (21 January 1991): 1, 4.

51. Many question the use of Secret Service raids when the actual crimes are so vaguely defined. As a *Business Week* article on *Operation Sundevil* pointed out, "And a prosecutor involved in the investigation, who didn't want to be quoted by name, says chances are 'extremely high' that most of the cases will be dropped—as quietly as possible." Lewyn and Schwarts, "Legion of doom," 31.

52. K. Hafner, "A superhacker meets his match," *Newsweek*, 27 February 1997, pp. 61–63.

53. "Mitnick pleads guilty to illegally using phones, violating probation," *The Associated Press* [Lexis-Nexis] 23 April 1996; D. Smith, "Famed hacker pleads guilty to 1 federal charge," *Los Angeles Times*, 23 April 1996, p. 4.

54. Flanagan and McMenamin, "Playground bullies," 184.

55. V. Edelman, "Primed for crime on the Internet," *Inc.* (November 1995): 18.

56. K. J. Higgins, "Swarming your sites," *Communications Week* (8 April 1996): 37.

57. Edelman, "Primed for crime," 18.

58. B. Violino, "Pentagon caught in its own net," *Information Week* (27 May 1996): 32.

59. Aho, "This thing of darkness," 30.

60. L. Kehoe, & S. Stephens, "A hacker's paradise," *Financial Times*, 16 April 1996, p. 13.

61. L. Kehoe, & S. Stephens, "Computer invasions growing with Internet," *The Financial Post*, 17 April 1996, p. 54.

62. N. Wice, "Companies challenge computer hackers to break codes," *CNN News*, [Transcript 313–4], [Lexis-Nexis] (13 April 1996).

63. E. Weise, "Computer-savvy buddies hack their way into federal prison," *Los Angeles Times*, 14 April 1996, p. 1.

64. J. Bjorhus, "Suspect arrested in library hacking," *The Seattle Times*, 10 April 1996, p. A1.

65. J. Bjorhus, "Hacker attacks just tip of the iceberg," *The Seattle Times*, 10 April 1996, p. A9.

66. A. Stefora, & M. Cheek, "Hacking goes legit," *Industry Week, 243* (7 February 1994): 43–45.

67. C. Wilder, & B. Miolino, "Online theft—trade in black-market data is grow-

ing problem for both business and the law," *Information Week* (28 August, 1995): 30.

68. "FBI braces for hackers," *Information Week* (27 November 1995): 24.

69. "Government unwilling to relax software encryption limits," *Investor's Business Daily*, 2 January 1995, A6. This article details the latest hearings on encryption policy. It is documented that hackers are increasingly able to break 40-bit keys.

70. J. Markoff, "In search of computer security," *The New York Times*, 2 January 1996, p. 15.

71. B. McMenamin, "Fallen hacker," *Forbes, 153* (20 June 1994): 12.

72. J. Markoff, "Computer hacker in Britain said to enter U.S. systems," *The New York Times*, 24 October 1988, p. D1.

73. M. Alexander, "Hacker may have penetrated Pentagon," *Computerworld, 25* (16 September 1991): 14.

74. J. Daly, "Netherlands, Mexico chase after hackers," *Computerworld, 26* (13 July 1993): 14.

75. "Hackers raid U.S. lab file," *The New York Times*, 18 June 1988, pp. 45(L), 29(N).

76. J. Markoff, "Arrests in computer break-ins show a global peril," *The New York Times*, 4 April 1990, pp. A1, A16.

77. I. Brodie, & G. Gamini, "U.S. agents pursue hacker of secrets across cyberspace," *The New York Times*, 1 April 1996, p. 45 [Lexis-Nexis].

78. P. Thomas, & E. Corcoran, "Argentine, 22, charged with hacking computer networks," *The Washington Post*, 30 March 1996, p. A4.

79. Bird, "Inside track"; Freedman, "The goods on hacker hoods"; M. Alexander, "Hackers paradise?" *Computerworld, 24* (1991): S26–S27.

80. Aho, "This thing of darkness," 31.

81. Wilder and Miolino, "Online theft," 30.

82. T. Forester, & P. Morrison, *Computer ethics: Cautionary tales and ethical dilemmas in computing*, (Cambridge, MA: MIT Press, 1993).

83. Marie Christine-Leps offered a Foucaultian thesis as a working assumption in her book *Apprehending the Criminal: The Production of Deviance in Nineteenth Century Discourse*. "The second working hypothesis is that there exists an inter-referential network between institutions producing hegemonic knowledge: power does not originate in a specific locus—such as the legal, penitentiary, or police systems, or schools, families, or armies—but in the web of reciprocal validation and authentication existing between these various institutions." M. Christine-Leps, *Apprehending the criminal: The production of deviance in nineteenth century discourse* (Durham, NC & London: Duke University Press, 1992), 4.

84. Campbell, *Writing security*.

85. Ibid., 195.

86. Realist John J. Mearsheimer made exactly this argument. He argued that there will be an increase in major crises in Europe now that the Cold War has receded. J. J. Mearsheimer, "Why we will soon miss the Cold War," *The Atlantic Monthly*, August 1990, pp. 35–50.

87. Campbell, *Writing security*, 19.

88. Ibid., 196.

89. Ibid., 56.

90. Ibid., 70; R. K. Ashley, "Living on borderlines: Man, poststructuralism, and war," in *International/intertextual relations: Postmodern readings of world politics*, eds. J. D. Derian & M. J. Shapiro (Lexington, MA: Lexington Books, 1989), 303.

91. Campbell, *Writing security*, 71.

92. A recent interview with Steven Levy makes this point in relation to corporate security. Levy argued that hackers should not be blamed for poor security problems and that making hackers scapegoats does little to address the substantive issues. Kelleher, "The hacker as scapegoat," 80–81.

93. Campbell, *Writing security*, 209.

94. C. Bromberg, "In defense of hackers," *The New York Times*, 21 April 1991, p. 45.

95. Ibid.

96. Rosemary Coombe presented an excellent analysis of the harmful effects of more tightly controlled ownership of intellectual property. See: R. Coombe, "Objects of property and subjects of politics: Intellectual property laws and Democratic dialogue," *Texas Law Review, 69* (1991): 1853–1880.

97. Christine-Leps, *Apprehending the criminal*, 2.

6

Authors in the Information Age

Understanding authorship is critical to understanding intellectual property laws. Without a clear owner, it is difficult to control the exchange of information. Copyright was originally designed so the English Crown could keep track of who was saying seditious things. Today, it plays the function of policing the proprietary boundaries of cultural production. We cannot talk about copyright law without also talking about authorship. However, authorship is not the stable unidimensional concept the law would have it be. Authorship is complex and fraught with tension. Many types of people can assume the identity of author. Authors can be writing the most profound literary novel of the century or they can be writing pulp fiction by recycling story lines in order to produce more books. Authors, in a modern sense, have been defined as those who make a living from their creative work. How authorship is intertwined with intellectual property is an important relationship to uncover.

As the print-dominated age wanes, digitized information requires new perspectives and new rules. The proprietary framework that has dominated intellectual property law has not been capable of dealing with the new relationships between the author, the reader, and the text that emerge with the introduction of computer technology. More importantly, there is a fundamental clash between the legal discourse of copyright, which is interested in preserving the economic aspects of intellectual products, and the theoretical discourse of authorship with its emphasis on exchange and creativity. Exciting work is being done in literary and cultural theory on the function of authorship, yet copyright law, which governs the use and exchange of intellectual property, is failing to address these possibilities. Instead, copyright law has served to preserve an 18th-century notion of proprietary ownership best (if at all) suited for the print/analog age.

The Internet and computer technology facilitates the fragmentation of authorship, and the hypertexting of texts, even as copyright law has attempted to push these new approaches to intellectual property and creativity back within the boundary of the traditional economic model. The battle that emerged is best described by Peter Jazi: "On the one side are those who see its potential as a threat to traditional notions of individual proprietorship in information, and who perceive the vigorous extension of traditional copyright principles as the solution. On the other side are those who argue that the network environment may become a new cultural commons, which excessive or premature legal control may stifle."[1] A discourse intent on establishing copyright control over the uses of technology new and old, is emerging. The story that emerges is one that attempts to locate technology generally, and cyberspace specifically, within the traditional boundaries of the sovereign state and copyright law.

Copyright, much like all legal concepts, is an unstable idea relying heavily on litigation and legal definition for continued support. The overemphasis of ownership is the logical outcome of the existing law that assumes the author is a coherent identity, that the text never changes, and that ownership is the best method for facilitating creativity. Copyright, if only superficially, was constructed to protect the author from unauthorized use of a work. Thus, paying attention to the already existing literary theory about authorship can help explain why copyright may not be the most appropriate method for facilitating creation. Additionally, looking at how technology is changing authorship is helpful in understanding why copyright no longer offers the type of protection it was originally designed to provide. This chapter looks more closely at the concept of *authorship*, as well as the possibilities for authorship made available by new technology.

READERS, WRITERS, AND AUTHORS

The concept of *authorship* should not be taken for granted. Is there such a thing as original genius? Is a concept of *originality* the product of the enlightenment, much like the concept of *progress*? Does creativity have more to do with the cultural context within which the author works than any inspired thought? How is it possible to account for great authors? For great literature? For inspired poetry? Finally, what motivated great authors and poets to write? Was it the money they hoped to make? Was it a system of copyright? Was it a creative drive? These questions illustrate how complex the issue of authorship can be. What, then, is an author?

As Mike Shapiro noted, "Authors are, therefore, sovereignty functions, among other things."[2] Authors are political in that they help cement ownership. Authors are the product of an economic system, not the product of creative minds. The designation of an individual author who can take credit for a tangible work is critical to a functioning copyright law. The author acts as a boundary for the text. Foucault's seminal essay "What is an Author?" sheds light on the author function. Foucault wrote, "We can conclude, that, unlike a proper name, which moves from the interior of a discourse to the real person outside who produced it, the name of the author remains at the contours of texts—separating one from the other, defining their form, and characterizing their mode of existence."[3] Foucault elaborated on the boundary function of the author by arguing that the role of the author is to "characterize the existence, circulation, and operation of certain discourses in our society."[4] In modernity, the author–work relation is institutionalized. Rose explained: "The author–work relation is embedded in library catalogues, the indexes of standard literary histories, and such basic reference tools as *Books in Print*. It is pervasive in our educational system, where students are typically taught from the canon of major works by major authors. It is also institutionalized in our system of marketing cultural products."[5] The author thus serves a function not directly related to creativity. The author is both a boundary and a controlling mechanism for the text. The author helps control a system of book production. Literature is created through such a system where some authors should be read and some ignored.

Copyright institutionalizes the author–text relation, a link made clear by Rose: "No institutional embodiment of the author–work relation, however, is more fundamental than copyright, which not only makes possible the profitable manufacture and distribution of books, films, and other commodities but also, by endowing it with legal reality, helps to produce and affirm the very identity of the author as author."[6] The author function is reinforced by the authorizing function, meaning privilege is given to some interpretations (by professionals) and not to others. A text is given a boundary by its author and title and an interpretation by experts. Ultimately, authors and interpretations work together to form a discourse network.[7] Simply put, authorship is a method through which writing can be harnessed and owned. As Foucault wrote, "A text has an inaugurative value precisely because it is the work of a particular author, and our returns are conditioned by this knowledge."[8]

Although the author function is all pervasive in society, it obscures several important points about creativity. First, the author function obscures the interconnectedness of texts. Texts draw from each other. In a sense, they merge and blend through the process of quotation and referencing. The myth of an autonomous text, created by the author function, co-exists with the interconnectedness of texts and ideas. The author function helps us forget the interconnectedness in favor of the autonomous author. Additionally, the reader can be a writer and is inspired by the ideas he or she might read. The reader uses other texts as a springboard. Nobody creates in a vacuum, we are all dependent on the ideas of others.

Second, collaborative writing, not the work of an autonomous individual author is the norm, not the exception. Woodmansee touched on this critical aspect of authorship when she observed:

> In their recent study of professional writing practices, Andrea Lunsford and Lisa Ede have found that most of the writing that goes on today is in fact collaborative. Indeed, one comes away from their investigation of how people actually write in business, government, industry, the sciences and social sciences with the impression that there is but one last bastion of solitary origination: the arts and humanities. What gives their study such urgency is the fact that, this powerful collaborative trend notwithstanding, the assumption that writing is inherently and necessarily a solitary, individual act still informs both the theory and practice of the teaching of writing.[9]

Despite efforts to isolate texts via authors, writing tends to be collaborative in nature.[10] A novel is not written in isolation, it goes through drafts and has numerous editors. Any movie in production is worked on by hundreds of people. A book is not the work of an individual, even though only one name appears as author and said author is to have contributed something original to the discipline.

Jaszi argued that the "persistence of the notion of 'authorship' in American copyright law makes it difficult for any new legal synthesis, which would focus on the reality of collective creativity, to emerge."[11] The protection for joint authorship in the Copyright Act, although arguably about collective authorship, really takes the individual author and assumes each individual will contribute a portion. There is no room for collective and collaborative writing. Jaszi continued, "Far from acknowledging the extent to which participation in a corporate, creative enterprise entails the surrender of individual prerogative, copyright law implicitly assumes the continued relevance of the Romantic vision of 'authorship' to this domain.[12] The result is a complete lack of understanding when it comes to collaborative works.[13]

Theories of authorship obscure the collaborative trend in writing. Forcing authorship into the folds of copyright renders it nearly impossible to accommodate collaborative writing within a property system designed to protect the individual author.[14] The system is biased toward a specific notion of author—the individual proprietary author.

The author function also tends to obscure the differences between authorship and the process of writing. French feminist and literary critic Helene Cixous helped provide some depth to the notion of writing as differentiated from authorship. She argued that there is an immense difference between the author and the book written. As she put it, "We don't know the authors, we read books and we take them for authors. We think there must be an analogy or identification between the book and the author. But you can be sure there is an immense difference between the author and the person who wrote; and if you were to meet that person, it would be someone else."[15] Focusing on authorship provides one with a different framework from which to theorize than focusing on writing.

For Cixous, writing is about the expression of thoughts. For her, writing is not only a creative experience but a soul-searching one that cannot be bound into the human form of an author. She wrote, "A writer has no children; I have no children when I write. When I write I escape myself, I uproot myself, I am a virgin; I leave from within my own house and I don't return. The moment I pick up my pen—magical gesture—I forget all the people I love; an hour later they are not born and I have never known them."[16] Writing is not about ownership or even authorship but about creative expression. This viewpoint speaks to the power of writing and creativity and is reflected in what Trinh Minh-Ha called *body writing*, or writing from the body. Body writing escapes authorship and becomes expression. As Minh-Ha pointed out, "Moreover, more and more women see writing as *the* place of change, where the possibility of transforming social and cultural structures is offered. Going beyond the convention Presence-God-Author and feeling the urgency of a decentralizing movement, they take up speech not to identify it with themselves or to possess it, but to deliver it from its enslavement to mastery."[17] Writing is different from authorship. Writing expresses ideas, authorship owns them. Much like putting a title on a work to describe its contents, an author describes its ownership. The distinction between writing and authorship is critical because it produces very different results.

For Cixous, the most powerful book, the abominable book, is that which has no author. "The imund book is the book without an author. It is the book written with us aboard, though not with us at the steering wheel. It is the book that makes us experience a kind of dying, that drops the self, the speculating self, the speculating clever 'I.' "[18] Such a book may have hundreds of authors, or just one. The creative process of writing, from this point of view, is the resistance to the author function. Instead of focusing on the author as a boundary and owner of the text, it is quite possible to understand writing as the process of giving up ownership.

In attempting to distinguish the author function from writing, I do not wish to romanticize writing. Writing, although possibly being all that Cixious described it as being, is still a manifestation of a relationship between the author and the historical context in which the writer writes. Writing must be contextualized as emerging from within the culture in which it was produced. What must be brought from the discussion of writing and authorship is that there are diverse facets to the authorial personality. There are the aesthetic/creative facets that produce writing; there are the legal facets that produce copyrights; and there are the author-function facets that produce boundaries.[19] In modern discourses, the author-function aspect of the authorial personality is used to replace the aesthetic/creative aspects, and solidify ownership as the method for dealing with literary work.

Literary work itself, however, must also be deconstructed. Romanticism suggests that the "literary work itself comes to be seen as a mysterious organic unity."[20] Literature emerges in a romantic form because social conditions in industrializing countries fostered a climate in which " 'imaginative creation' can be offered as an image of non-alienated labor; the intuitive, transcendental scope of the poetic mind can provide a living criticism of those rationalist or empiricist ideologies enslaved to 'fact.' "[21] The author function works to incorporate even this last bastion of imaginative creation within the scope of production.

The author is so embedded in our thought processes that we look to the author as owner instead of looking behind the role of authorship to the production of discourses in society. The author becomes the boundary of a text, "separating one from the other, defining their form, and characterizing their mode of existence."[22] Additionally, centering the author changes the focus from what is written to who writes it. This change takes us further from the process of writing described by Cixous. Foucault's analysis suggests that the text is not a stable fixed entity, but is made so through the author function.[23] New technologies help illuminate the relationship between authorship and intellectual property by challenging the notion of authorship. The next section evaluates the potential challenge to authorship presented by the information age.

THE CHALLENGE OF AUTHORSHIP IN THE INFORMATION AGE

There is a critical difference between intellectual property and tangible property—intellectual property can be shared and used by more than one person simultaneously. It is difficult to conceptualize ownership in ideas and expressions because once an idea is shared it becomes the property of all.[24] Property theory cannot adequately describe knowledge, ideas, the communication of ideas, or the motivations for exchange of ideas. However, in the United States, there is no alternative to the intellectual property regime framework. Copyright has become our only option. Our language is encased in notions of "property," "intellectual work," "intellectual products," and "proprietary ideas." Copyright law helps solidify the notion of authorship as a textual boundary.

Computer technology can substantially alter authorship. Computer technology highlights the communal nature of intangible property because it is easier to exchange information, ideas, and expressions, than to own them. In the face of new technologies it becomes increasingly difficult to solidify the boundaries of ownership. This new electronic environment thus provides a mechanism for disruption of the traditional copyright story. This disruption takes the form of new definitions of authorship and originality.

In the electronic age, individuals are increasingly aware of who owns information and knowledge.[25] The electronic age also provides numerous opportunities for the average American to subvert the intellectual property system. Most Americans do not place importance on intellectual property in the same way those who own the copyrights do. Instead, they see the tangible item (the book or record) as their personal property to use as they wish. Instilling a notion of respect for intellectual property has become a critical task for the owners of intellectual property rights, however, the subversion of this system is easily accomplished in everyday life through cultural appropriation.

Those who consider themselves authors find it impossible to control their work once it enters the electronic realm. The author function is diluted as texts move freely from one electronic account to another. Because each individual can reproduce data easily, electronic media fosters exchange of information through multiplication. People on the Internet, like people in face-to-face situations, communicate by sharing information, stories, and news. Anyone with experience using e-mail has seen the chains of addresses at the top of the message indicating all the previous readers. Additionally, anyone who uses e-mail can pass along an interesting item to friends.

Authors are faced with several serious problems as they bypass the industry and connect with communities of readers via technology. First, authors lose control over their work much faster than in print. Authors, in order to engage in the exchange of ideas, place their ideas in the public. Once engaged in exchange, control is minimized, if not lost. If an author exchanges even one text, it can cross the globe and reach thousands of people within the space of a few minutes. The scope of readership for even the most basic of papers can be expanded beyond what is capable for traditional print. Additionally, it is much easier for readers to begin a conversation with the author. Through e-mail, an author is easy to contact. If someone feels proprietary about their work, the loss of control can signal a significant loss in revenue.

Authors can probably survive the loss of distribution control, after all they have very little control over distribution in the present system. However, a second problem with technology is that authors lose more control over authentication and reward, which are better protected under traditional copyright law. Over the Internet, authentication is virtually impossible. Anyone can alter texts, change authorship, or appropriate the ideas without the knowledge of the initiating author. In the case of discussions, the texts can mingle until it is difficult to know who said what. The brackets designed to differentiate new text from the old can lose meaning completely after three or four exchanges and it is easier to get lost in the dialogue than to worry about who is talking.

Although technology that provides for authentication may soon be widespread, the environment allows for the out-of-control, communal exchange of information. Making cyberspace secure means making it easy to track and authenticate information in order to reward the owner. Currently, no system exists that provides the originator of an idea with monetary reward. Conversely, there is no system through which to track infringement of copyright, although one may expect this type of system to be available in the near future. As a document moves across the Internet, the infringer becomes virtually impossible to track. The sovereignty response will be to develop technology that can charge a fee for reading information or using programs via the Internet. In such a system, everything could be commodified and owned.[26]

Given the current discourse on intellectual property, the loss of control, and the inability to authenticate and reward authors, exchange via the Internet is met with fear, hostility, and a sense of crisis by those advocating a traditional copyright story. Bruce L. Flanders described the crisis best in his article appropriately entitled, "Barbarians at the Gate." He stated:

> What we have is a classic example of the "loss of identifiable boundaries of works on which copyright has relied to distinguish 'yours' from 'mine.' " In this informal and often unpredictable intellectual collaboration, authorship is frequently unrecorded. One of the goals of the soon-to-be-realized National Research and Education Network (NREN) is the implementation of ultra high-speed telecommunications to make it easier for immense quantities of data to travel rapidly between users. This will only exacerbate the copyright problem.[27]

What one might see as a positive step—unpredictable intellectual collaboration—Flanders viewed as a troublesome threat. We have reached a significant crossroad in our understanding of intellectual property. It is this threat that can be transformed into a positive challenge if we can reconceptualize authorship. It is important to look at the possibilities of authorship in the information age.

THE TRANSFORMATION OF AUTHORSHIP

Transfer from Author Function to Dialogue

The first possible potential for authorship is to replace the emphasis on authorship with an emphasis on dialogue. In the Middle Ages, texts were viewed as instruments to incite action. Authorship was important in order to know who to hold accountable. The short history of copyright outlined in chapter 1 illustrated the switch from the text as an act to the text as an original and aesthetic creation. This transformation corresponded with the assertion of author's rights and copyright.[28]

We are seeing a new transformation emerge in which the text loses its bounded quality and becomes part of a larger informational network. Authorial works can be conceived as connections between everyone, moving and changing to meet the needs of those involved in the dialogue. The possible transformation is from the text as an individual creation to the text as a dialogue produced in a community. Exchange provides different understandings of authorship as it separates this concept from its relation with proprietary ownership. Collaborative constructions are facilitated by the ease with which electronic data can be manipulated. Authorship in an electronic age can embrace facets of community, intertextuality, and instability. This perspective has qualities of an older age when dialogue with a text was carried out in the margins. It also has uniquely modern qualities of which the loss of a substantive form is only one.[29]

Discourse, not authorship can become the emphasis. Doug Brent explained, "In short, with electronic communication the notion of the static and individually owned text dissolves back into the communally performed fluidity of the oral culture. . . . In the electronic world as in the oral, the latent intertextuality of print is raised to consciousness: it becomes more obvious that originality lies not so much in the individual creation of elements as in the performance of the whole composition."[30] Individually owned texts can be the products of a carefully managed discourse about intellectual property. As this shared vision dissipates in the face of electronic communication, the stage is set for a transformation in authorship and originality. If discourse becomes the focus, there is also the potential that authorship can develop in a noncommodified manner where monetary incentive is not the motivating force behind creation.

Currently, the Internet is a connection of individuals who show little concern for the economic rationale offered by copyright. More important is the potential for dialogue and exchange made possible in this new public sphere. If our language centers the identity of owner as the important part of intellectual property, then loss of control is likely to be the inevitable result. However, if one centers the potential for creation and exchange, the Internet and other forms of electronic communication become an exciting and valuable realm for discourse and communication. The potential for transformation lies in substituting a discourse emphasizing dialogue for the discourse emphasizing the economic incentive of taming cyberspace for "real" authors. The medium helps the former in the sense that electronic communication is an assault on the distinction "between *mine* and *thine* that the modern authorship construct was designed to enforce."[31] Hypertext, an electronic presentation of text, is a perfect illustration of this potential breakdown.

Hypertext, which is the foundation of the Web, is a form of interaction with a document that allows the reader to transgress the boundary of a text by following themes of interest that may not always remain in a single text. A linear presentation is circumvented by the ability to "point and click" your way through a document. A person can go from document to document without ever depending on the author function to legitimate the text. For example, a paragraph introducing the director of a particular university research group may have several highlighted words. The user can click the mouse on any of the highlighted words and the screen will change to provide the desired text, picture, or sound. The user can choose to follow an interesting link outside the text of the document to another text, or to another university. This method of interacting with a text gives the reader more freedom to move from topic to topic. George P. Landow argued that hypertext creates metatexts: "In the future there will be more metatexts formed by linking individual sections of individual works, although the notion of an individual, discrete work becomes increasingly undermined and untenable within this form of information technology, as it already has within much contemporary critical theory."[32] The success of hypertext in the form of the Web is evidence of the possibilities of metatexts formed by linking a variety of works together. The result is a discourse where individual voices can be lost in the cacophony of many voices.

Additionally, hypertext reconfigures the role of readers and writers. As Landow said, "First of all, the figure of the hypertext author approaches, even if it does not entirely merge with, that of the reader; the functions of reader and writer become more deeply entwined with each other than ever before."[33] The reader plays an active role in this story. A variety of texts, pictures, and sounds are available to the reader connected via hyperlinks. As the reader in a hypertext document moves through the links they produce a meaning that surpasses a single text.

As someone links documents together in a hypertextual fashion the links are creating not only a linear story, but the possibility of much more as well. What results inside the reader's head is the acquisition of knowledge, but not necessarily knowledge garnered from the linear progression of an argument by an original author. The relationship of reader to text is made clearer through the technology of hypertext. By focusing on the text as dialogue and the function of the reader, the author function is diminished in importance and the possibilities of a dialogue via hypertext is made possible.

As the electronic communication and the methods for communicating become more commonplace, it could lead to a transformation in the manner in which information is communicated. The reader can become part of the writing process. It is easy to continually add and subtract from an electronic document and to a dialogue. Anyone using a word processor understands this. As Woodmansee pointed out, "By contributing his or her commentary, the reader becomes an overt collaborator in an unending process of reading and writing which reverses the trajectory of print, returning us to something very like the expressly collaborative writing milieu of the Middle Ages and the Renaissance with which we began."[34] This return occurs with the corresponding loss of the author function. The negative consequence could be the further fragmentation of knowledge. The positive outcome is a greater degree of interactivity between the text and the reader.

Loss of Individual Authorial Control

Second, and closely related to the transformation of the text to a dialogue, is the resulting loss of authorial control. This can occur through the process of collective authorship that transforms the subject and the way authorship is interpreted. It can also occur by destabilizing the authenticity of the author's text. To quote Landow again:

> There's more than one way to kill an author. One can destroy (what we mean by) the author, which includes the notion of sole authorship, by removing the autonomy of the text. One can also achieve the same end by de-centering text or by transforming text into a network. Finally, one can remove limits on textuality, permitting it to expand, until Nietzsche, the edifying philosopher, becomes equally the author of *The Gay Science* and laundry lists and other such trivia—as indeed he was.[35]

There is much to suggest that hypertext begins the process of decentering texts as well as speeding up the loss of authorial control. Foucault would most likely see hypertext as a mechanism that speeds up the death of the author.

Mark Poster was among the first to discuss the transformation of authorship via technology. Poster argued that the traditional subject is destabilized via electronic writing. In other words, the subject is destabilized through new avenues of collective authorship.[36] From simply passing the same disk from person to person or taking a text received from the Internet and changing the words before sending it on, it is clear that once text becomes electronic its stability and authorial authenticity is reduced, if not lost. For example, if a copy of this chapter is sent via e-mail to a listserv, there is nothing I can do to stop anyone on the list from changing my words, or appropriating the work as their own.

Such collaborative authorship, as we have seen, is certainly not new. However, although copyright can only define the author as an individual (or a couple of individuals who can identify their specific contribution to a collaborative work), computers make collaborative work easier and the distinctions between authors more difficult to make. The implications radically affect how the author is perceived. First, works can become collective in a manner not anticipated or understood by copyright law. How does one assign ownership to a document when no one knows who exactly did what? Second, an individual author cannot maintain control over his or her words. This can happen quite unintentionally. When using Eudora's "redirect" command, for example, a message that is forwarded looks as if it comes from the person who forwarded the message, not the original sender. This can make it quite difficult to identify who sent what and who should be attributed, and thus causes confusion about who is the author.[37] Phil Agre illustrated with the following example:

> If someone forwards a message from me to a mailing list, the listserv might reject the message (because I'm listed in the From: field even though I'm not on the list of authorized users of the list) and send me an error message, or it might accept the message and tell the whole list that I sent it. Even worse, Jane (who really sent the message to the list) might have added her own text without it being clear whether the text was mine or hers.[38]

Obviously, identifying an author under these circumstances becomes difficult. The technology itself mingles authorship to the point where it becomes practically meaningless. By decentering the author, all that is left is the text. The author loses control over the text. This has implications for those who wish to ensure that their authorial integrity is intact. However, even if a name appears in the body of the text, at the point where a message has been forwarded a dozen times, figuring out who authored the text is often harder than it might appear.

Still, many people embrace the instability of electronic communication. As Doug Brent put it, "When knowledge inhabits a print space, it seems natural to want to own it. When it enters electronic space, it seems equally natural to surrender it."[39] Uploading a file to the Internet is an act acknowledging an absence of control over the ideas that are written about. A written work can be altered by numerous other individuals who come into contact with it. To participate in this form of exchange is to give up sovereignty over intellectual property almost completely.

Electronic communication provides the unique opportunity for authorship to be separated from the text. Furthermore, it is easy to lose sight of the author with so much information on any topic available. If one engages in a discussion at some point the author is separated from the arguments, especially if one does not know the participants personally. Consequently, there is a challenge to traditional notions of authorship waiting to be embraced on the Internet.

Democratic Authorship

Technology also revolutionizes authorship by providing an outlet for virtually anyone with access to have the ability to be heard. A very real possibility is the downfall of traditional publishing, and thus the traditional system of copyright law. Publishers have acted as a centralizing mechanism controlling access to the marketplace of ideas. Mainstream media has been a most successful method for delivering messages to the public, in a "one-to-many" format. The result was commercialized television where critical thinking tended to be scorned and consumerism became the surrogate for substantive dialogue.[40]

Electronic media challenges everything about publishing and authorship from selection to ownership to distribution. The Internet allows anyone with a story, poem, book, or manifesto to find an audience. Traditional publishers can be completely bypassed as authors take their work directly to the public. The National Writers Union, a group dedicated to protecting the rights of authors (which can sometimes be at odds with the rights of publishers), clearly defined the potential of new technology:

> They say that freedom of the press only applies to those who own one. And as presses have become more and more expensive, publishing has been concentrated into fewer and fewer hands. With the new information technologies we have the opportunity to reverse that historical trend. The technology exists for the new electronic marketplaces to be implemented so that individual authors, small presses, and writer co-ops can publish on the network, and have their payments and royalties electronically collected and transferred to them,

> without their having to invest in equipment beyond their financial means or pay prohibitive usage and carrier fees.[41]

Thus, authorship can be radically democratized as the centralized world of publishing becomes the decentralized world of the Web.[42]

The decentralized nature of information exchange also provides a more critical role for readers. Each individual can become responsible for his or her own material. The one-to-many format of mass communication where the recipient has little control is reversed into a format where the recipient has complete control over the messages received. The result is that each information receiver is responsible for filtering information and the author as authority loses its centrality. Although the Internet is no panacea for healthy subjects, its "many-to-many" format provides a form of access and dialogue missing from mainstream media.

The potential of democratic authorship provides room for everyone who wants to exchange ideas with others to become an author. "Real" authors, those who make money writing, find this prospect frightening because it diminishes their authority. As the potential for transforming authorship clashes with a system for legitimating expertise and institutionalizing the production of printed work, the loss of control experienced by the publishing companies spurs the sovereignty function and the need to make the information superhighway safe for authors. The manner in which authorship might be transformed has been explored in order to illustrate that there is potential for authorship outside the highly commodified definition of the author that is the framework for the current copyright regime. As Barlow noted, "As we return to continuous information, we can expect the importance of authorship to diminish. Creative people may have to renew their acquaintance with humility."[43]

The democratic effects of the Internet illustrate that although the potential for a switch to dialogue and the instability of authorship exist (Possibilities 1 and 2), the author is far from dead. Instead, what we see is a clash between the interests of authors who want to exchange and authors who want proprietary control over their work. Of course, it is probably true that most authors fall somewhere in the middle. The interest in author's moral rights, or the ability to control the integrity of a work once it has entered public exchange, brought on by the sudden ability to exchange information seems to attest to authorial interest in proprietary rights.[44] The inability to control proprietary work has led some authors to become paranoid about their ideas reaching the public. Already the assertion that inadequate protection will dampen the incentive to create can be heard.[45]

It would seem it is incompatible for democratic authorship and exchange to exist in the same environment as proprietary authorship interested in monetary rewards. There is bound to be a blurring of the boundaries when proprietary works are exchanged without reward. This can represent an intolerable situation for traditional creators and producers.

The greater danger, however, is to those who wish to engage in a noncommodified, democratic form of authorship. Those who have little respect for original authorship, but much respect for making a quick buck, are most likely to take ideas that are exchanged for free and turn them into profit-making enterprises. Although some authors may willingly set their ideas free on the Internet waves, there are many people willing to profit from ideas they find but did not create. The problem then, does not lie in the fact authors are unwilling to share ideas unless compensated. It lies in the fact that a system that commodifies knowledge produces a powerful logic that quickly overshadows any alternative system. This does not make it normatively better. It simply makes it more aggressive. It allows those within it to appropriate ideas donated to the public good for personal profit.[46]

If we follow the path of democratizing authorship, the author as authority and boundary is decentralized. From this perspective, democracy is about balancing the needs of authors with the needs of readers and the general public. Democratic authorship removes authorship from the confines of author-as-expert and creates a situation where everyone can exchange ideas, some of which will be individually authored. Even democratic authorship can serve as a boundary. However, these boundaries will be defined by exchange instead of sovereignty. Advancing some form of democratic and decentralized authorship might help avoid the current trends toward increased ownership of authorial work.

Computers as Authors

Our notions of creativity are also affected by technology. Increasingly, computer programs can create "art." Computer-generated fractals are an example. These designs embody mathematical precision and artistic beauty, although they involve very little human input. The personality that traditionally is responsible for making art is lacking from computer-generated images. Our understanding of creativity is challenged in the process. Sam Ricketson made this argument in light of copyright protection and how authorship and originality should be defined in the future.

> My [Ricketson] thesis will be that this concept (authorship) has now developed close to the breaking point. While it still embodies the values of personal creation traditionally central to copyright law, these values have now reached the point at which they are being steadily

> undermined and debased. To adopt the terminology used in the title of the lecture, the choice is rapidly becoming one between people and machines.[47]

If machines can produce artistic works, what does creativity as an outgrowth of human personality mean? What are the implications for intellectual property? Who owns the literary or artistic work created by a machine?

We have always accepted that human authorship is needed to define creation.[48] In her analysis of photography as art, Jane M. Gaines made clear the requirement for some form of human input. She stated:

> Crucial to Edelman's theory is the idea that in order for the law to protect the photographic work, the photographer (the creative subject who had disappeared into the machine), had to be reintroduced into the equation; a soul had to be found in the mechanical act, the "soulless labor" of operating a camera. The subject (and here all of the grand potential of humanism's "Man" is unfolded) "invests" the photograph with something of himself, with the combination of humanness and particularity that we have come to call the "original conception."[49]

In this original concept the creative spirit of the human is seen through the product of the machine, which then becomes the intellectual property of the creator. Modern technology, which takes the creative power of machines even further than the camera, is much more problematic for copyright. If all a human agent does is press a button, how is the personality of the human endowed in the ultimate product? As artificial intelligence becomes increasingly sophisticated and capable of acts traditionally considered creative, who will own the results? A copyright system and authorship that requires that a human endeavor in which human labor or human personality manifests itself in a creative medium is being stood on its head.

Giving copyright to machines is one method for dealing with this problem. A second possibility is to embrace the cultural nature of all creative work and to accept a creative work as a public good instead of something done for private advantage. Of course, as with the example of photography, the resilience of the law to incorporate new forms of human authorship within its folds may provide avenues for the human soul to take control over these products as well. As Gaines stated, "So Edelman's account reminds us, new technologies may 'surprise' old categories, but only to be reformed according to existing conceptions of the world. Science and engineering may produce technologies that outstrip human capabilities, but these strange inventions are soon reconceived—domesticated and humanized—as they are put to use."[50]

CONCLUSION: THE POSSIBILITIES OF AUTHORSHIP

The possibilities of authorship and creativity are multiple. New technology blurs boundaries that have been discursively drawn and accepted for many years. New technology helps deconstruct the traditional copyright story by undermining authorship as the work of an individual and original creation as the work of a human agent.

Our future can be a place where authorship is not the boundary of texts, and where multiple authors and dialogues exist. The future could be a place where everyone can put their thoughts, ideas, stories, and music on the Internet for anyone's use. Authorial control is likely to diminish in the face of free exchange, or if the commodification of ideas is diminished. Currently, cyberspace is a place where commodification remains unimportant. However, traditional authors and traditional industries are seeing vast market potential for their products. In making this market safe for proprietary goods, the possibilities for a democratic alternative may lose out.

The prospects for decentralization are not high. Without a concerted effort to respect democratic relations, old notions of ownership will prevail. To quote Doug Brent:

> Moreover, given the economic structure that we have painstakingly built on the back of print-induced linearity and specialization, it will take more than a new attitude toward texts to make us stop wanting to charge for knowledge. In fact, the very technology that has made certain aspects of replication so easy as to make old-fashioned copyright unenforceable has simultaneously brought into existence new possibilities of charging by the byte for using information—a process that Moulthrop calls "information capitalism." For every move in the economic game there is a countermove, and knowledge has been so closely tied to economics for so long that it may never be dislodged.[51]

However, if knowledge is to stand a chance of being dislodged from economics, it must start through the process of recognizing the benefits of a new system and establishing a way of talking about knowledge that avoids the pitfalls of an economistic discourse. So far, as new technologies have fostered increased dialogue between authors, texts, and audiences, the law has been used to decrease dialogue and extend traditional notions of ownership to new mediums. Faced with the largess of corporate power and governmental policing, it is difficult to see how new technologies will be able to transform the boundaries that have been established by print. But as new technologies permit the acquisition and exchange of knowledge within the privacy of one's home, it has become unclear whether one can sustain the traditional copyright story without compromising constitutional rights of privacy and free expression.

NOTES

1. P. Jaszi, "On the author effect: Contemporary copyright and collective creativity," *Cardozo Arts & Entertainment* (1992): 320.

2. M. J. Shapiro, "Sovereignty and exchange in the orders of modernity," *Alternatives, 16* (1991): 460.

3. M. Foucault, "What is an author?" in *Language, counter-memory, practice: Selected essays and interviews*, trans. D. F. Bouchard & S. Simon (Ithaca: Cornell University Press, 1977), 123.

4. Ibid., 124.

5. M. Rose, *Authors and owners: The invention of copyright* (London & Cambridge, MA: Harvard University Press, 1993), 1.

6. Ibid.

7. A discourse network is a system of learning that developed in the wake of printing.

> A system in which knowledge was defined in terms of authority and erudition, in which the doctrine of rhetoric governed discursive production, in which patterns of communication followed the lines of social stratification, in which books circulated in a process of limitless citation, variation, and translation, in which Universities were not yet state institutions and the learned constituted a special (often itinerant) class with unique privileges, and in which the concept of literature embraced virtually all of what was written. (This is the discourse network of the 1800's).

See: F. A. Kitler, *Discourse networks: 1800/1900*, trans. M. Metteer (Stanford: Stanford University Press, 1990), XVIII. This quote is from the introduction written by David E. Wellbery.

8. Foucault, "What is an author?" 136.

9. M. Woodmansee, "On the author effect: Recovering collectivity," *Cardozo Arts & Entertainment* (1992): 288–289.

10. Ibid.

11. Jaszi, "On the author effect," 295.

12. Ibid., 315.

13. "At base, however, the law is not so much systematically hostile to works that do not fit the individualistic model of Romantic 'authorship' as it is uncomprehending of them. Such works are marginalized or become literally invisible within the prevailing ideological framework of discourse in copyright—even to the point of literal invisibility." Ibid., 302.

14. The Copyright Act only deals with collaborative work in terms of co-ownership. Each author is recognized as autonomous and the ultimate creation is called a *joint work*. The language of collaboration, which suggests the inability

to separate out the individual work of any one person, is missing from the Copyright Act. See: 17 U.S.C.A 201(a).

15. H. Cixous, *Three steps on the ladder of writing*, trans. S. Cornell, & S. Sellers (New York: Columbia University Press, 1993), 20.

16. Ibid., 21.

17. T. T. Minh-Ha, *When the moon waxes red: Representation, gender and cultural politics* (New York & London: Routledge, 1991).

18. Cixous, *Three steps*, 156.

19. I am appropriating the language of authorial personalities from: D. Saunders, & I. Hunter, "Lessons from the literatory: How to historicise authorship," *Critical Inquiry* (Spring 1991): 479–509.

20. T. Eagleton, *Literary theory: An introduction* (Minneapolis: University of Minnesota Press, 1983).

21. Ibid., 19.

22. Foucault, "What is an author?" 123.

23. The lack of a stable text is reflected on in the works of many theorists working in literary theory and computer science. This notion is the foundation for George P. Landow's work on hypertext. He discussed the convergence of literary and social theory in the work of Derrida, Deluze and Guittari, and Foucault with that of computer scientists. See: G. P. Landow, *Hypertext/text/theory* (Baltimore, MD & London: The Johns Hopkins University Press, 1994).

24. E. Mansfield, Intellectual property, technology and economic growth, in *Intellectual property rights in science, technology, and economic performance*, eds. F. W. Rushing & C. G. Brown (Boulder, San Francisco, & London: Westview Press, 1990), 23.

25. One of the better and more recent evaluations of ownership of all types of intellectual property was conducted by Anne Wells Branscomb. See: A. W. Branscomb, *Who owns information? From privacy to public access* (New York: Basic Books, 1994).

26. This possibility is evaluated in the final chapter.

27. B. L. Flanders, "Barbarians at the gate," *American Libraries* (July/August 1991): 669.

28. M. Rose, "The author in court: *Pope v. Curll* (1741)," *Cardozo Arts & Entertainment* (1992): 475–493.

29. "Bolter (Jay David) likens this new incarnation of the book to a medieval manuscript the margins of which 'belonged to the scholarly reader'—were for 'conducting a dialogue with the text.' During generations of copying this text could migrate from the margins into the center, as the glosses of readers made their way into the original text." See: Woodmansee, "On the author effect," 290–291.

30. D. Brent, "Oral knowledge, typographic knowledge, electronic knowledge: Speculations on the history of ownership," *Ejournal* [On-line], Available: DA-BRENT@ACS.UCALGARY.CA. (November 1991).

31. Woodmansee, "On the author effect," 290.

32. G. P. Landow, *Hypertext: The convergence of contemporary critical theory and technology* (Baltimore, MD & London: The Johns Hopkins University Press, 1992), 40.

33. Ibid., 71.

34. Woodmansee, "On the author effect," 290.

35. Landow, *Hypertext*, 74.

36. M. Poster, *The mode of information: Poststructuralism and social context* (Chicago: University of Chicago Press, 1990), 115.

37. This example comes from P. Agre, *The Network Observer* (TNO) [On-line], Available: rre-maintainers@weber.ucsd.edu. (1995).

38. Ibid.

39. Brent, "Oral knowledge."

40. See: I. I. Mitroff, & W. Bennis, *The unreality industry: The deliberate manufacturing of falsehood and what it is doing to our lives* (New York & Oxford: Oxford University Press, 1993).

41. National Writers Union, *Electronic publishing issues, a working paper* [On-Line], Available: University of Maryland Gopher <anon@info.umd.edu>. (30 June 1993).

42. The National Writers Union predicts the demise of the traditional printing industry: "Tomorrow, however, desktop publishing and the electronic marketplace will eliminate the need for typesetting, printing, binding, trucking, warehousing, shelf-stocking, and inventory maintenance. If electronic distribution is implemented to allow individual authors, or small writer co-ops, access to the world electronic marketplace, what then is the need or purpose of publishers?" Ibid.

43. J. P. Barlow, "*The economy of ideas: A framework for rethinking patents and copyrights in the digital age, Wired, 2.03* [On-Line], Available: http://www.wired.com/wired/2.03/features/economy.ideas.html (Visited 2/20/98).

44. K. Aoki, "Adrift in the intertext: authorship and audience 'recoding' rights—comment on Robert H. Rotstein 'Beyond metaphor: Copyright infringement and the fiction of the work,' " *Chicago-Kent Law Review* (1993): 818–820.

45. Keith Aoki predicted this argument in his article. See: Aoki, "Adrift in the intertext," 830.

46. The profiteering motivations of the U.S. pharmaceutical industries abroad is a perfect example. These companies take indigenous knowledge about traditional healing, bring it into their laboratories and patent the resulting drugs. It is a clash between a culture that sees medicine as a communal good to be shared as communal knowledge with a culture that only sees private profit as a motivating factor. For a recent look at this and related controversies see: M. B. Snell, "Bioprospecting or biopiracy," *Utne Reader* (March/April 1996): 83.

47. S. Ricketson, "The 1992 Horace S. Manges lecture—people or machines: The Berne convention and the changing concept of authorship," *Columbia VLA Journal of Law & the Arts, 16* (1991): 3.

48. Ibid., 11.

49. J. M. Gaines, *Contested culture: The image, the voice, and the law* (Chapel Hill & London: The University of North Carolina Press, 1991), 46–47.

50. Ibid., 47. An example of the domestication of the new technology of the Internet under existing copyright law can be read in: E. A. Cavazos, & G. Morin, *Cyberspace and the law: Your rights and duties in the on-line world* (Cambridge & London: MIT Press, 1994). A more sensitive look at the problems of copyright and the Internet is provided in M. E. Katsh, *Law in a digital world* (New York & Oxford: Oxford University Press, 1995).

51. Brent, "Oral knowledge."

7

The Future of Intellectual Property Law

From its beginnings, copyright law has been shaped by technology. Each new technology renewed the debate over the ideal balance between public sharing and private control. The newest challenge to copyright, however, is making it increasingly clear that the traditional copyright story might be incapable of addressing the global exchange of information. Emphasizing the possibilities of new technology is one method to help construct a democratic vocabulary that endorses the free flow of information. The impulse to freely exchange information can be used to challenge information and cultural ownership because it defies the boundaries copyright owners wish to create between themselves and the public.

The preceding chapters have described how the traditional copyright story has been used, constructed, and defended. These chapters illustrate how the boundary of property has been expanded to include computer technology and how an attempt is underway to clearly commodify other dimensions of intellectual property uses in the information age. These property boundaries are extended through a process that relies heavily on narrative strategies where a particular notion of property is asserted as truth.

The traditional copyright narrative is not without its fractures. Copyright itself is balanced between sovereignty and exchange systems. It takes immense effort in the form of litigation and the construction of deviance to maintain this particular system of sovereignty. The copyright system has helped create a unified notion of authorship and creativity that can help enforce the boundaries of ownership and is currently being used to further expand and cement ownership. Copyright turns the author into a conceptually coherent subject when the reality is the opposite.

People working as authors, readers, professors, and creators are multiple and diverse, their reasons for creating are many, and the way they share, appropriate, and own information varied. As noted in chapter 6, when technology makes it possible to exchange, collaborate, borrow, and steal like never before, the notion of authorship inevitably changes. Copyright, however, continues to force the dialogue into that occupied by the individual authorial subject who is protected by a system of rights. Although absolute control will ultimately be impossible, what may be done, or attempted, in the name of controlling property in the digital world is a significant threat worth watching.

From the preceding chapters, it becomes obvious that a concerted effort exists to further expand copyright. In this chapter, I make some observations about the assumptions of our current copyright system. Additionally, what the future of intellectual property might look like is important to evaluate. Not only is it important to discuss our probable future if those advocating strict ownership of information prevail, but alternative methods for conceptualizing intellectual property need to be developed. The goal of this book has been to get the reader to critically assess the expansion of copyright and to heighten awareness about how the narrative process works in order to help foster a movement toward creating alternative narratives to deal with creative work. It is not within the scope of this book to fully outline an alternative plan. However, unless we carefully think about the future of intellectual property, we may end up with an approach to exchange in the digital world that is stifled at best.

SOME OBSERVATIONS ABOUT COPYRIGHT LAW

In the United States, and throughout the globe, cultural symbols are increasingly in the hands of a few giant producers.[1] Additionally, in order to better control the market in copyrighted products, copyright has been extended over virtually all possible applications of a copyrighted work. Many uses of copyrighted work considered illegal today, such as a public performance of a copyrighted work, would have been legal 100 years ago. Each new addition to the copyright law, including additions related to computer technology, extends control over the use of creative work. Although copyright is intended to strike a balance between public access and monopoly privileges, this balance is tilted in favor of private ownership. As each new copyright "right" is added, the exchange of cultural symbols becomes more difficult. Given these conditions, it is fair to say the law is not neutral, but favors owners of copyright over public use of copyrighted works. Copyright owners tend to be favored because it is difficult to make normative claims within the boundaries of statutory interpretations. The law is about how the statutes should be interpreted, not about who should be protected.

A normative claim such as, "a day care ought to be able to put Mickey Mouse on its walls because it brings joy to the children" has no standing.[2] The day-care center is a cultural pirate, illegally copying the property of the copyright owner. Any well-meaning intentions on the part of the day care are unimportant and the infringer is transformed into a criminal and free rider. If interpreted through the lens of the copyright law, the only salient fact is that the day care's use of Mickey Mouse was a copyright infringement. There is no space for normative voices to ask how such tight control over cartoon characters benefits society as a whole, or provides Walt Disney with the incentive to produce new characters, or why cultural appropriation and public use should be made so difficult and expensive. In fact, if the rubric of statutory copyright is accepted, there is little room for normative claims to be made at all. It is possible, however, to draw out the assumptions copyright law is premised on and try to denaturalize the copyright story.

A first important assumption undergirding U.S. copyright law is that protection spurs invention and creation. This is one of the most commonly asserted facts about copyright law. It is asserted that the protections given to authors provide an atmosphere in which authors will exchange ideas. The logic of copyright suggests that only if given property rights will authors share and innovate. It could be suggested that the exact opposite occurs. Once property rights are given, sharing is less likely and lawsuits to protect property boundaries are more likely. Ultimately, it is a questionable assertion at best. It is not creation that is protected, but the production of creative materials.

There are two dimensions to the question of who creates and why. The first dimension is the archetype copyright is designed to protect—the individual author. Everyone, of course, can be defined as an author. Most people have some form of creative outlet that allows them to express themselves. This creativity is not a commodity, but a part of being human. Within the general drive to create, there exists a subset of people who consider themselves "artists" and hope to make a living at their art. Certainly, those individuals engaged in creative occupations hope to be paid for their contributions. However, it must be recognized that payment is secondary to creation.

At the risk of essentializing artistic expression, it is important to recognize that most creative people would continue to create even if they could not make a living.[3] The starving artist attitude is exemplified by Jeff Seaver, president of the Graphic Artists Guild. He testified, "Sure it's true that I'd continue to draw even if I wasn't being paid according to a value for value exchange; but I sure as hell wouldn't be drawing the proverbial 'whale of a sale' or even illustrations for magazines. I'd be forced to make a living—pay my rent and buy food and clothes another way, I'd save my creative output for my personal ideas and projects."[4] What is at issue is what types of creation occur within the copyright system, not the lack of creation without copyright. Seaver's statement indicates that the type of creative work would differ, but that the incentive to create would continue to exist. Somehow creation exists outside the economic rubric of copyright law.

If the artist continues to paint, write, or perform without the protection of a decent income, despite the desirability of one, what does copyright protect? Copyright becomes important, not in the process of creation, but in the process of distribution. An artist wants to be paid for his or her creative work. In order to be paid, one of two things must happen. First, the artist might sell a work directly to a buyer. For example, a freelance writer might sell a story to a news magazine at which point the writer will typically sign over the copyright to the news magazine as well. Thus, the author loses control over the work in exchange for a flat fee or royalties paid based on the number of copies sold. Second, an artist may be hired to produce a creative work. Under this contractual relationship, the creative product is a "work made for hire" and is owned by the person hiring the artist, not the artist. The artist can expect an hourly wage or a commission for the work. In both cases, copyright does not protect the author, it protects the person or company who owns the copyright. The traditional story of copyright operates under the guise that individual authors are protected, whereas the law in reality is predominantly used to protect large corporations that strategically keep authors in the forefront of their battles.[5]

Copyright, especially in the modern world, protects a system of production, not the individual author. It is copyright in its industrial capacity that is the second dimension of the law. Does copyright law provide an incentive for corporations to innovate? Industry is vocal about its need for copyright protection in order to spark innovation. However, the effect on the production of creative work by industry in the absence of strong intellectual property laws is negligible. The fact that companies research, market, and distribute products reliant on intellectual property laws despite the fact that piracy is rampant illustrates that there are other motivations for production besides copyright. For example, despite rampant piracy, computer companies continue to invest a great deal of money in programs and export to countries where piracy is commonplace. Why would they engage in this activity if the lack of intellectual property law inhibited their production? Perhaps because intellectual property law is merely one tool that provides protection for industry.

Intellectual property has little to do with research and development. In order to be competitive in the market, a company will continue to research. Copyright provides companies with exclusive control over their products and potential markets. Copyright is about establishing boundaries around a given product. The law is continually redefined to better protect products in the marketplace and copyright gives companies a claim to potential markets as well. If a pirate sells copies of a copyrighted work for a reduced price he or she is tapping a market reserved exclusively for the copyright owner. Even if the people buying the cheaper product could not afford the regular item (and would never buy it), the infringer is taking prospective sales away from the company and must be stopped. Thus, current business practices provide evidence that research and development will not stop, nor will creative production. Copyright is used as a club to eliminate all unauthorized uses of intellectual property not as an incentive to increase innovation.

The enlightenment notion of exchange of ideas has been replaced with a right to monopoly. In no other aspect of trade is a monopoly conferred to provide the first entry with exclusive rights. However, under copyright, cultural producers expect a monopoly over all aspects of a cultural work.[6] The result is litigation to stop what many feel is valuable cultural appropriation or at the very least a form of creative expression.[7] The traditional story helps obscure how authorial creation has been replaced with industrial sovereignty.

A second assertion about modern copyright that can be drawn from this discussion is that a balance exists between public access and authorial protection. The constitutional mandate of intellectual property protection in the United States is to furnish adequate protection to the author so the public can benefit from the creation. As Brown and Rushing noted in their introduction to *Intellectual Property Rights in Science, Technology, and Economic Performance*, "The essential problem is to strike a balance; enough protection to sustain incentives to the innovator, but not too much protection to allow for the maximization of the social good."[8] Intellectual property is valuable as a public good. Ownership must be balanced with exchange within what is popularly called the *marketplace of ideas*. The assumption is that a balance exists, the current reality is that ownership is overemphasized to the detriment of the public good.

Unfortunately, the language of the public good has been completely subsumed under the language of private protection. The argument has been twisted to make any potential benefit to the public an outcome of private protection. Thus, instead of emphasizing innovation to better serve the needs of humanity, the narrative allows for the profit motive to become the primary drive and public benefit to become important only if the public can afford to pay the property owners. Promoting the needs of the public, part of the enlightenment tradition, has been replaced with an interpretation of copyright law that privileges private ownership and control.

When a copyrighted work is illegally copied what has been taken? What constitutes the theft? Obviously, the ideas are still intact. "What is being stolen is not the object nor a property of the object, but rather a market for the object or the possibility of being able to exploit the commercial potential of the object."[9] As ideas become increasingly commodified, even though they are prone to being shared, copyright infringement becomes a larger issue. As discussed in chapter 4, market control benefits the largest cultural producer, in this case the United States. On a national and international level, the United States takes an active role in defining intellectual property to ensure its continued dominance in intellectual property-related markets.[10]

The political economy of intellectual property is evident in the contrast between approaches taken by the United States and the developing world. As Brown and Rushing noted, "Developing countries think of intellectual property—the results of science and technology—as a public good. On the other hand, industrial countries view intellectual property primarily as a means of maintaining a competitive edge in the marketplace as well as of providing monetary returns to the individual investor."[11] The balance between public good and private gain is tenuous at best, and how it is viewed is a product of standpoint and levels of development.[12] As technological innovation becomes an important aspect of development, as well as a tightly controlled commodity, the developing world will have even more about which to worry.

Third, separating any one creation from a larger social context is not as easy as copyright law assumes. Copyright laws exist because the courts have deemed it possible to distinguish between ideas and expression. The result is a clearly defined text that can be infringed. However, what is the idea and thus not protected versus what is protected expression is often a political distinction. Is it possible for a uniquely creative piece to result from copying a specific "expression" directly?[13]

Courts tend to ignore that most cultural works are dependent on the appropriation and transformation of other works. To use a phrase Rosemary Coombe borrowed from M. de Certeau—creation is usually "textual poaching." Textual poaching is at the heart of cultural dialogue, without which our culture would stagnate. Coombe suggested,

> As Michel de Certeau and Paul Willis argue, consumption is always a form of production and people continually engage in cultural practices of *bricolage*—resignifying media meanings, consumer objects, and cultural texts in order to adapt them to their own interests and make them fulfill their own purposes. These practices are central to the political practices of those in marginal or subordinated social groups who forge "subcultures" with resources foraged from the mediascape.[14]

When large industries own the key cultural symbols, and rigorously defend their use, the culture as a whole suffers.

What is unique about property in expressions and ideas is that once distributed they cannot be returned. Jeremy Waldron defined this unique characteristic as "crowdable" and "noncrowdable" objects of property. "The striking thing about intellectual products is that they are noncrowdable. Although only one person can read a given copy of a novel at a given time, any number of people may enjoy the prose contained therein without diminishing anyone else's enjoyment, and of course it's the prose not the physical book that is the subject of intellectual property."[15] Ideas can only be controlled if they are not shared. The minute they are communicated, enforcing a property right becomes virtually impossible. What is important is the dialogue fostered by the sharing of ideas. However, copyright law emphasizes the importance of property boundaries instead.

The tension between sovereignty and exchange is perhaps greatest in cultural production and reproduction. Coombe argued that tightly controlled intellectual property boundaries, with little or no room for cultural interpretation, strips us of our humanity by depriving us of the ability to appropriate and use cultural symbols for our own uses.[16] She made an excellent point about how boundaries created by intellectual property deny access to signs and freezes cultural evolution. She stated, "What I am suggesting here is that intellectual property laws may deprive us of the optimal *cultural* conditions for dialogic practice. By objectifying and reifying cultural forms—freezing the connotations of signs and symbols and fencing off fields of cultural meaning with "no trespassing" signs—intellectual property laws may enable certain forms of political practice and constrain others."[17] By depriving us of dialogue, or the option of building on the creation of others, we deprive ourselves of an essential element of cultural growth.

The unintended (or perhaps intended) consequence of intellectual property law is to further control ownership of ideas in such a manner that makes new creation or appropriation difficult. Legal attitudes toward intellectual property have important implications within this framework:

> If both objective social worlds and subjective desires, identities, and understandings are constructed with cultural resources, then legal attitudes toward cultural forms may have profound implications. Laws creating and enforcing intellectual property rights permit, maintain, and perpetuate the commodification of cultural texts and images by securing their market value. . . . Copyright laws restrict the social flow of texts, photographs, music, and most other symbolic works. All these forms retain their cultural qualities, however, and in a world where mass media tends to monopolize the dissemination of signi-

> fying forms, the cultural resources available to us (and within us) are increasingly the properties of others.[18]

Intellectual property relies on the sovereignty impulse and the political dynamics created by this impulse are damaging to cultural change.

Finally, the assumption of copyright law is that an individual author exists. This assumption takes up the issues of authorship discussed in chapter 6. U.S. copyright law is heavily reliant on the notion of proprietary author that emerged in the 18th century. In U.S. law, a literary work is defined as anything from a book to a computer program and thus proprietary authorship extends to expressions in any medium.[19] Copyright is culturally shored up by our impression of authorship as an individual occupation. To label someone a literary author, an artist, or musician, is to produce a powerful cultural image—a creative genius working to produce the masterpieces of the century, often under harsh conditions. In reality, copyright in the United States protects the major cultural industries far better than the individual author. Most cultural products are not the property of the creator, but of their employers.[20] Highlighting a method in which the author confers legitimacy to some texts and not to others is the beginning of a literary critique important for copyright. The discourse works to privilege the owners of information. It works to smooth over assumptions about authorship and to reaffirm the traditional copyright story. Exchange is defined as theft—a fact that became increasingly clear in the discussion about hackers and pirates.

Robert Rotstein noted that although patent courts make every effort to bring the latest techniques in any given field into the court to aid in making decisions, the courts have not extended this courtesy in the realm of literary criticism and its applicability to copyright.[21] Literary criticism challenges the modern understanding of authorship and originality. U.S. law, because of its utilitarian approach, has fairly low standards of originality. However, the decision in *Feist Publications Inc. v. Rural Telephone Service Co.* where Rural was accused of violation of Feist's copyright because they had copied the data from its phone book, proves a spark of creativity is needed.[22] In accepting the proprietary author as the creator of something original, a distinguishing characteristic of the modern author, the commodification of literary texts is accepted.[23] The boundary between texts of any kind, contrary to legal definitions, are permeable and unstable. However, texts in the information age are especially difficult to place boundaries around. The individual proprietary author is in many ways a myth of the copyright system that ignores the way cultural production operates.

These observations about the manner in which copyright is used are instructive in understanding the power of the copyright narrative. The power of this narrative and how it is used to expand intellectual property boundaries have very real implications for the future. It is possible to resist the copyright narrative as constructed in modernity. The final sections of this chapter outline the implications of copyright law if they are continued to be used the way they have been used to date. When discussing our probable intellectual property future, it is a useful experiment to take uncritical adherence to the law to its logical (if not extreme) conclusions. If we take absolute adherence to current copyright to its logical conclusion, we end up with a future that is dismal at best. Obviously, the totalizing forces of property ownership cannot prevail in their entirety however, the future as seen in the extreme highlights some of the characteristics of the intellectual property regime that we uncritically embrace today. I am not speculating on the reality of this future, only that our current intellectual property trends make it a possible one.

THE LOGICAL EXTENSION OF CURRENT COPYRIGHT PRACTICES

As the end of the 20th century nears, several claims about intellectual property and the future can be made.[24] First, intellectual property is becoming one of the most important exchangeable commodities supporting late industrial societies.[25] Second, cultural symbols, as well as day-to-day products, are increasingly privatized and unavailable for public appropriation.[26] Privatization of information and ideas will only become more expansive because no incentives exist to alter the system in favor of more equitable access or freedom of information. Third, new technology can transform the way information and creative work is owned, made, and exchanged.[27] In fact, this transformation is potentially so radical that our understanding of intellectual property that developed in a print-dominated age cannot adequately protect intellectual works in an electronically dominated age.[28] Fourth, in order to enforce intellectual property rights, it is increasingly important to resort to the law and education to convince people that ideas can be private property.[29] As the stakes grow, so do the penalties for noncompliance.

One final statement about intellectual property: The only way we think about creative work is as private property. Our language does not allow for other possibilities and our economic system provides such extensive monetary incentives (or the possibility of them) that to think of creative work as anything but personal property is foolish and naive. If you are unwilling to accept profits for your intellectual work, there are others willing to take the idea and use it for their own personal gain.[30] Once the assumptions of intellectual property regimes are accepted and one speaks the statutory language of the law, there is no alternative but to see the expression of intangible thoughts and ideas as property. Given this context, it is important to stake out the ground created by intellectual property law as we enter a technologically driven future.

Neal Stephenson offered an excellent description of the not too distant future where our current approach to information is taken to its logical conclusion and the United States relies on its intellectual property industries.

> This is America. . . . When it gets down to it—talking trade balances here—once we've brain-drained all our technology into other countries, once things have evened out, they're making cars in Bolivia and microwave ovens in Tadzhikistan and selling them here—once our edge in natural resources has been made irrelevant by giant Hong Kong ships and dirigibles that can ship North Dakota all the way to New Zealand for a nickel—once the Invisible Hand has taken all those historical inequities and smeared them out into a broad global layer of what a Pakistani brickmaker would consider to be prosperity—y'know what? There's only four things we do better than anyone else: music, movies, microcode (software), high-speed pizza delivery.[31]

No generation has seen the accumulation of information as property to such a great extent as current generations. Although detailed information about individuals has been privately owned and sold for some time,[32] we can look forward to the further commodification of our minds and bodies as they become owned and traded like any other commodity.[33] Corporations already own patents and copyrights in genes, biotechnology, plants, and potentially life-saving drugs. They will also increasingly own personal information about people, and public documents will be privatized by "adding value" in the form of headers and commentary. Intellectual property translates into profits, often times at the expense of the bodies the information describes, or the people who would use the products if they could afford them.

The commercialization of knowledge will soon permeate the university system. Traditionally, faculty have been required to contribute to their disciplines in order to contribute to human understanding and knowledge. In the future, all copyrighted and patented works will be considered "work made for hire" by university administrators and all potential profits will become the property of the university. Innovation in the world of academics will also be placed within the profit-driven paradigm of intellectual property law. This paradigm switch will impact the types of research considered legitimate. Additionally, it provides universities with a mechanism for censoring controversial work. It is already common to sign waivers of all rights to inventions made during employment to a specific company in the private sector. This logic will soon permeate the university system as well.

Ownership of information leads to the need for secrecy and an increase in perceived insecurity. In such a world, industrial espionage will run rampant and the lagging power of the state will be renewed in an attempt to protect the corporate secrets of those falling within state boundaries while ferreting out the secrets of corporations located in other states.[34] The heightened awareness of the proprietary aspects of ideas will lead to increased secrecy and policing of property. The more prevalent the idea of creative work as property becomes, the less willing people will be to share freely. The logical conclusion of treating ideas as property is that people will become less likely to want to share their innovations.

The future of the Internet could be one of total commercialization. We can expect the current avenues for free information to be turned into the equivalent of the home shopping network. Already, debate about taxing businesses on the Internet is afoot. The greatest problem will be how to define business. Perhaps business will be broadly construed as all communication. Most people in the United States will soon have access to some form of the Internet as technologies integrating television and computers develop and become cheaper. However, there will be an increased push to make this information one-sided and commercialized. Thus, it will be easy to download a movie for a fee and watch it, but it may be reasonable to expect a system of licensing to emerge to control who has access to the Internet. Just as the FCC regulates access to the publicly owned airwaves and thus controls who can broadcast information, we can expect the government to attempt to regulate the Internet by establishing a licensing system. Although this system will ostensibly be designed to halt the exchange of pornography and fight Internet-related crime, it will ultimately result in more traditional mass media industries gaining control of the Internet and its content. The majority of the U.S. population will live with an artificial sense of empowerment when in reality information is still controlled by a few individuals who own both the information and the technology through which the information passes. The future will be a world dominated by the information elite, a world of global capital where the trade of dollars, information, and bits of data make some rich at the expense of the environment, the developing world, and the poor.

Within this framework what will happen to creation and authorship? Copyright protection will most likely be expanded to include ideas. Not only will it be possible to own a specific expression of an idea, but the idea itself will be property. Many avenues of creativity will be eliminated by strict adherence to copyright law and the tendency to protect copyrights. Current examples already exist. Artist Jeff Koons, for example, had taken a photograph entitled "A String of Puppies" and used it to create a sculpture of the same scene. The copyright owner of the photograph sued Koons for copyright violation. Koons' argument was that his sculpture, exhibited in a show about American Banality, was a postmodern approach to illustrating the banality of art in an "image-saturated society." Koons used a technique called "appropriation" to bring this point home. He lost.[35]

Originality will continue to be an important aspect of copyright even though it is becoming increasingly obvious that there is little original in the products produced by mass culture. The original author creating a U.S. masterpiece is a legal fiction used to shore up the culture industry. Even as the electronic world attempts to rip authorship apart, introduce alternative voices, connect texts in a hyperlinked "metatext," and pull creativity in directions the copyright law will not be able to address, there will be a serious attempt to halt these creative potentials and keep traditional notions of authorship, creation, and the text intact through a variety of policing mechanisms.

If copyright is extended uncritically into the information age, the author will remain essentially untransformed by new technology, despite the possibilities of democratic authorship made available by the Internet. Because education will continue to be used to impart the truths of the traditional copyright narrative most people in the future will behave as legal citizens. Despite some trouble during the transitions, major intellectual property industries will successfully use the law to maintain boundaries around creative property. They will increase their hunts for potential infringers and stop at nothing to protect their property rights. Everything will be exchanged for a price. Nothing in the future, as constructed through the traditional property narrative, will be exchanged freely or for the public good. However, the language that the public good is best protected by ensuring the property rights of copyright owners will be firmly entrenched.

The courts will continue to play a role in protecting copyright from unlawful infringement and we can expect the penalties to be harsher. People will be sued for exchanging newspaper articles, pictures, or music with copyrights attached over the Internet. Fair use will be curtailed in the electronic arena because exchange is too easy and uncontrollable. Additionally, because there is little likelihood that fair use will survive, it becomes possible to sue a person for using even small snippets of information. Copyright will be operating as a form of censorship as well as a form of property. Because all court cases are decided on the merits of the Copyright Act, there is no room for questions that fall outside the proprietary framework. The law ensures that everyone plays by the rules and the rules enforce a property regime.

Pirating and hacking will be the most notorious of the crimes against intellectual property and will result in the most severe sentences. There will be a significant increase in cybercops—security officers dedicated to stopping computer theft in all its manifestations. Security for all types of intellectual property will be the defense issue of the future. Although the 1990s saw some computer raids, where private security forces invaded pirate strongholds, the 21st century will see an enormous crackdown on private bulletin board operators inside and outside the United States for offenses ranging from exchanging illegal software to maintaining a site where copyrighted materials can be sent and discussed. The crackdown will include arresting citizens and confiscating their computer equipment, a practice already in play today.[36] The United States will use its role as the global police to ensure its version of intellectual property is enforced. It will persuade all other countries to deal with copyright violators according to U.S. law. The success of these policing tactics is questionable. Already, reverse engineering, cracking, pirating, and exchanging computer software is virtually unstoppable.[37] It needs to be reemphasized that what is at issue here is not the potential that exchange will be truly halted, but how far the attempt will go to halt exchange, how much invasion of privacy will be allowed, and how little value will be placed on civil rights in a world designed to halt piracy and hacking.

Intellectual property litigation will also have to deal with the ownership of artificial intelligence. Many futurists believe cyborgs will be the next step in human evolution.[38] Cyborgs will also be intellectual creations subject to property laws. Although owning bodies is not new to the legal system, the next legal battles will concern defining human from nonhuman and drawing a line between what can and cannot be owned. Cyborgs, mixtures of human and machine, will be a future challenge to intellectual property. The creation of viable artificial intelligence will also challenge property rights. How does one treat a scientifically created sentient creature? Although these questions might seem to be better suited to science fiction, they will be the legal dilemmas of the not so distant future.

The law helps us move forward and provides redress for those injured. However, the logic of the law is firmly entrenched in the concept of private property. As such, it is not capable of offering a transformative alternative. The implications of a future that uncritically embraces the property narrative to understand creative work is not a happy future. Describing this future in such gloomy terms helps to highlight the problems with the traditional copyright narrative. It is important to note, however, that it will be virtually impossible to eliminate all forms of creative exchange. The problem for the future becomes the problem of dealing with the harsher laws and penalties handed down by a sovereignty system intent on maintaining stricter copyrights. Exchange will continue to occur, but it may be increasingly criminalized in the future. Thus, clearly outlining alternative narratives to that created by private property is essential for understanding the potential of the Internet and the free exchange of ideas.

ALTERNATIVE NARRATIVES AND THE FUTURE

A truly transformational future might be possible if we can give up our reliance on a discourse of property. The decentralized nature of the Internet can make a fresh approach toward intellectual property possible. The fragments of the old and tattered intellectual property system can be discarded and replaced with something more appropriate for the information age. In part, this replacement must be done rhetorically. Just as the current copyright story is extended through a variety of narrative strategies, a new narrative could help construct an alternative understanding of creative work. What could the replacement be? What other language could we speak in order to escape the limited discourse of private property?

Copyright law is entirely too rigid to sustain the requirements of a technological world with a viable free flow of information. In constructing an alternative narrative for understanding the function of information it is important to embrace the potential of the existing technology. Because complete information is better than incomplete information, the hacker slogan: "Information should be free and plagiarism saves time,"[39] helps clarify the radical potential of alternative discourse. Ultimately, the sharing and total exchange of information is the scenario that best stands in opposition to current intellectual property practices and is thus the subject of this section. This narrative already exists and is fully embraced by those who see the futuristic implications of the Internet.

Computer programs can serve as an example for how information sharing can best work in the future. There is certainly room for creative people in a world where writing computer code is a form of art. However, computer programs are best created with the understanding that others will take what has been written and expand, pull apart, rewrite, and improve it. The future can be one where this same attitude exists toward all creative things. Ultimately, it could be possible for cultural appropriation and transformation to be at the foundation of a new way of approaching ideas and information. A communitarian dialogue focusing on the text as creation absent the author function is possible. The author, as a group or individual, will have meaning but it will be a radically decentralized meaning that will recognize the lack of boundaries between ideas and allow them to move freely. Because the boundaries of the text will not be so tightly guarded, everyone can feel free to add, experiment, appropriate, and use information. The author is better balanced between a proprietary person and a communitarian person. Information can reach a state of movement, if not freedom.

The transformation that must occur is one from competition to cooperation. In a future premised on a narrative of sharing, competition must be tempered by the pursuit of cooperation. Sharing is especially appropriate for what is currently called *intellectual property*. Sharing ideas is different from sharing tangible goods because ideas can dwell in more than one mind simultaneously. They cannot be an exclusive possession. Ideas, by definition, cannot be owned once shared. Expressions, also, become more developed with each new contributor. Each expression of an idea creates other expressions and other possibilities. As Ursula Le Guin noted in *The Dispossessed*, "It is the nature of the idea to be communicated: written, spoken, done. The idea is like grass. It craves light, likes crowds, thrives on crossbreeding, grows better for being stepped on."[40]

What would the world look like if intellectual property rights were replaced by sharing and mutual responsibility for the betterment of humankind? This would be a communitarian future. In such a future, narrative power would be used to enhance the public good through sharing instead of through property protection. Such a standpoint assumes that human freedom can be best realized through the promotion of the collective welfare instead of the facilitation of personal profit.[41]

Law, as practiced today, would need to be significantly transformed. Intellectual property law is about protecting property and this function of the law would no longer be needed. Laws like copyright limit the flexibility of the creative work and reduce its ownership to an individual or corporation. In constructing an alternative narrative it is important to emphasize that texts, and creation generally, are for the public good. Because it is recognized that people create for a variety of reasons, rewards could be diverse, and often as cheap as public recognition for an excellent idea.

Texts come in a variety of shapes and sizes and can be shared freely. Electronic networks are put to their best use by providing links on links to countless voices that exist in a world where textuality does not have to be owned. Exchange will be given precedence over the sovereignty of ideas and this exchange will occur in an environment where all individuals can realize their potential as authors. Individuals who saw the Internet as a possibility for new forms of authorship will prevail. The sharing of information takes precedent over the owning of information. Although names will continue to be placed in conjunction with a work, the use of an authorial name will not function as a boundary that marks one text from another. Texts will rarely be the work of a single person and names will not necessarily indicate ownership.

Authorship is not a profession in a world based on sharing. Everyone participates in the creation of art and information. Many people utilize their creative capacity by linking and developing already existing works. Because creation is premised on facilitating cultural development and not on monetary rewards, new possibilities are opened up. It would be recognized that originality is always culturally dependent and great ideas do not appear from nowhere. Rather, everything is connected, including creation.

Within this future, the possibilities of collective authorship can be fully realized. Sometimes a collective work will be the culmination of a vast number of contributors who have no knowledge of each other outside the work. Ideas, expressions, and all creative work will develop organically and dialogically. This means authorship will be less important and the dialogue will become more important. It is possible to preserve a sense of individuality within this collective approach. Every person will be acknowledged for his or her contribution. The reward is in the promotion of the collective good rather than private compensation. Creativity is something every person can make a part of his or her life. It is not a commercialized entertainment industry, but a form of cultural cohesion.

Copyright law bastardized the relationship between the author and the text by transforming the idea into property that could be stolen. The problem of criminality and theft would be eliminated by switching to a narrative of sharing. Problems over intellectual works would arise, but they would not be couched in terms of property. What is absent is the overwhelming emphasis on material accumulation and the logic that if intellectual property is not protected someone else will unjustly benefit. What is present in a narrative that emphasizes sharing is a sense of solidarity and freedom, a place where ideas can flourish. In a narrative based on sharing there is no intellectual property and it becomes impossible to steal.

Sharing is a utopia based on a transformational discourse instead of the law. The law is helpful as long as prearranged definitions are followed. Many people might respond that we do not need an alternate discourse on intellectual property, that thinking about creative and informational works in terms of copyright is fine. These people would argue that over the centuries the courts have developed a balance between protection and public use. However, if new ways of thinking about what we call intellectual property are to be found, we must move outside the law and into other modes of speaking. In a world where the concept of *private ownership* is replaced with the concept of *sharing* everything would be changed.

My point in writing a narrative that emphasizes sharing is to highlight how the language of property, and the legal system that constructs property, impacts how we think about creative work. Such a narrative will most likely provoke a strong reaction from people who make it their job to understand the importance of copyright. In part, rejecting the sharing narrative will occur because the benefits to copyright owners under the current system are quite extensive and offer little justification for change. Additionally, most people have never attempted to think about creative work outside the box of intellectual property law. However, new technology is posing a significant challenge to the traditional notion of authorship, to the traditional notion of the text, and to the traditional notion of intellectual property. These are exciting and positive challenges that must be critically assessed and embraced.

The present response to the challenges of the information age—to shore up the boundaries of intellectual property law and extend property rights to new areas of ownership—will only work for a short while. There are other possibilities, if we are allowed to enter a creative dialogue. A communitarian narrative is designed to point out that thinking about creative work only in terms of intellectual property does little to make the future brighter. It only facilitates the mass production and mass consumption made possible by the culture industry that seems emptier with each passing day. Without a view of the future that provides for cultural dialogue, technology will continue to be a tool for domination and the protection of property.

CONCLUSION: SOME TENTATIVE RECOMMENDATIONS

Copyright is out of control in the United States. Under the guise of protecting authors, we have created a system that preserves the interests of major copyright holders—software companies, publishers, music producers, and movie makers. From the outset, copyright law was designed to protect the property of the copyright owner, not the author. Copyright is an excellent example of how the law works to protect property and not people.

Although it is not within the scope of this book to do so, the most extreme conclusion—to abolish copyright law—should be examined. Copyright does very little to protect authors from plagiarists bent on copying their work. Copyright is significantly better at preserving the integrity of a work if the copyright owner has money to sue and the copyright infringer is worth suing. Copyright is used as a threat and as a censor, as illustrated by the manner in which the Church of Scientology attacks its critics. If we abolish copyright law, creativity will not come to a halt. Rather, we could see a radical decentralization of creativity as much of what is preserved as copyright becomes available for appropriation and reproduction.

I do not advocate the complete loss of protection for creative work.

After all, within a competitive capitalist economy it is only to be expected that someone will attempt to profit off a good idea. However, in order to appropriately strike a balance between the public good and private gain, this copyright law should be severely limited. If we must have copyright law, it should be the minimal necessary to protect a creative work. Ultimately, given modern technology, there is no reason for the author to sign away the rights to his or her work. The Internet will soon be the best method to distribute ideas (if it isn't already) and can bypass traditional copyright owners. Thus, the author should retain rights to a creative work and the "work made for hire" doctrine should be eliminated. If copyright is designed to protect authors as the creators of work, then it should do so. The Internet makes it possible to bring items directly to the public with the author retaining control.

Any new copyright law would severely limit the rights an author holds instead of expanding them. Instead of increasing the years of potential copyright ownership and increasing the ownership over all possible uses of a work, any new copyright legislation should allow for virtually all forms of creative uses. Protecting an author's right to achieve a return on his or her creative work is acceptable, but allowing for this creative work to be a monopoly right that extends into all aspects of its use is an inappropriate balance between the public good and private gain. Unless a creative work is copied directly there should be no copyright infringement. For example, if a song appropriates snippets from another song, there should be no infringement, or if a coffee shop plays the radio there should be no copyright infringement. What may be required is an acknowledgment of the author in order to preserve a sense of indebtedness when possible, however the creative uses of a work will be left as free as possible.

Instead of fostering the creation of new thoughts, by making ideas property, we become more secretive and less likely to share our ideas. In a world where ideas are money there is no sense of sharing. This bizarre property practice thwarts creation. Education in the area of copyright is needed. It is important to teach people not to plagiarize the works of others. However, and more importantly, it is important to teach people that everyone is culturally indebted and that originality owes more to cultural dialogue than to individual creation. It is important to teach that everyone operates within a discursive environment that facilitates their ideas and expressions. It is important to communicate that sharing is the manner in which creation is best facilitated, not secrecy fostered by property boundaries.

These words must be said in part because few people appear willing to question the assumptions of copyright. The debate needs to be diversified. A progressive perspective in the world of copyright is lacking. If nothing else results from this book, perhaps it can bring to the intellectual property debate a voice of dissent regarding the direction the United States is currently headed.

NOTES

1. B. Badikian, *The media monopoly*, 4th ed., (Boston: Beacon Press 1992). In this book, Badikian outlined the trend toward increased centralized ownership of the media. See also: H. Schiller, *Culture Inc.: The corporate takeover of public expression* (New York: Oxford University Press, 1989). Schiller's book is an excellent work focusing on corporate America's hold over cultural artifacts and their display via museums and public art.

2. In 1989, one of Disney's more notorious copyright actions was to force three Hallandale Florida day-care centers to paint over their murals of Disney characters. See: "Disney characters removed; Day-care center follows park's order," *The Orange County Register*, 3 August 1989, p. A25.

3. See chapter 6 where the writing of Helene Cixous is discussed.

4. *OTA report on intellectual property rights in an age of electronics and information: Joint hearing of the subcommittee on patents, copyrights, and trademarks of the senate committee on the judiciary and the subcommittee on courts, civil liberties, and the administration of justice of the house committee on the judiciary*, 99th Cong., 2nd Session (16 April 1986). Testimony by the Graphic Artists Guild Regarding Receipt of the Report of the Office of Technology Assessment, 91.

5. Walt Disney is a classic example. Disney ensured that his cartoonists remained anonymous, were paid hourly and usually small wages, and that his name figured prominently in all productions even though he never drew a cartoon. Although Disney was (and his company still is) a vociferous litigator when someone infringed on his work, he made sure that the authors were emotionally removed from their creations. David Kunzle, writing the introduction to the English Edition of Dorfman's and Mattelart's *How to Read Donald Duck* made this clear:

> The system at Disney Productions seems to be designed to prevent the artist from feeling any pride, or gaining any recognition, other than corporate, for his work. Once the contract is signed, the artist's idea becomes Disney's idea. He is its owner, therefore its creator, for all purposes. It says so, black and white, in the contract: "all art work prepared for our comics magazines is considered work done for hire, and we are the creators thereof for all purposes." There could hardly be a clearer statement of the manner in which the capitalist engrosses the labor of his workers. In return for a small fee or wage, he takes from them both the profit and the glory. . . . While the world applauds Disney, it is left in ignorance of those whose work is the cornerstone of his empire: of the immensely industrious, prolific and inventive Ub Iwerks, whose technical and artistic innovations run from the multi-plane camera to the character of Mickey himself; . . . And of course, Carl Barks, creator of Uncle Scrooge and many other favorite "Disney" characters, of over 300 of the best "Disney" comics stories, of 7,000 pages of "Disney" artwork paid at an average $11.50 per page, not one signed with his name; while his employers, trying carefully to keep him ignorant of the true extent of this astonishing

> commercial success, preserved him from individual fame and from his numerous fans who inquired in vain after his name.

A. Dorfman, & A. Matterlart, *How to read Donald Duck: Imperialist ideology in the Disney comic,* trans. D. Kunzle (New York: International General, 1975), 17.

6. For example, the International Olympic Committee (IOC) sued the San Francisco Arts and Athletics Committee over the use of the phrase "Gay Olympics" arguing the IOC held exclusive rights to the word *Olympics.* See: *International Olympic Comm. v. San Francisco Arts and Ath.*, 781 F.2d 733 (9th Cir. 1986).

7. Another Disney example is a suit against a satire using Mickey Mouse. D. Newdorf, "Disney is no fairy tale in court: Mickey's new lawyer continues tough stance," *Legal Times* (29 July 1991): 16. See also: *Walt Disney Productions v. Air Pirates,* 581 F.2d 751 (9th Cir. 1978).

8. C. G. Brown, & F. W. Rushing, "Intellectual property rights in the 1990s: Problems and solutions" In *Intellectual property rights in science, technology, and economic performance* eds. F. W. Rushing, & C. G. Brown (Boulder, CO, San Francisco, & London: West View Press, 1990), 2.

9. C. Lind, "The idea of capitalism or the capitalism of ideas? A moral critique of the Copyright Act," *Intellectual Property Journal, 7* (December 1991): 69.

10. An excellent example of U.S. domination in copyright and its willingness to protect its economic market in ideas is seen in how the United States is dealing with China over copyright. Historically, China has had little if any copyright protection. This has made China, as with many Asian countries, prone to piracy of copyrighted works. The United States, in order to crack down on this economic activity, and control the markets for ideas, has offered China the following options: develop a copyright protection law or suffer U.S. trade sanctions. China has opted for the former. See: M. Sidel, "The legal protection of copyright and the rights of authors in the People's Republic of China, 1949–1984: Prelude to the Chinese copyright law," *Art and the Law, 9* (1985): 477–508. See also: chapter 4, this volume.

11. Brown and Rushing, "Intellectual property rights in the 1990s," 4.

12. The gap between developed and developing countries in technology is not a new problem. Strictly controlled intellectual property rights hinder the ability of LDCs to modernize. The tension between sovereignty and exchange is highly visible in this confrontation. LDCs need a high degree of exchange in order to develop. Developed countries require a high degree of control over ideas in order to make a profit. See: R. P. Benko, *Protecting intellectual property rights: Issues and controversies* (Washington, DC: American Enterprise Institute for Public Policy Research, 1987), 27–30.

13. M. Buskirk, "Appropriation under the gun," *Art in America, 80* (June 1992): 37–39.

14. R. Coombe, "Author/izing the celebrity: Publicity rights, postmodern politics, and unauthorized genders," *Cardozo Arts and Entertainment* (1992): 377.

15. J. Waldron, "From authors to copiers: Individual rights and social values in intellectual property," *Chicago-Kent Law Review, 68* (1993): 871.

16. R. Coombe, "Objects of property and subjects of politics: Intellectual property laws and Democratic dialogue," *Texas Law Review, 69* (1991): 1870.

17. Ibid., 1866.

18. Ibid.

19. The Copyright Act of 1976 devotes its first five sections to defining the subject matter of copyright. In Section 102, works of authorship include literary works; musical works, including any accompanying words; dramatic works, including any accompanying music; pantomimes and choreographic works; pictorial, graphic, and sculptural works; motion pictures and other audiovisual works; sound recordings; and architectural works. 17 U.S.C.A. § 102.

20. D. Vaver, "Some agnostic observations on intellectual property," *Intellectual Property Journal, 6* (6 September 1990): 130. In most cases, copyright is in the hands of the publishers. Another condition that divides creator and owner is in work made for hire. See: 17 U.S.C.A. § 201b.

21. R. H. Rotstein, "Beyond metaphor: Copyright infringement and the fiction of the work," *Chicago-Kent Law Review, 68* (1993): 725.

22. In *Feist Publications, Inc. v. Rural Telephone Service Co.*, 111 S.Ct. 1282 (1991), the court ruled that the phone book was not copyrightable because it was a compilation of facts and did not meet the requisite standard of originality. The court stated that,

> The *sine qua non* of copyright is originality. To qualify for copyright protection, a work must be original to the author. Original, as the term is used in copyright, means only that the work was independently created by the author (as opposed to copied from other works), and that it possesses at least some minimal degree of creativity. To be sure, the requisite level of creativity is extremely low; even a slight amount will suffice.

Quoted in P. Goldstein, *Copyright, patent, trademark and related state doctrines: Cases and materials on the law of intellectual property*, 3rd ed. (Westbury, NY: The Foundation Press, 1993), 584.

23. M. Rose, *Authors and owners: The invention of copyright* (London & Cambridge MA: Harvard University Press, 1993), 1.

24. For other intellectual property scenarios based on these same premises see: D. Halbert, "The future of intellectual property law," *Technological Forecasting and Social Change* (June/July 1997): 147–160.

25. A. Toffler, *Powershift: Knowledge, wealth, and violence at the edge of the 21st century* (New York: Bantam Books, 1990).

26. "In the current climate, however, intellectual property laws stifle dialogic practices—preventing us from using the most powerful, prevalent, and accessible cultural forms to express identity, community, and difference." Coombe, "Objects of property and subjects of politics," 1855.

27. This is the conclusion of the Office of Technology Assessment on this issue. *OTA Report on Intellectual Property Rights in an Age of Electronics and Information.*

28. This claim is contested. There are many intellectual property lawyers who believe current law is adequate with a few simple adjustments. For an example of the logic behind this brief see: E. A. Cavazos, & G. Morin, *Cyberspace and the law: Your rights and duties in the on-line world* (Cambridge & London: Massachusetts Institute of Technology, 1994).

29. If anyone doubts the types of punishment that the legal system attempts to assign to crimes dealing with intellectual property one only has to look to the

documentation on hackers, pirates, and data theft to understand that a full-fledged legal battle designed to create property rights is being fought. K. Hafner, & J. Markoff, *Cyberpunk: Outlaws and hackers on the computer frontier* (New York & London: Simon & Schuster, 1991).

30. Copyright notices are springing up due to the desire to exchange information, which corresponds with the desire to see this information used properly. Such notices state that the information within the electronic message is copyrighted but can be freely exchanged as long as it is always credited to the original author and a profit is not made from the material. Of course, there is no enforcement. However, it speaks to the willingness of authors to exchange ideas in a noncommodified manner while being all too aware that many less idealistic people do not think the same way.

31. N. Stephenson, *Snow crash* (New York: Bantam Books, 1993), 2.

32. A. W. Branscomb, *Who owns information? From privacy to public access* (New York: Basic Books, 1994).

33. For those who might doubt this possibility, I site a few examples here. One recent trend is challenging ownership of ideas that have not been expressed yet. Traditionally, copyright only protects the expression of ideas. However, as corporations make bids on key employees and people change jobs, industry is becoming more concerned with the ideas stored in a person's head. Thus, lawsuits are emerging over who owns the ideas that transfer with a person to a new company. As James Bennet pointed out, " 'If it's your invention or idea, it belongs to the employer if you were hired to come up with those kinds of inventions or those kinds of ideas,' said Stephen L. Carter who teaches intellectual property law at the Yale University Law School." J. Bennet, "Who owns ideas and papers, is issue in company lawsuits," *The New York Times*, 30 May 1993, p. 27. The commodification and selling of the body and body functions is also documented in: A. Kimbrell, *The human body shop: The engineering and marketing of life* (San Francisco: Harper-Collins, 1993).

34. Chapter 4 briefly discusses the trend toward increased industrial espionage.

35. Buskirk, "Appropriation under the gun," 37–39.

36. In 1984, Congress authorized a civil court procedure called an "ex-parte search and seizure with expedited discovery." This procedure allows private parties (such as the Church of Scientology or Microsoft) along with an "officer of the court" to search a person's property for copyrighted materials. This type of search has been used to confiscate computers and software from people's homes that is said to violate a company's copyright. A. S. Bauman, "Only police may search your home, right? Guess again," *Seattle Times*, 24 October 1995, p. A 1.

37. See: "Fravia's page of reverse engineering," http://fravia.org/.

38. "The greatest social consequence of the Darwinian revolution was the grudging acceptance by humans that humans were random descendants of monkeys, neither perfect nor engineered. The greatest social consequence of neo-biological civilization will be the grudging acceptance by humans that humans are the random ancestors of machines, and that as machines we can be engineered ourselves." K. Kelly, *Out of control: The rise of neo-biological civilization* (Reading, MA: Addison-Weseley, 1994), 55.

39. G. Branwyn, "Street noise," *Mondo 2000* (1992): 30.

40. U. Le Guin, *The dispossessed* (New York: Harper & Row, 1974), 79.

41. There are a number of feminist utopias built on this basic assumption of sharing, including Le Guin, *The dispossessed*; M. Piercy, *Woman on the edge of time* (New York: Fawcett Crest 1976); J. Slonczewski, *A door into ocean* (New York: Avon Books, 1986).

Bibliography

Agre, P. (1995). *The Network Observer* (*TNO*) [On-line]. Available: rre-maintainers@weber.ucsd.edu

Agreement on trade-related aspects of intellectual property rights, including trade in counterfeit goods [On-line]. (1994). Available: http://itl.irv.uit.no/trade_law

Aho, J. (1994). *This thing of darkness: A sociology of the enemy*. Seattle & London: University of Washington Press.

Aldrich, J. (1990). Push button felonies. *The Epic Project* [On-line]. Available: jefrich@well.sf.ca.us.

Alexander, M. (1989, February 20). Hacker victims heartened by convictions. *Computerworld, 23*, 1, 12.

Alexander, M. (1989, February 20). Prison term for first U.S. hacker-law convict. *Computerworld, 23*, 1, 12.

Alexander, M. (1990, March 12). Computer crime: Ugly secret for business. *Computerworld, 24*, 1, 104.

Alexander, M. (1990, March 19). Complex crimes stall enforcers. *Computerworld, 24*, 4.

Alexander, M. (1991). Hackers paradise? *Computerworld, 24 (Suppl.)*, S26–S27.

Alexander, M. (1991, January 21). Morris case impact slight. *Computerworld, 25*, 1, 4.

Alexander, M. (1991, June 24). Hackers promote better image. *Computerworld, 25*, 124.

Alexander, M. (1991, September 16). Hacker may have penetrated Pentagon. *Computerworld, 25*, 14.

Alford, W. P. (1992). Intellectual property, trade and Taiwan: A GATT-fly's view. *Columbia Business Law Review*, 97–107.

Alford, W. P. (1995). *To steal a book is an elegant offense: Intellectual property law in Chinese civilizations*. Stanford, CA: Stanford University Press.

Alleged hacker is ordered not to talk about computers. (1996, April 5). *The Orlando Sentinel*, p. A12.

Anderson, B. (1991). *Imagined communities: Reflections on the origin and spread of nationalism* (2nd ed.). London & New York: Verso.

Aoki, K. (1993). Adrift in the intertext: Authorship and audience "recoding" rights—comment on Robert H. Rotstein "Beyond metaphor: Copyright infringement and the fiction of the work." *Chicago-Kent Law Review*, 805–840.

Apple Computer Inc. v. Franklin Computer Corp. 714 F.2d 1240, (1983).

Apple Computer Inc. v. Microsoft Corporation. 821 F.Supp. 616, (N.D. Cal. 1993).

Ashley, R. K. (1989). Living on borderlines: Man, poststructuralism, and war. In J. D. Derian & M. J. Shapiro (Eds.), *International/intertextual relations: Postmodern readings of world politics.* Lexington, MA: Lexington Books.

Ashton-Tate Corporation v. Richard Ross. 916 F. 2d 516. (1990).

Attacking the pentagon. (1996, May 24). *The Commercial Appeal*, 12a.

Awanohara, S., & Lincoln, K. (1991, September 5). Patently hostile: Washington set to impose sanctions on China. *Far Eastern Economic Review*, 69–70.

Badikian, B. (1992). *The media monopoly* (4th ed.). Boston: Beacon Press.

Bahktin, M. M. (1993). *Toward a philosophy of the act* (V. Liapunov, Trans.). Austin: University of Texas Press.

Barlow, J. P. The economy of ideas: A framework for rethinking patents and copyrights in the digital age. *Wired, 2.03* [On-line]. Available: http://www.wired.com/wired/2.03/features/economy.ideas.html(Visited2/20/98).

Barthes, R. (1972). *Mythologies.* (A. Lavers, Trans.). New York: Hill and Wang.

Basic Books Inc. v. Kinko's Graphics Corporation. (1989). In K. D. Crews, *Copyright, fair use, and the challenge for universities: Promoting the progress of higher education.* Chicago & London: University of Chicago Press.

Bauman, A. S. (1995, October 24). Only police may search your home, right? Guess again. *Seattle Times*, A1.

Beam, A. (1990, August 1). Free the Sun Devil 6! (Why?). *The Boston Globe*, 55.

Behar, R. (1993, February 8). Surfing off the edge. *Time, 141*, 62–63.

Benhabib, S. (1991). On Hegel, women and irony. In M. L. Shanley & C. Pateman (Eds.), *Feminist interpretations and political theory* (pp. 129–145). University Park: The Pennsylvania State University Press.

Benko, R. P. (1987). *Protecting intellectual property rights: Issues and controversies.* Washington, DC: American Enterprise Institute for Public Policy Research.

Bennet, J. (1993, May 30). Who owns ideas and papers, is issue in company lawsuits. *The New York Times*, 1, 27.

Berger, P., & Luckman, T. (1996). *The social construction of reality: A treatise in the sociology of knowledge.* Garden City, NJ: Doubleday.

Bird, J. (1992, June). Inside track on hackers. *Management Today*, 78–82.

Bjorhus, J. (1996, April 10). Hacker attacks just tip of the iceberg. *The Seattle Times*, A9.

Bjorhus, J. (1996, April 10). Suspect arrested in library hacking. *The Seattle Times*, A1.

Blizzard, C. (1998, January 3). Pirates in cyberspace: The internet is creating a generation of software thieves. *The Toronto Sun*, 17.

Bourdieu, P. (1977). *Outline of a theory of practice.* (R. Nice, Trans.). Cambridge: Cambridge University Press.

Bromberg, C. (1991, April 21). In defense of hackers. *The New York Times,* 45.

Branscomb, A. W. (1990). Computer software: Protecting the crown jewels of the information economy. In F. W. Rushing & C. G. Brown (Eds.), *Intellectual property rights in science, technology, and economic performance.* Boulder, San Francisco, & London: Westview Press.

Branscomb, A. W. (1994). *Who owns information? From privacy to public access.* New York: Basic Books.

Branwyn, G. (1992). Street noise. *Mondo 2000,* 30.

Brent, D. (1991, November). Oral knowledge, typographic knowledge, electronic knowledge: Speculations on the history of ownership. *Ejournal* [On-line]. Available: DABRENT@ACS.UCALGARY.CA.

Brodie, I., & Gamini, G. (1996, April 1). US agents pursue hacker of secrets across cyberspace. *The New York Times,* 45. [Lexis-Nexis].

Bromberg, C. (1991, April 21). In defense of hackers. *The New York Times,* 45.

Brown, C. G., & Rushing, F. W. (1990). Intellectual property rights in the 1990's: Problems and solutions. In F. W. Rushing, & C. G. Brown (Eds.), *Intellectual property rights in science, technology, and economic performance.* Boulder, San Francisco, & London: West View Press.

Bruner, J. (1991, Autumn). The narrative construction of reality. *Critical Inquiry,* 4–5.

Burgess, J. (1990, January 9). Hackers case may shape computer security law. *The Washington Post,* A4.

Buskirk, M. (1992, Spring). Commodification as a censor: Copyrights and fair use. *October,* 83–109.

Buskirk, M. (1992, June). Appropriation under the gun. *Art in America, 80,* 37–39.

Butler, M. A. (1991). Early liberal roots of feminism: John Locke and the attack on patriarchy. In M. L. Shanley & C. Pateman (Eds.), *Feminist interpretations and political theory* (pp. 74–94). University Park: The Pennsylvania State University Press.

Campbell, D. (1992). *Writing security.* Minneapolis: University of Minnesota Press.

Cavazos, E. A., & Morin, G. (1994). *Cyberspace and the law: Your rights and duties in the on-line world.* Cambridge & London: Massachusetts Institute of Technology.

Chetham, A. (1997, December 11). Rewards to catch pirates. *South China Morning Post,* 2.

The China IPR agreement. (1996, May 3). *Congressional Record* (Vol. 142, No. 60, p. S4672–S4675). Washington, DC: U.S. Government Printing Office.

China's violations of United States intellectual property rights. (1996, May 7). *Congressional Record* (Vol. 142, No. 62, p. H4435). Washington, DC: U.S. Government Printing Office.

Christine-Leps, M. (1992). *Apprehending the criminal: The production of deviance in nineteenth century discourse.* Durham & London: Duke University Press.

Churchill, J. I. (1994, June 1). Patenting humanity: The development of property rights in the human body and the subsequent evolution of patentability of living things. *Intellectual Property Journal, 8,* 249–284.

Cixous, H. (1993). *Three steps on the ladder of writing* (S. Cornell & S. Sellers, Trans.). New York: Columbia University Press.

Clapes, A. L. (1993). *Softwars: The legal battles for control of the global software industry*. Westport, CT & London: Quorum Books.

Cobb, S., & Rifkin, J. (1991). Neutrality as a discursive practice. *Politics and Society, 19*, 69–91.

Cohen, Y. (1997, December 27). Software pirates pile up profits in afflicted Asia. *Christian Science Monitor*, 1.

Computer Associates International, Inc. v. Altai, Inc. 775 F.Supp. 544 (E.D.N.Y. 1991).

Computer game maker sues U.S. government over office raid. *Wall Street Journal*, B7.

Computer hacker ring with a Bay area Link. (1990, May 9). *San Francisco Chronicle*, A30.

Computers and intellectual property: Hearings before the subcommittee on courts, intellectual property and the administration of justice of the committee on the judiciary, House of Representatives. 101st Cong., 1st, & 2nd Session. (1989).

Coombe, R. (1991). Objects of property and subjects of politics: Intellectual property laws and democratic dialogue. *Texas Law Review, 69*, 1853–1880.

Coombe, R. (1992). Author/izing the celebrity: Publicity rights, postmodern politics, and unauthorized genders. *Cardozo Arts and Entertainment*, 365–395.

Copyright Act of 1976. 17, U.S.C.A.

Copyright Bills. Joint hearing of the courts and intellectual property subcommittee of the House judiciary committee and Senate judiciary committee. (1995, November 15). *Federal News Service*. [Lexis-Nexis].

Copyright Law. (1998, October 12). Red Rock Eater News Service. http://commons.somewhere.com/rre/idex.html.

Copyrights, PTO, Copyright office praise bill to direct traffic on information superhighway. (1995, November 15). *Daily report for executives*. 1995 DER 221 d43. [Lexis-Nexis].

Court, R. (1998, February 12). Inventor stakes claim to MS fortunes. *Wired News*. [On-line]. Available: http://www.wired.com/news/news/business/story/10251.html.

Daly, J. (1993, March 1). Hackers switch sides, offer security package. *Computerworld, 27*, 6.

Daly, J. (1993, July 13). Netherlands, Mexico chase after hackers. *Computerworld, 26*, 14.

The database investment and Intellectual Property Antipiracy Act of 1996. (1996, May 23). *Congressional Record* (Vol. 142, No. 74, p. e890). Washington, DC: U.S. Government Printing Office.

De Certeau, M. (1984). *The practice of everyday life* (S. Rendall, Trans.). Berkeley, Los Angeles, & London: University of California Press.

Dettmer, J. (1997, October 5). Clinton Friendly spying scandal. *Scotland on Sunday*, 21. [Lexis-Nexis].

Digital Communications Associates, Inc. v. Softklone Distributing Corp. 659 F.Supp. 449, (N.D. Ga. 1987).

Disney characters removed; Day-care center follows park's order. (1989, August 3). *The Orange County Register*, A25.

Dorfman, A., & Matterlart, A. (1975). *How to read Donald Duck: Imperialist ideology in the Disney comic* (D. Kunzle, Trans.). New York: International General.

Doyle, L. (1991, July 2). Majoring in the arts and crafts of spying. *The Independent*, 10.

Dreier, D., & Herger, W. (1990, May 19). No harmless hacker he. *The Washington Post*, A23.

Ducking the issue of the little black duck. (1995, February 21). *Honolulu Advertiser*, B1.

Eagleton, T. (1983). *Literary theory: An introduction*. Minneapolis: University of Minnesota Press.

Earle, E. (1991, September 6). The effect of romanticism on the 19th century development of copyright law. *Intellectual Property Journal, 6*, 269–290.

Eco, U. (1992). Between author and text. In S. Collini (Ed.), *Interpretation and over interpretation*. Cambridge, New York, Port Chester, Melbourne, & Sydney: Cambridge University Press.

Edelman, V. (1995, November). Primed for crime on the internet. *Inc.*, 18.

Edge, A. R. (1994, Fall). Preventing piracy through regional trade agreements: The Mexican example. *North Carolina Journal of International Law and Commercial Regulation, 20*, 175–204.

Elmer-Dewitt, P. (1991, April 8). Cyberpunks and the constitution. *Time, 137*, 81.

Ely, J. W., Jr. (1992). *The guardian of every other right: A constitutional history of property rights*. New York & Oxford: Oxford University Press.

Engardio, P. (1992, February 3). Yankee traders breath a sigh of relief. *International Business, 39*, 42.

Erikson, K. (1966). *Wayward puritans: A study in the sociology of deviance*. New York, London, & Sydney: Wiley.

Executive summary and recommendations from intellectual property and the national information infrastructure. The report of the working group on intellectual property rights. (1995, September 6). *Daily Report for Executives*. [Lexis-Nexis].

FBI braces for hackers. (1995, November 27). *Information Week*, 24.

FBI links 23 countries to economic espionage. (1988, January 12). *The Buffalo News*, 5A.

Feist Publications Inc. v. Rural Telephone Company. 111 S.Ct. 1282. (1991).

Fish, S. (1989). *Doing what comes naturally: Change, rhetoric, and the practice of theory in literary and legal studies*. Durham & London: Duke University Press.

Flanagan, W. G., & McMenamin, B. (1992, December 21). The playground bullies are learning how to type. *Forbes, 150*, 184–189.

Flanders, B. L. (1991, July/ August). Barbarians at the gate. *American Libraries*, 669.

Fleming, C., & Giles, J. (1995, January 16). Jimi, rest in peace. *Newsweek*, 64–65.

Foreign spies hurt American business. (1998, January 13). *Newsday*, A43.

Forester, T., & Morrison, P. (1993). *Computer ethics: Cautionary tales and ethical dilemmas in computing*. Cambridge, MA: MIT Press.

Foster, M. (1989, April 3). U.S. firms battle the pirates of Taiwan. *Electronic Business*, 83–84.

Foucault, M. (1977). What is an author? In D. F. Bouchard & S. Simon (Eds. & Trans.), *Language, counter-memory, practice: Selected essays and interviews*, (pp. 113–138). Ithaca, NY: Cornell University Press.

Freedman, D. H. (1993, September 3). The goods on hacker hoods. *Forbes ASAP, 152,* 32–40.

Frohock, F. M. (1992). *Alternative medicine, spiritual communities, and the state.* Chicago & London: University of Chicago Press.

Gaines, J. M. (1991). *Contested culture: The image, the voice, and the law.* Chapel Hill & London: The University of North Carolina Press.

Garcia, D. L. (1987, April 22–24). *The OTA report on intellectual property rights. Intellectual property rights in an electronic age: Proceedings of the Library of Congress network advisory committee meeting.*

Garfinkle, S. L. (1996, January 4). Making an arrest in cyberspace. *The Christian Science Monitor,* 13.

GCA Corp. v. Chance. 217 U.S.P.Q. (BNA) 718, 720 (N.D. Cal. 1982).

George, D., & Ford, L. L. P. (1994, Spring). Legal bytes. *Cu Digest, 6.62, File 1,* [On-line]. Available: gdf@well.sf.ca.us

Ginsburg, J. C. (1990). Creation and commercial value: Copyright protection of works of information. *Columbia Law Review, 90,* 1865–1936.

Goldberg, D., & Bernstein, R. J. (1995, November 17). The white paper's proposed amendments to the act. *New York Law Journal.* [Lexis-Nexis].

Goldstein, P. (1992, Spring). Copyright. *Law and Contemporary Problems,* 79–91.

Goldstein, P. (1993). *Copyright, patent, trademark and related state doctrines: Cases and materials on the law of intellectual property* (3rd ed.). Westbury, NY: The Foundation Press.

Goldstein, P., Kitch, E., & Perlman, H. S. (1994). *Selected statutes and international agreements on unfair competition, trademark, copyright and patent.* Westbury, NY: The Foundation Press.

Gopinath, K. (1992, August 29). Computer software and intellectual property rights: Issues at stake for developing countries. *Economic and Political Weekly, 27,* m101–m104.

Gordon, W. J. (1992, February). On owning information: Intellectual property and the restitutionary impulse. *Virginia Law Review, 78,* 149–171.

Gorman, R. A. (1993). The *Feist* case: Reflections on a pathbreaking copyright decision. *Intellectual Property Law Review, 25,* 355–396.

Gorman, R. A., & Ginsburg, J. C. (1993). *Copyright for the nineties: Cases and material.* Charlottesville: The Michie Company Law Publishers.

Government unwilling to relax software encryption limits. (1995, January 2). *Investor's Business Daily,* p. A6.

Gurdon, H. (1997, March 29). Humiliations tarnish CIA's reputation. *The Ottawa Citizen,* A16.

Habermas, J. (1989). *The structural transformation of the public sphere: An inquiry into a category of bourgeois society* (T. Burger, Trans.). Cambridge, MA: MIT Press.

Hackers raid U.S. lab file. (1988, June 18). *The New York Times,* 45(L), 29(N).

Hafner, K. (1995, August). Kevin Mitnick, unplugged. Computer hacker. *Esquire, 80.* [Lexis-Nexis].

Hafner, K. (1997, February 27). A superhacker meets his match. *Newsweek,* 61–63.

Hafner, K., & Markoff, J. (1991 December). Conversations: Cyberpunk authors

Hafner and Markhoff talk about investigating hackers, tricksters, and international computer spies. *Compute, 13,* 16.

Hafner, K., & Markoff, J. (1991). *Cyberpunk: Outlaws and hackers on the computer frontier*. New York & London: Simon & Schuster.

Halbert, D. (1997). Discourses of danger and the computer hacker. *The Information Society, 13,* 361–374.

Halbert, D. (1997, June/July). The future of intellectual property law. *Technological Forecasting and Social Change,* 147–160.

Halbert, D. (1997). Intellectual property piracy: The narrative construction of deviance. *International Journal for the Semiotics of Law, 10*(28), 55–78.

Halbert, D. (in press). Poaching and plagiarizing: Intellectual property and feminist futures. In A. Roy & L. Buranen (Eds.), *Perspectives on plagiarism and intellectual property in a postmodern world*. Albany: State University of New York Press.

Helpman, E. (1993, November 16). Innovation, imitation, and intellectual property rights. *Econometrica, 16,* 1247–1280.

Hernadi, P. (1980, Autumn). Afterthoughts on narrative. I: On the how, what, and why of narrative. *Critical Inquiry,* 201–206.

Hernstein Smith, B. (1980, Autumn). Afterthoughts on narrative. III: Narrative versions, narrative theories. *Critical Inquiry,* 213–236.

Hesse, C. (1988). Enlightenment epistemology and the laws of authorship in revolutionary France, 1777–1793. *Representations, 30,* 109–137.

Higgins, K. J. (1996, April 8). Swarming your sites. *Communications Week,* 37.

Hoffman, G. M. (1989). *Curbing national piracy of intellectual property. The report of the international piracy project*. Washington, DC: The Annenberg Washington Program.

Horbulyk, T. M. (1993). Intellectual property rights and technological innovation in agriculture. *Technological Forecasting and Social Change, 43,* 259–270.

Horn, J. (1998, February 19). Mickey in middle of copyright fight. *Columbus Dispatch,* 8E.

Huang, A. (1997, September 8). Made in Taiwan: A high-tech revolution pirates' paradise goes legit to become formidable competitor. *The Ottawa Citizen,* C4.

Hubco Data Products, Corp. v. Management Assistance Inc. 219 U.S.P.Q. (BNA) 450, 454 (D. Id. 1983).

Hughes, J. (1988). The philosophy of intellectual property. *The Georgetown Law Journal, 77,* 287–366.

Huus, K. (1995, January 19). Back to normal: U.S.–China trade war looms closer. *Far Eastern Economic Review,* 52.

Ignatin, G. R. (1992). Let the hackers hack: Allowing the reverse engineering of copyrighted computer programs to achieve compatibility. *University of Pennsylvania Law Review,* 1999–2050.

Information Infrastructure Task Force. (1994, July). *Intellectual property and the national information infrastructure: A preliminary draft of the report of the working group on intellectual property rights.* http://www.uspto.gov/web/offices/com/doc/ipnii/

Information Infrastructure Task Force. (1995, September). *Intellectual property and the national information infrastructure: The report of the working group on in-*

tellectual property rights. http://www.uspto.gov/web/offices/com/doc/ipnii/

Intellectual property and international issues. Subcommittee on intellectual property and judicial administration of the House Judiciary Committee. 102nd Cong., (1991, May 15 and 16).

Intellectual property . . . is theft. (1994, January 22). *The Economist, 330,* 72–73.

International Olympic Comm. v. San Francisco Arts and Ath. 781 F.2d 733 (9th Cir. 1986).

International piracy involving intellectual property. Hearing before the subcommittee on trade, productivity, and economic growth of the joint economic committee. 99th Cong., (1986, March 31).

Jaszi, P. (1992). On the author effect: Contemporary copyright and collective creativity. *Cardozo Arts & Entertainment,* 293–320.

Jobs through anti-piracy. Hearing before the subcommittee on economic policy, trade and environment of the committee on foreign affairs. 103rd Cong., (1994, May 3).

Johnson-Laird, A. (1997, Spring). Copyright owners' rights and users' privileges on the internet: The anatomy of the internet meets the body of the law. *University of Dayton Law Review,* 465–505.

Johnston, O. (1990, December 6). Experts call for better computer security. *Los Angeles Times,* A29.

Karpinski, R. (1990, August 6). Charges dropped against alleged Bell South hacker. *Telephony, 219,* 12–13.

Katsh, M. E. (1989). *The electronic media and the transformation of law.* New York & Oxford: Oxford University Press.

Katsh, M. E. (1995). *Law in a digital world.* New York & Oxford: Oxford University Press.

Kaye, L. (1995, March 9). Trading rights: Beijing exacts a high price for copyright accord. *Far Eastern Economic Review,* 16.

Keefe, P. (1992, June 22). Portrait of hackers as young adventurers not convincing. *Computerworld, 26,* 33.

Kehoe, L., & Stephens, S. (1996, April 16). A hacker's paradise. *Financial Times,* 13.

Kehoe, L., & Stephens, S. (1996, April 17). Computer invasions growing with internet. *The Financial Post,* 54.

Kelleher, J. (1989, October 23). The hacker as scapegoat. *Computerworld, 23,* 80–81.

Kelly, K. (1994). *Out of control: The rise of neo-biological civilization.* Reading, MA: Addison-Weseley.

Kiely, T. (1992, February). Cyberspace Cadets. *CIO,* 70.

Kilborn, R., & Hanson, C. (1998, January 13). News in brief. *Christian Science Monitor,* 2.

Kimbrell, A. (1993). *The human body shop: The engineering and marketing of life.* San Francisco: Harper-Collins.

Kitler, F. A. (1990). *Discourse networks: 1800/1900* (M. Metteer, Trans.). Stanford, CA: Stanford University Press.

Kroupa, P. (1993, November). Memoirs of a cybernaut. *Wired, 1,* 59.

La Croix, S. J. (1994, December). *Intellectual property rights in ASEAN and the*

United States; Harmonization and controversy, private investment and trade opportunities (PITO) economic brief. Honolulu: East–West Center.

Ladd, D., & Joseph, B. G. (1987). Expanding computer software protection by limiting the idea. *The Journal of Law and Technology, 2*, 5–15.

Lai, E. (1997, December 2). Leading the war to end software piracy. *South China Morning Post*, 10.

Landow, G. P. (1992). *Hypertext: The convergence of contemporary critical theory and technology*. Baltimore & London: The Johns Hopkins University Press.

Landow, G. P. (1994). *Hypertext/Text/Theory*. Baltimore & London: The Johns Hopkins University Press.

Lange, D. (1992, Spring). At play in the fields of the work: Copyright and the construction of authorship in the post-literate millennium. *Law and Contemporary Problems*, 139–152.

Le Guin, U. (1974). *The dispossessed*. New York: Harper & Row.

Levy, S. (1984). *Hackers: Heroes of the computer revolution*. Garden City, NY: Anchor Press.

Lewyn, M., & Schwartz, E. I. (1991, April 15). Why the legion of doom has little to fear of the feds. *Business Week*, 31.

Lind, C. (1991, December). The idea of capitalism or the capitalism of ideas? A moral critique of the Copyright Act. *Intellectual Property Journal, 7*, 65–84.

Litman, J. (1992, Spring). Copyright and information policy. *Law and Contemporary Problems*, 185–209.

Littman, J. (1993, September 12). The last hacker. *Los Angeles Times*, 18–23, 64–65.

Littman, J. (1996). *The fugitive game: The inside story of the great cyberchase*. Boston, New York, Toronto, & London: Little, Brown.

Long, P. O. (1991, October). Invention, authorship, "intellectual property," and the origin of patents: Notes toward a conceptual history. *Technology and Culture*, 846–884.

Lotus Development Corp. v. Borland International Inc. 116 S. CT. 1062; U.S. (1995).

Lotus Development Corp. v. Paperback Software Intl. 740 F. Supp. 37 (D. Mass. 1990)

Lubman, S. (1997, October 19). There's no rushing China's slow march to a rule of law. *Los Angeles Times*, M2.

Lyotard, J. F. (1984). *The postmodern condition: A report on knowledge* (G. Bennington & B. Massumi, Trans.). Minneapolis: University of Minnesota Press.

Macchiarola, F. J. (1993). Copyright protection: Has look and feel crashed? *Cardozo Arts and Entertainment Law Journal*, 721–763.

Maiorana, D. M. (1996, October). Privileged use: Has Judge Boudin suggested a viable means of copyright protection for the non-literal aspects of computer software in *Lotus Development Corp. v. Borland International? The American University Law Review*, 149–188.

Mansfield, E. (1990). Intellectual property, technology and economic growth. In F. W. Rushing & C. G. Brown (Eds.), *Intellectual property rights in science, technology, and economic performance*. Boulder, San Francisco, & London: Westview Press.

Marke, J. J. (1998, May 18). Proposed legislation on digital copyright. *Law Journal Extra!*, http://www.ljextra.com:80/copyright/0519digcplegis.html.

Markoff, J. (1988, October 24). Computer hacker in Britain said to enter U.S. systems. *The New York Times*, D1.

Markoff, J. (1990, April 4). Arrests in computer break-ins show a global peril. *The New York Times*, A1, A16.

Markoff, J. (1992, June 24). Ruling restricts software copyright protection. *The New York Times*, D1 (L).

Markoff, J. (1996, January 2). In search of computer security. *The New York Times*, 15.

Maskus, K. E. (1990, September). Normative concerns in the international protection of intellectual property rights. *World Economy*, 387–409.

Maskus, K. E., & Penubarti, M. (1990, September). *How trade-related are intellectual property rights?* Unpublished manuscript.

Mazer v. Stein, 74 S.Ct. 460.

McMenamin, B. (1994, June 20). Fallen hacker. *Forbes, 153*, 12.

Mearsheimer, J. J. (1990, August). Why we will soon miss the Cold War. *The Atlantic Monthly*, 35–50.

Merry, S. (1990). *Getting justice and getting even: Legal consciousness among working class Americans*. Chicago: University of Chicago Press.

Meyer, G., & Thomson, J. (1990, June 10). *The baudy world of the byte bandit: A postmodern interpretation of the computer underground* [On-line]. Available: http://www.eff.org/pub/Net_info/Net_culture/ Cyberpunks_hackers/ Publications/Papers/

Meyer, M. (1995, December 4). Is the hacker evil or merely misunderstood? *Newsweek*, 60.

Meyer, M., & Underwood, A. (1994, November 14). Theft on the infohighway. *Newsweek*, 47.

Mickey Mouse back in China. (1993, November 4). *Far Eastern Economic Review*, 46.

Midway Manufacturing Co. v. Strohon. 564 F. Supp. 741, 750 (N.D. Ill. 1983).

Miller, P. (1998, May 20). Final meeting on the conference on fair use. *NCC Washington Update*, vol. 4, no. 19, H-Net Distribution List for NCC Reports. H-NCC@h-net.msu.edu.

Miller, P. (1998, May 20). Senate passes digital copyright law 99–0. *NCC Washington Update*, vol. 4, no. 19, H-Net Distribution List for NCC Reports. H-NCC@h-net.msu.edu.

Minh-Ha, T. T. (1991). *When the moon waxes red: Representation, gender and cultural politics*. New York & London: Routledge.

Mitnick pleads guilty to illegally using phones, violating probation. (1996, April 23). *The Associated Press* [Lexis-Nexis].

Mitroff, I. I., & Bennis, W. (1993). *The unreality industry: The deliberate manufacturing of falsehood and what it is doing to our lives*. New York & Oxford: Oxford University Press.

Mody, A. (1990). New International environment for intellectual property rights. In F. W. Rushing & C. G. Brown, (Eds.). *Intellectual property rights in science, technology, and economic performance*. Boulder, San Francisco, & London: Westview Press.

Moorhead, C. J. (1995, December 3). Protect copyright holders and the internet will grow. *The Washington Times*, B2.

Moran, J. M. (1996, January 2). The antidote: Learn more about computers. *The Buffalo News*, p. 7E.

Mungo, P., & Clough, B. (1992). *Approaching zero: The extraordinary underworld of hackers, phreakers, virus writers, and keyboard criminals.* New York: Random House.

National Writers Union. (1993, June 30). *Electronic publishing issues, a working paper* [On-line]. Available: University of Maryland Gopher <anon@info.umd.edu>

Nedelsky, J. (1990). *Private property and the limits of American constitutionalism: The Madisonian framework and its legacy.* Chicago & London: University of Chicago Press.

Nelson, J. (1998, January 12). More spies targeting U.S. firms. *The Dallas Morning News*, 1D.

Newdorf, D. (1991, July 29). Disney is no fairy tale in court: Mickey's new lawyer continues tough stance. *Legal Times*, 16.

No Electronic Theft (NET) Act. (1997, November 4). *Congressional Record, 143* (152), H9887.

Nowell-Smith, S. (1968). *International copyright law and the publisher in the reign of Queen Victoria.* Oxford: Clarendon Press.

O'C. Hamilton, J. (1990, April 23). Who told you you could sell my spleen? *Business Week*, 38.

Office of Technology Assessment. (1986, April). *Intellectual property rights in an age of electronics and information, summary* (OTA-CIT-303). Washington, DC: U.S. Government Printing Office.

OTA report on intellectual property rights in an age of electronics and information: Joint hearing of the subcommittee on patents, copyrights, and trademarks of the senate committee on the judiciary and the subcommittee on courts, civil liberties, and the administration of justice of the house committee on the judiciary. 99th Cong., 2nd Session. (1986, April 16).

Oyejide, T. A. (1990, September). The participation of developing countries in the Uruguay round: An African perspective. *World Economy*, 427–444.

Patterson, L. R. (1968). *Copyright in historical perspective.* Nashville, TN: Vanderbilt University Press.

Paul, E. F., & Dickman, H. (Eds.). (1989). *Liberty, property, and the foundations of the American constitution.* Albany: State University of New York Press.

Perry, J. M. (1991, April 23). What publishers call quoting, computer firms call piracy as industries face off on Capitol Hill. *Wall Street Journal*, A24.

Peterzell, J. (1989, March 20). Spying and sabotage by computers. *Time, 133*, 25–26.

Piercy, M. (1976). *Woman on the edge of time.* New York: Fawcett Crest.

Playboy Enterprises, Inc. v. George Frena., U.S. Dist. [Lexis-Nexus 19165].

Porn on the Internet. (1995, July 3). *Time*, 38.

Posner, S. (1993). Can a computer language be copyrighted? The state of confusion in computer copyright law. *Intellectual Property Law Review, 25*, 485–518.

Poster, M. (1990). *The mode of information: Poststructuralism and social context.* Chicago: University of Chicago Press.

Prescott, P. (1989). The origins of copyright: A debunking view. *European Intellectual Property Review*, 453–455.

Preston, W., Jr. (1988). *Hope and folly*. Minneapolis: University of Minnesota.

Price, M. E., & Pollock, M. (1994). The author in copyright: Notes for the literary critic. In M. Woodmansee & P. Jaszi, (Eds.), *The construction of authorship: Textual appropriation in law and literature*. Durham & London: Duke University Press.

Probe Focuses on Entry, Theft by Computers. (1990, May 10). *Chicago Tribune*. [Lexis-Nexis].

PTO, copyright office praise bill to direct traffic on the information highway. (1995, November 16). *BNA Washington Insider*. [Lexis-Nexis].

Rabinow, P. (Eds.). (1984). *The Foucault reader*. New York: Pantheon Books.

Reeve, A. (1986). *Property*. London: MacMillan.

Reid, C. (1996, April 15). Free speech or piracy?: Copyright ruling favors Scientologists. *Publishers Weekly*, 14.

Religious Technology Center v. Arnaldo Pagliarina Lerma, Digital Gateway Systems, The Washington Post, Marc Fisher, and Richard Leiby. 1995 U.S. Dist. [Lexis 16799].

Religious Technology Center v. Arnaldo Pagliarina Lerma, Digital Gateway Systems, The Washington Post, Marc Fisher, and Richard Leiby. 1995 U.S. Dist. [Lexis 17833]. (Memorandum Opinion).

Religious Technology Center and Bridge Publications Inc. v. Netcom On-Line Communication Services, Inc., Dennis Erlich, Tom Klemesrud, Clearwood Data Service. 1995 U.S. Dist. [Lexis 18173].

Ricketson, S. (1991). The 1992 Horace S. Manges lecture—people or machines: The Berne convention and the changing concept of authorship. *Columbia VLA Journal of Law & the Arts, 16*, 1–37.

Rodau, A. G. (1986). Protecting computer software: After *Apple Computer Inc. v Franklin Computer Corp.*, 714 F.2d 1248 (3rd Cir. 1983), does copyright provide the best protection? *Intellectual Property Law Review*, 413–438.

Rose M. (1988, Summer). The author as proprietor: *Donaldson v. Becket* and the genealogy of modern authorship. *Representations, 23*, 51–85.

Rose M. (1992). The author in court: *Pope v. Curll* (1741). *Cardozo Arts & Entertainment*, 475–493.

Rose M. (1993). *Authors and owners: The invention of copyright*. London & Cambridge, MA: Harvard University Press.

Ross, P. E. (1996 September 9). Cops versus Robbers in Cyberspace. *Forbes*, 134–139.

Rotenberg, M. (1990, March). Prepared testimony and statement for the record on computer virus legislation. *Computers and Society, 20*, 19.

Rotstein, R. H. (1993). Beyond metaphor: Copyright infringement and the fiction of the work. *Chicago-Kent Law Review, 68*, 725–804.

Samuelson, P. (1989, Winter). Information as property: Do *Ruckelshaus* and *Carpenter* signal a changing direction in intellectual property law? *Catholic University Law Review, 38*, 365–400.

Samuelson, P. (1992, Spring). Computer programs, user interfaces, and section 102(b) of the Copyright Act of 1976: A critique of *Lotus v. Paperback. Law and Contemporary Problems*, 311–353.

Samuelson, P. (1994, December). The NII intellectual property report: National information infrastructure. *Communications of the ACM, 37,* [Lexis-Nexis].

Saunders, D., & Hunter, I. (1991, Spring). Lessons from the literatory: How to historicise authorship. *Critical Inquiry,* 479–509.

Schatz, W. (1990, June 24). The terminal men: Crackdown on the legion of doom ends an era for computer hackers. *Washington Post,* H1, H6.

Schiller, H. (1989). *Culture Inc: The corporate takeover of public expression.* New York: Oxford University Press.

Schultz, D. A. (1992). *Property, power, and American democracy.* New Brunswick & London: Transaction.

Schwartz, E. I., Rothfeder, J., & Lewyn, M. (1990, August 6). Viruses? Who you gonna call? Hackerbusters. *Business Week,* 71–72.

Scientology finds refuge in white paper. (1995, September 25). *Information Law Alert: A Voorhees Report.* [Lexis-Nexis].

Sega Enterprises v. Accolade, Inc. 1992 U.S. Dist. [LEXIS 4028].

Sega Enterprises Ltd. v. Maphia. 857 F.Supp. 679, 683 (N.D. Cal. 1994).

Sell, S. (1998). *Power and ideas: North-South politics of intellectual property and antitrust.* Albany: State University of New York Press.

Shapiro, M. J. (1991). Sovereignty and exchange in the orders of modernity. *Alternatives, 16,* 447–477.

Shapiro, M. J. (1993). *Reading "Adam Smith": Desire, History and value.* Newbury Park, London, & New Delhi: Sage.

Sherman, B., & Strowel, A. (1994). *Of authors and origins: Essays on copyright law.* Oxford: Clarendon Press.

Sidel, M. (1985). The legal protection of copyright and the rights of authors in the People's Republic of China, 1949–1984: Prelude to the Chinese copyright law. *Art and the Law, 9,* 477–508.

Siegan, B. H. (1989). One people as to commercial objects. In E. F. Paul & H. Dickman (Eds.), *Liberty, property, and the foundations of the American Constitution.* Albany: State University of New York Press.

Sirius, R. U. & St. Jude. (1996). *How to mutate and take over the world.* New York: Ballantine Books.

Slonczewski, J. (1986). *A door into ocean.* New York: Avon Books.

Smith, D. (1994, June 26). News: Corporate losses due to international copyright piracy. *Cu Digest, 6.57,* file 1.

Smith, D. (1996, April 23). Famed hacker pleads guilty to 1 federal charge. *Los Angeles Times,* 4.

Snell, M. B. (1996, March/April). Bioprospecting or biopiracy. *Utne Reader,* 83.

Solutions emerge as U.S. sanctions loom. (1996, May 23). *South China Morning Post,* p. 6.

Steele G. L., Jr. (1991). Confessions of a happy hacker. In R. Eric (Ed.), *The New Hacker's Dictionary* (pp. 413–420). Cambridge, England, & London: MIT Press.

Stefora, A., & Cheek, M. (1994, February 7). Hacking goes legit. *Industry Week, 243,* 43–45.

Stephenson, N. (1993). *Snow crash.* New York: Bantam Books.

Sterling, B. (1992). *Hacker crackdown: Law and disorder on the electronic frontier.* New York: Bantam Books.

Stern Electronics, Inc. v. Kaufman. 669 F.2d. 852 (2nd Cir. 1982).

Stoll, C. (1989). *The cuckoo's egg: Tracking a spy through the maze of computer espionage*. New York & London: Doubleday.

Stowe, D. W. (1995, November/December). Just do it. *Lingua Franca*, 32–42.

Subramanian, A. (1991). The international economics of intellectual property right protection: A welfare-theoretic trade policy analysis. *World Development, 19*, 45–55.

Supra-national response to networked world. (1995, March 2). *Computer Weekly*.

Synercom Technology, Inc. v. University Computing Co. 462 F.Supp. 1003 (N.D. Tex. 1978).

Terry, N. P. (1994). GUI wars: The windows litigation and the continuing decline of look and feel. *Arkansas Law Review*, 93–157.

Thomas, J., & Meyer, G. (Eds.). (1994, October 2). *Computer Underground Digest, 6*, file 3,4.

Thomas, P., & Corcoran, E. (1996, March 30). Argentine, 22, charged with hacking computer networks. *The Washington Post*, A4.

Tigar, M. E. (1984). The right of property and the law of theft. *Texas Law Review, 62*, 1443–1475.

Toffler, A. (1990). *Powershift: Knowledge, wealth, and violence at the edge of the 21st century*. New York: Bantam Books.

United States of America v. David LaMacchia. 871 F.Supp. 535; U.S. Dist. (1994).

United States v. Zod. (1990, September 1). *The Economist, 316*, 23–24.

U.S. Constitution, Article I § 8, clause 8.

Vault Corp. v. Quaid Software Ltd. U.S. Dist. [Lexis, 1180].

Vaver, D. (1990, September 6). Some agnostic observations on intellectual property. *Intellectual Property Journal, 6*, 125–153.

Violino, B. (1996, May 27). Pentagon caught in its own net. *Information Week*, 32.

Waldron, J. (1993). From authors to copiers: Individual rights and social values in intellectual property. *Chicago-Kent Law Review, 68*, 842–887.

Wall, W. (1993). *The imprint of gender: Authorship and publication in the English renaissance*. Ithaca & London: Cornell University Press.

Waller, S. W., & Byrne, N. J. (1993). Changing view of intellectual property and competition law in the European community and the United States of America. *Brooklyn Journal of International Law, 20*, 1–24.

Walt Disney Productions v. Air Pirates. 581 F.2d. 751 (9th Cir. 1978).

Weise, E. (1996, April 14). Computer-savvy buddies hack their way into federal prison. *Los Angeles Times*, 1.

Wells, S. (1990). Narrative figures and subtle persuasions: The rhetoric of the MOVE report. In H. W. Simons (Ed.), *Rhetorical turn: Invention and persuasion in the conduct of inquiry*. Chicago: University of Chicago Press.

Whelan v. Jaslow Dental Laboratory, Inc. 797 F.2d. 1222 (3rd Cir 1986).

White, H. (1980, Autumn). The value of narrativity. *Critical Inquiry*, 5–28.

Wice, N. (1996, April 13). Companies challenge computer hackers to break codes. *CNN News*. [Transcript #313–4]. [Lexis-Nexis].

Wilder, C., & Miolino, B. (1995, August 28). Online theft-trade in black-market data is growing problem for both business and the law. *Information Week*, 30.

Will we need fair use in the 21st century? [On-line]. Available: http://www.utsystem.edu/OGC/intellectual property/confu.htm [Visited 2/13/98].

Williams Electronics Inc. v. Artic International Inc. 685 F.2d. 870, 876–77. (3rd Cir. 1982).

Williams, P. (1991). *The alchemy of race and rights: A diary of a law professor.* Cambridge, MA & London: Harvard University Press.

Woodmansee, M. (1984, Summer). The genius and the copyright: Economic and legal conditions of the emergence of the author. *Eighteenth Century Studies, 17,* 425–448.

Woodmansee, M. (1992). On the author effect: Recovering collectivity. *Cardozo Arts & Entertainment,* 279–292.

Xerox Corp. v. Apple Computer Inc. U.S. Dist. [LEXIS, 8622] (1989).

Yarbrough, J. (1989). Jefferson and property rights. In E. F. Paul, & H. Dickman (Eds.), *Liberty, property, and the foundations of the American Constitution.* Albany: State University of New York Press.

Index

About the Author

DEBORA J. HALBERT is Assistant Professor of Political Science at Otterbein College. She has specialized in intellectual property issues, and her articles on the topic have appeared in *International Journal of the Semiotics of Law*, *The Information Society*, and *Technological Forecasting and Social Change*.